THE CRAFT OF POE'S TALES

THE CRAFT OF POE'S TALES

D. Ramakrishna

GYAN PUBLISHING HOUSE
NEW DELHI-110002

THE CRAFT OF POE'S TALES
(*Literature*)

ISBN : 81-212-0697-9

Published in 2000 in India by
Gyan Publishing House,
5, Ansari Road, Darya Ganj
New Delhi-110 002

Phone: 3282060, 3261060 Fax: (011)-3285914
E-mail: gyanbook@del2.vsnl.net.in
Visit Our Web Site At http://www.gyanbooks.com

Laser Typesetting at A.S. Printers, Delhi

Printed at Mehra Offset Press, Delhi

TO
SRINIVASA

CONTENTS

FOREWORD

It is a great pleasure for me to recommend Dr. Ramakrishna's book–the product of many years of appreciative reading and intensive research devoted to the works of Edgar Allan Poe. In this volume will be found evidences of his delight in perceiving Poe's aims and techniques and in presenting his many insights into Poe's originality and imaginative power. It seems clear to me that the Indian scholar's distance from Poe's milien has given to him the advantage of a particularly comprehensive and panoramic vision. Dr. Ramakrishna has made a close study of the Poe texts and also of the critical literature about them emanating from his admirers in many countries, such as France, which regards Poe as "one of its own." But, it is the universality of Poe's creative appeal which has made his works the subjects of the outstanding artists of the country, such as Manet, Odilon Redon, Doré, and Gauguin. This is true also for the German artist Alfred Kubin; the British artists, John Tenniel, Aubrey Beardsley, and Harry Clarke; the Belgians, James Ensor and René Magritte; the Czech, Frantisek Kupka; and the Americans, James Whistler, Albert Ryder, and Edward Hopper. Hundreds of others have left graphic testimonies to the manifold attractions of Poe's texts: their Gothic mysteriousness or strangeness, their comic ebullience, their strong rationalism even in the ambiance of extreme terror and anguish, and their rigid sense of scientific curiosity applied to life–endangering crises. It is this multiplicity of aims, techniques, and atmospheres, so well presented by Dr. Ramakrishna, that has tempted musicians from many countries to seek out Poe texts for choral pieces, songs, instrumental works, tone poems, symphonies, and operas: Debussy for his unfinished

"Fall of the House of Usher," Dominick Argento and Phillip Glass for two widely performed operas, Rachmaninoff for his symphony on "The Bells," humorous operas by Lualdi and Tosatti, ballet or dance drama scores by holbrooke and Milhaud, and many more, to the tune of over 800 composers throughout the world.

The adaptability of Poe's works to the varied approaches of other media, such as the drama, or fiction, as in the works of Stephen King and A.S. Byatt, as well as to the theories and approaches of different schools of critic is tacitly shown through Dr. Ramakrishna's book of commentary; it is organized around a "variety of modes," without too artificially separating one from another. It is clear that the author has a firm grasp of the major views about Poe's intentions and his controlling tenets without adopting a slavish or narrow adherence to any one. The positive achievements of Poe in each mode are recognized, along with infelicities and weaknesses in particular tales. Poe is here shown to be a genius with the faults of a harassed mortal, holding to his basic aims and ideals with occasional lapses. The wide gamut of his *oeuvre*, ranging from the austere and supernal to the trivial, is implicit in the articles which follow. Dr. Ramakrishna's open-minded attitude toward Poe as a multiple artist will provide all readers with new ideas and stimulating conclusions.

New York City **Burton R. Pollin**

PREFACE

Edgar Allan Poe is a literary theorist and one of the seminal minds of America in the nineteenth century. He has a theory of the tale put forth in some detail in his letters, marginalia, reviews, and articles, and in his own compositions attempts to put his principle into practice. His critical writings contain numerous statements concerning such fictional aspects as the beginning, middle, and end, character, setting, plot, author–reader relationship, and point of view. An attempt has been made in this study to comment on each of the fictional elements and to relate it to the overall strategy of the tale. In the course of the analysis of Poe's statements the principles of some of the major theorists, both classical and modern, have been taken into account.

The main concern of the present study has been a systematic application of Poe's theory to his practice. Surely, the best way to judge a writer is to interpret him in the light of his own artistic goals. Sometimes one might notice considerable divergence between a writer's intentions and his actual achievement: he might fall short of his ideals or achieve results not immediately anticipated by the theory.

Deconstruction and Reader–Response Criticism have minimized the author and his intentions. But the more recently prevalent New Historicism takes into account the overall historical context including the author and his attitudes.

Poe as a writer of the tale aims at a great diversity of "effect"–a concept adopted from A.W. Schlegel and S.T. Coleridge–and employs a strategy appropriate to each kind of the tale that he has composed. According to him, each of his tales is a unique composition. He wrote to P P Cooke about his *Tales* of 1845:

> ...I do not consider any one of my stories *better* than another. There are a vast variety of kinds and in degrees of value, these kinds vary–but each tale is equally good *of its kind.*

Thus not only does each type–Gothic, Grotesque, Ratiocinative, the Visionary and the Beautiful–exploit a specific narrative method, but each individual tale of any particular type is unique in its own particular strategy. Although it is difficult to maintain that no two of Poe's tales are alike, there are several tales with strictly individual traits. Poe's own classification of his tales into four broad categories is based largely on thematic considerations. But some of the tales do not fall under any known category; they adopt strictly individual techniques while thematically containing the traits of more than one type. In his letter of July 20, 1835 to Thomas W. White, Poe says, "many contradictory opinions had been formed in relation to my *Tales.*" This state of Poe criticism seems to prevail even today in spite of a multitude of interpretations including the Deconstructionist and Reader–response studies. The grouping of the tales by earlier critics like W.H. Auden, Richard Wilbur, Edward H. Davidson, Patrick F. Quinn, and Stephen L. Mooney takes into consideration the larger thematic unities. Even recent critics like G.R. Thompson, David Halliburton, Daniel Hoffmann, and David Ketterer have looked at Poe's works in the light of concepts like Romantic Irony, Phenomenology, or the cosmological unity of *Eureka.* While these studies are excellent in themselves, they seem to miss the real focus of Poe's tale–writing–the diversity and variety of theme and technique. Stuart Levine sees in his book, *Edgar Poe: Seer and Craftsman* a basic unity in the writings of Poe in the light of the theory of Beauty. However, Daniel Hoffman is more convincing when he says:

> When we consider his work as a whole, his *oeuvre*, we can't help but be struck by the *particularity of its parts.* Oh yes, we can link together the images in one tale with those in another or with those in a poem or poems, and connect the ideas in the imaginative writings with the theories in the criticism... but it's damned near

> impossible to bolt the whole shebang together into *one unitary whole*...

What really appeals in Poe to the modern reader is the fragmented vision presented through the "diversity and variety" of his tale–writing. In order to embody such fragmentation, the techniques employed too may tend to be multiple. I have attempted in this book a grouping of the tales based on the technical features of the compositions, without forcing the entire work of Poe into the poetic or the symbolistic framework. T.S. Eliot says in his essay, "From Poe to Valery" that the general difference between the way the French poets have taken Poe and the way of the American and the British critics is "the attitude of the former toward Poe's *oeuvre,* toward his work as a whole. Anglo–Saxon critics are, I think, more inclined to make separate judgments of the different parts of an author's work." Under the influence of the French symbolists, Poe scholarship has generally tried to discover the underlying unities in the tales and poems. Even the recent Deconstructionist studies of Poe's writings following the French interpretations by Jacques Lacan and Jacques Derrida have not done justice to the author or his works. An approach based on Poe's own attitude toward the "vast variety of kinds" in his writings will be very much in the tradition of the Anglo–Saxon criticism.

My study aims to analyze each tale for its own effect and to estimate the author's technical success or failure in terms of the peculiar problems of its subject. This has naturally made it necessary to consider as many tales as possible, under each group, in an attempt to see how the composition in each case takes effect. In addition, I have indicated wherever certain tales do not fall into any known category.

Poe has given us a variety of critical distinctions such as "effect wrought by incident," "effect wrought by tone," and "effect wrought by ordinary incidents and peculiar tone, or the converse, or by peculiarity both of incident and tone"– distinctions that emphasize the predominance of a specific fictional element in each tale. I have kept these distinctions in mind while analyzing the tales under each type. In addition, while determining the nature of the effect, specific terms like "plot," "atmosphere," "tone," "Gothic," "Grotesque," and "parody and burlesque" we must analyze in the light of Poe's own meaning.

In the chapter on "The Fictional Principle," I have analyzed Poe's theory of the tale (put together from his letters, marginalia, reviews, and critical essays) in the light of literary theory from the classical to the recent times. The second chapter on "The Terror of the Soul" is devoted to an analysis of the Gothic tales. In this chapter, tales have been grouped under the heads "Atmosphere and Suspense" and "Character and Situation" to focus upon the significant technical features of the individual tales. Poe's much–disputed "Comic Sense" has been considered in the third chapter. While the "Grotesque" is a region between the Gothic terror and the purely humorous, the "Parody and Burlesque" constitute a lighter comic vein. Contrary to a general misunderstanding, there are tales like "Three Sundays in a Week" and "The Spectacles" in the latter category. Poe's intellectual gymnastics have been observed in the fourth chapter entitled "The Rational Stance." Crime detection in Poe is not based merely on the armchair reasoning of Dupin. In a much–neglected tale like "Thou Art the Man", Poe emerges as a precursor to the great line of detective–fiction writers from Conan Doyle to Gardner in presenting the process of detection in dramatic terms. There is a tendency on the part of critics like Stuart Levine to apply Poe's theory of Beauty to all of his prose compositions, including the tales of terror and of ratiocination. In fact, only a few of the tales are visionary and poetic in theme and technique, as Poe understood the terms. I have treated these tales in the sixth chapter entitled "The Visionary and the Beautiful." In his critical comments on fiction Poe considers the question of the short and the long compositions. He emphatically states that a longer narrative is a contradiction in terms. Ironically, his own attempts at writing longer fiction have been unsuccessful. In both *The Narrative of Arthur Pym* and *The Journal of Julius Rodman,* he tries to create character, however unsuccessfully, since the narratives are fragmentary. Either Poe is not constitutionally suited to the writing of sustained narratives or, responding to the contemporary magazine requirements, he felt that his true forte lay in the shorter composition only. The last chapter of this study deals with this aspect of Poe's fiction.

Though the main approach of the present study is Formalistic, an attempt has been made to take into account certain important aspects of the recent Deconstructionist and Reader–Response interpretations since the essential drama of Poe's creative imagination arises from a tension between the subjective and the objective, the intentional and the affective.

Warangal **D. Ramakrishna**

ACKNOWLEDGMENTS

The author is grateful to various scholars and institutions who encouraged research on "The Craft of Poe's Tales" over the years. The dissertation written with initial encouragement from Professors V.K.Chari and Shiv K. Kumar was awarded the Ph.D. degree by Kakatiya University in 1980.

A series of post–doctoral research grants awarded by the American Studies Research Centre in Hyderabad facilitated revision and updating of the work with a view to publication. The encouragement from Professor Isaac Sequeira of the American Studies Research Centre at this stage was of great help.

Thanks are due to the Editors of *The Emerson Society Quarterly* and *The Explicator* in the U.S. for publishing parts of the manuscript.

The award in 1992 of the Senior U.S. Government/Fulbright Post–Doctoral Fellowship by the U.S. Educational Foundation in New Delhi and the Council for International Exchange of Scholars in Washington resulted in further enrichment of the manuscript on intensive research in Peo Collections at the University of Texas at Austin and New York Public Library.

The leading Poe Scholar, Professor Burton R. Pollin of the City University of New York kindly offered detailed comments on the revised manuscript, helping the author to prepare the work for publication, the scholarship having been updated to 1998. Prof. Pollin has also been generous to write a Foreword to the book.

Finally, grateful thanks are due to M/s Gyan Publishing House, New Delhi for publishing book.

D. Ramakrishna

1

CLASSIFICATIONS AND INTERPRETATIONS

Edgar Allan Poe's contemporaries and successors, theorists and practitioners of tale-writing, have immensely benefited from the work he has left. As Arthur Conan Doyle puts it, his tales "have been so pregnant with suggestion, so stimulating to the minds of others, that it may be said of many of them that each is a root from which a whole literature has developed."[1] Each of the several literatures that have developed from the several roots of Poe's writing has a theory that is unique. The sixty eight tales that he had composed either conform to the principles enunciated in his own letters, marginalia, reviews, and critical essays, or in the absence of explicit statements, themselves imply a distinctive theory of the tale. In his letter of August 9, 1846 to P. P. Cooke, Poe emphasizes the diversity of this writing–his "mind in its various phases"–

> ...one of my chief aims has been the widest diversity of subject, thought, & especially *tone* & manner of handling. Were all my tales now before me in a large volume and as the composition of another–the merit that would principally arrest my attention would be the wide *diversity and* variety.[2]

Poe maintains that his *ouevre* is multifaceted. This diversity and variety of his writing can be observed in the light of his own pronouncements on the writing of the tale. Such a study may bring out what is traditional and what is experimental in Poe's writing.

The question of the classification of Poe's tales has presented a number of difficulties to scholars. As the central focus in a Poe tale is the "effect" as Poe conceived it, a definition of its precise nature, and the method of treatment adopted to achieve it must precede an analysis of the technique of each tale. A proper classification of Poe's tales would necessarily involve such a definition; it would seek to identify the categories in terms of the kind of effect of each tale, but it would also bring out the variations of emphasis, tone, and manner of handling.

Poe himself has provided the broad lines on which such a classification may be based. In his letter of April 30, 1835 to Thomas W. White, he defines four different categories based on the nature of the effect aimed at:

> ...the ludicrous heightened into the grotesque: the fearful colored into the horrible: the witty exaggerated into the burlesque: the singular wrought into the strange and mystical.[3]

In the same letter, Poe also says: "No two of these Tales will have the slightest resemblance one to the other." Although he draws a distinction between the grotesque and the burlesque, both these belong to the comic art. Therefore we may derive distinct categories from the above: (i) the Gothic romance or the horror tale. This would represent "the fearful colored into the horrible." (ii) the comic tale which includes the grotesque and the burlesque varieties and also the literary satires. (iii) the visionary and poetic pieces in which a "singular (an uncommon, extraordinary) incident or experience" is worked out into an effect of the mystical or the strange and the beautiful. However, these categories do not include the ratiocinative tale which is a major class of composition in Poe. Despite the fact that Poe does not speak of it here we know for certain that he thought of it as a distinct mode. He classifies his tales like "The Gold Bug" and the mystery tales as "tales of ratiocination." Also in his letter of August 9, 1846 to P. P. Cooke, speaking in defense of the character of Dupin, Poe says:

> You are right about the hair–splitting of my French friend–that is all done for effect. The tales of ratiocination owe most of their popularity to something in a new key. I do not mean to say that they are not ingenious–but people think them more ingenious than they are–on account of their method or air of method.[4]

It is well known that Poe took pride in his power of analysis which is represented in fiction and in cryptography in his essays. As he says in his latter of August 28, 1843 to Tomlin,

> "Much Curiosity was excited throughout the country by my solutions of these cyphers, and a great number of persons felt a desire to test my powers individually so that & was at one time absolutely overwhelmed."

Four major categories of composition emerge from the above two statements in Poe's letters, and these would represent four distinct kinds of effect: (i) horror; (ii) comic; (iii) mystery and ratiocination; (iv) poetic or visionary. Nearly all of Poe's narratives may be shown to belong to one or the other of these categories. Of course, a few defy any such classification. In addition to the strictly narrative pieces, Poe also wrote some dialogues and other pieces which do not possess a strict narrative structure and which may be called tales only be courtesy. Such are the compositions like "The Conversation of Eiros and Charmion," "The Colloquy of Monos and Una," "Mesmeric Revelation," and "The Power of Words," etc. *The Narrative of Arthur Gordon Pym, The Journal of Julies Rodman,* and *Light House* are adventure tales, being Poe's experiments in the longer form. They deserve a separate classification as they may not justifiably be included under any of the four categories mentioned above.

While the short–story devices like the opening, suspense, suggestion, point of view, climax, and denouement are largely applicable to the Gothic tales, Poe has not enunciated a systematic theory of the comic tale. However, an attempt will be made in the chapter on the Comic Sense to discuss the few remarks made by the author. In respect of the devices in the Ratiocinative tales, Poe has made explicit statements such as the opening paragraphs of "The Murders in the Rue Morgue" or "The Purloined Letter." These will be discussed in some detail in the chapter entitled "The Rational Stance."

Poe called the twenty-five stories of his two-volume edition of 1840 "The Tales of the Grotesque and Arabesque." However, he did not systematically define the terms "Grotesque" and "Arabesque", but for a few scattered remarks in his reviews. These terms will be considered at some length in the relevant chapters in the course of this study. Arthur H. Quinn thinks that, generally speaking, "the arabesques are the products of powerful imagination and the grotesques have a burlesque or satirical quality."[6] Quinn is justified in grouping together all of the Gothic tales under "Tales of the Arabesque," since they are products of powerful imagination. But the term "Arabesque" is perhaps too inclusive in its connotation. Quinn is led to include under this category both the Gothic romances and pieces like "Hans Pfaall" and "The Island of the Fay," which have quite different effects in the light of Poe's own definition. However, his classification of the three other categories, Grotesque, Ratiocinative, and the Landscape Studies follows on sound lines and keeps up the distinctions that Poe himself made in describing the various effects.

The classifications offered by others are even less satisfactory. According to Richard Wilbur, the tales may be grouped under Soliloquy, the Dramatic Monologue, the "Posthumous" tale, the Dialogue in Heaven, and the Dream Journey.[7] While there are certain elements of the Soliloquy and the Dramatic Monologue in Poe's tales, it is difficult to classify whole groups of tales under these categories since Poe has not successfully developed these forms. In fact, Wilbur's classification is largely based on dream symbolism. W.H. Auden offers two major and two minor groups. The Major groups are, (i) tales describing the state of wilful being:

The aggressive ego ("The Purloined Letter" and "The Imp of the Perverse"); and, (ii) *the passive ego* (e.g., *Pym* and "A Descent into the Maelstrom"). And the minor groups are, (i) The Great Good Place ("The Domain of Arnheim"); and (ii) the humorous–satiric group ("A Predicament").[8] But Auden's grouping, based on the subjective element, stands in no realistic relationship to Poe's own artistic intentions and is therefore unsatisfactory.

Equally unsatisfactory is the classification offered by Stephen LeRoy Mooney,[9] because in including tales like "The Black Cat," "William Wilson," and "The Man of the Crowd" under the ratiocinative type, it misses the whole point of the effect of these tales. Poe himself puts the categories in terms of the effect that they are intended to produce. Hence the most satisfactory classification would be one that is based on a consideration of the distinct effects that the tales are calculated to produce. However, as we have already observed, a few of the tales defy any classification.

The need for classification of Poe's tales, based on his own distinctions, is evident particularly in the context of interpretations (of his works) in the light of unitary concepts like Romanticism and Symbolism, done by critics like Edward H. Davidson and Patrick F. Quinn. Subsequently G.R. Thompson in *Poe's Fiction: Romantic Irony in the Gothic Tales* (1973)[10] suggests that Poe's ironic mode helps to explain the "paradoxical intertwining of the comic and the serious in his tales, and indeed the pattern of his career." He argues for thematic unity in Poe saying that the *grotesque* and *arabesque* "frequently occur together in Poe's writings in such a way as to suggest, predominantly, that they refer to a single psychological effect or response having to do with ambivalence, tension between opposites, and a sense of the transcendent ironic vision" (116-117). Thompson's study fails to recognize Poe's own insistence in his review of Hawthorne's *Twice–Told Tales* on "a vast variety of modes." It is difficult to read the ratiocinative tales from the point of view of the "absurdist," as Thompson understands the term. One should not fail to take into account Poe's evident sincerity and effort in "analyzing" his distinctions and aims. Thompson does not wish to take seriously Poe, one of America's most dedicated and objective critics. Daniel Hoffman in *Poe Poe Poe Poe Poe Poe Poe* (1972)[11] says the Poe, as a haunted man, worked his Oedipal and necrophilic obsessions into his poetry and fiction, wearing several masks: Horror–Haunted Poe, Edgar I Am Poet Poe, Edgar the Variety Artist Poe, Hoaxiepoe, and so on. Thus, in Hoffman's view, Poe's work coheres by the singleness of his personality as a man. Hoffman's approach parallels the biographical angle adopted by critics of the Freudian school like Marie Bonaparte, Joseph Wood Krutch, and Philip Lindsay. In *Edgar Poe: Seer and Craftsman* (1972)[12] Stuart Levine maintains that Poe's fiction reveals a fine craftsmanship consistent with his aesthetic theory. In Poe's prose fiction, Levine sees a seer who "can transcend the usual limits of consciousness to glimpse a deeper and more complex, but beautiful and unified reality which is the real source of both ultimate truth and artistic beauty." However, the visions of Poe's seers are bizarre and occult and different from the supernal beauty and ultimate reality defined in "The Poetic Principle." Levine appears to be stretching too far in applying the concept of beauty to the tales whereas Poe called it the sole province of poetry. David Ketterer in *the Rationale of Deception in Poe* (1979)[13] considers Poe as "a visionary." He says: "Operating on the belief that in relation to a sensed visionary reality everyday reality constitutes one gross deception, Poe finds himself in a better position to attack the false reality than to reveal the true. He hopes to destroy a deceptive reality by means of various technical and thematic deceptions of his own" (xii–xiii), However, Ketterer's interpretation of Poe as a "visionary," being close to John F. Lynen's, sees "a development from an immediately attainable reality to a unified reality in the future with some attempt to reconcile these alternatives." Thus Ketterer too looks for unities in Poe's writings. A more interesting interpretation is David Halliburton's *Edgar Allan Poe: A Phenomenological-logical View* (1973)[14] which emphasizes "the importance, not of the artist, but of the created work of art." Halliburton maintains that "the intention caught in the work is no longer purely subjective, though it arises from an intending subjectivity. Through the act of writing, subjectivity passes into objectivity, but without losing its subjective aspect. The work therefore can neither be equated with the subjectivity from which it emanates nor divorced from it" (27). The tension between the subjective and objective in Poe's writing makes it really fascinating.

While the studies by such critics as Edward H. Davidson, Patrick F. Quinn, Richard Wilbur, G.R. Thompson, and David Ketterer deal with the visionary unities in Poe's works, there are others that recognize the paradoxical nature of the writings. One of the earlier of the more objective studies is Leon Howard's *Literature and the American Tradition* (1960).*15* The simultaneous presence in Poe's writing of the romantic and the empirical is taken by Howard as the result of "the two extremes of his affected personalities" (106). However, Poe's works are not necessarily reflections of his own personality, but on account of his conscious artistry, they are the dramatizations of the mutually opposing tendencies like the emotional and the intellectual, the subjective and the objective. As Poe says in his essay on "The American Drama" (1845), "We wish now to suggest that, by the engrafting of Reason upon Feeling and Taste, we shall be able, and thus alone shall be able, to force the modern drama into the production of any profitable fruit." Applying the same standard it is possible to say that Poe tries to evolve a new type of fiction by fusing the subjective and the objective, by rejecting the traditional norms of romance. It is difficult to agree with Howard's view that even though Poe had shown an impulse toward the prevailing attitude of mind which had developed during the eighteenth century, he "had abandoned that solid ground of American thought in the desperate egotism of *Eureka*" (Howard, 156). What is really interesting in *Eureka* is not the romantic egotism alone but the mechanistic conception of the Universe juxtaposed with a romantic vision.

In *Poe: Journalist and Critic*[16] (1969) Robert D. Jacobs discusses the empirical aspect of Poe's mind. The empirical attitude is not necessarily an assumed role to ward off the romantic element but one that came to Poe through a disciplined training as writer and critic. As Jacebs argues, the eighteenth century philosophy of Commonsense was Prevalent during Poe's time and he definitely came under its influence. It has been established by scholars like Margaret Alterton and Killis Campbell that even the romantic symbols of Poe are a result of his reading. Killis Campbell has also given an account of Poe's reading in the classical literature. Thus his knowledge of the two styles helped him in presenting both the subjective and the objective in his literary compositions. N. Bryllion Fagin in *The Histrionic Mr. Poe* (1949)[17] discusses the dramatic strain in Poe's writing. He says, "The age of Romanticism supplied an appropriate setting for his histrionic personality and his particular form of art" (58). Like any other critic of the Romantic or the Psychoanalytical school, Fagin sees Poe in his writings when he says, "his own face and mood haunt his creations" (x). Without constantly feeling the presence of Poe's personality it is possible to recognize the dramatic element in his tales. The essential drama in his creative imagination arises from a conscious juxtaposition of the rational and the irrational, the subjective and the objective.

Among the earlier psychoanalytical interpretations of Poe, those of Joseph W. Krutch[18] and Marie Bonaparte[19] deserve attention. Krutch sees the source of Poe's genius in sexual impotence and takes creative activity as a compensatory mechanism for someone who was sexually inhibited and haunted by the threat of madness. Marie Bonaparte tries to interpret art in the light of Freudian theories. She maintains that Poe's art is the product of neurosis and that Poe was a "repressed sado–masochist and necrophilist" (299). If Poe did not posses the literary genius that enabled him to sublimate his dangerous impulses in art, he might have ended up as a murderer or a madman (209), dominated by a cruel psyche. Bonaparte also says that since Poe's work reflects the fantasies of his unconscious, its real significance is autobiographical. However, a more recent critic, Roger Forclaz is more convincing when he maintains that Poe is a conscious artist who makes deliberate use of literary borrowings. Forclaz rightly asserts, referring to the psychoanalytical studies: "A system that pretends to explain literature only by means of the unconscious and of early childhood, without taking into account literary movements or the intellectual climate of an era or of a country, can hardly be called scientific."[20] Poe was a psychologist before Freud and he was making a conscious use of dream symbolism for artistic effects. In *Freud and the Critic: the Early use of depth psychology in literary criticism,* Claudia C. Morrison says: "Unlike the practitioners of psychoanalytic criticism, the theorists for the most part seem to have agreed that although the artist himself might be neurotic, the impulse to create art was a healthy one."[21] The problem of art and neurosis has been widely debated and it may be interesting to read Poe's tales as works of art in the light of the early theory.

In the 1960s and 1970s Poe was read as a psycho–moral allegorist, a "psychal transcendentalist," and a German "Romantic Ironist and Absurdist." More recently Poe has also been interpreted in the light of Jungian psychology, "duplicity" and "hoaxing" as authorial intentions, and the structuralist view of fiction as an allegory for the writing process.

Recently, under the influence of European theories of Deconstruction and Post–structuralism, critics have focused on textuality and narratdogy, psychoanalytical criticism, and "philosophical" readings of literary texts. The Lacan–Derrida controversy over "The Purloined Letter"[22] has indeed been the starting point for the recent critical exercises of the American students of Poe. Several critics have analyzed Poe's works in their theoretical or philosophical implications–John Carlos Rowe, Joseph N. Riddle, J. Gerald Kennedy, and Michael Williams.[23] Basing his study on Derrida, Riddel discusses the *Library* as a metaphor in Poe's fiction and, in a comment on "The Murders in the Rue Morgue" and "The Purloined Letter," connects it to the theme of *madness:* "The library– is a pure house of fiction, hermetic yet multi–centered. It represents the 'madness' of a will to truth, the obsessive search for the 'same rare and remarkable volume' which is at the same time a search for a maximum luxury and security, a doubling of death."[24] The reference here is to the first meeting between Dupin and the narrator in "The Murders in the Rue Morgue." The library, instead of being the haven of the scholar, turns out to be a dangerous place where death is lurking in the nooks! Such an interpretation misses the central focus of the tale–the meticulously rational pursuit of the criminal by the reasoner, a death–defying activity, unravelling the causes for the murders.

In a major recent study entitled *Poe, Death and the Life of Writing*, J. Gerald Kennedy says that in an age obsessed by death, Poe's "projections of dread have become so ingrained in modern consciousness as to lose their singularity and prescience" and that his texts are "continuous with our psychic experience" (177). According to Kennedy, repression and fixation are located in Poe's texts as well as in our own responses to them. However, he says that his approach encompasses "old and new literary history, psychobiographical criticism, literary theory, and close examination of key texts with a concern for cultural history and the anthropology of death" (ix) Kennedy argues that Poe's work foreshadows that transformation of the writer's relationship to writing which would issue in "ecriture"–"inscription in the modern sense" (186). Jacques Derrida in *Of Grammatology* calls writing "the becoming–absent and becoming–unconscious of the subject," a process enabled by "the economy of death": "All graphemes are of a testamentary essence. And the original absence of the subject of writing is also the absence of the thing or the referent."[25] According to Kennedy, Poe's texts "mark a point of convergence" (29) of the acutely modern death anxiety and the new sense of writing.

Michael J.S. Williams in *A World of Words: Language and displacement in the fiction of Edgar Allan Poe*[25A] looks at the degree to which language itself is a topic of Poe's texts. According to Williams, Poe's fiction reflects on the nature of its signifying practices. He deals with issues like Poe's characterization of the relationship between author and reader as a struggle for authority and his awareness of the displacement of an "authorial writing self" by a "self as it is written" and his debunking of the redemptive properties of the romantic symbol.

Joan Dayan, in *Fables of Mind: An Inquiry into Poe's Fiction*[26] assumes that certain Poe texts have "deeply philosophical underpinnings" despite Poe's detestation of any recognizable theme "under the text. She discusses problematic or marginal works like "The Domain of Arnheim," "Landor's Cottage," "Loss of Breath," and "Eleonora" to elucidate the doubt and instability that characterize these "fables of thought." Unlike Richard wilbur and other transcendental or visionary critics, Dayan, with her skeptical and "materialist bent," analyzes Poe's fascination with mind and his complex response to various intellectual precursors. She maintains that Poe's interest in perception and knowledge links him to both the rationalism of Locke and Hume and the Calvinism of Jonathan Edwards. Dayan's interpretation seems to be an advancement over the studies of Leon Howard and robert D. Jacobs in that she recognizes mutually opposing tendencies of Poe's mind. However, she ignores totally the need for confirming evidence, e.g., his reading of Edwards and his clear adherence to cateridge's premises. In her Deconstruction, Dayan investigates the problem of lanquage and identifies Poe's "most original stylistic trait": the rhetoric of "convertibility," and offers ingenious but imtenable readings of the "really bizarre, apprently nonsensical, and most stylistically jarring tales" (8), dealing with both problems of diction and questions of human destiny.

Recent critical interpretations have obviously overstretched Poe's meaning in his works, sometimes ignoring the author and his works. In the light of what is on the critical air today, it may be worthwhile to listen to the saner counsel of a senior scholar like Burton R. Pollin: "...(Poe) was primarily creating narratives for the sake of the story line, for their entertainment or spell–binding value, not for their implied philosophical commentary on life or on man's 'condition.' It has been necessary to consider and evaluate the many critical theories about Poe's deliberate or implied or subconscious 'purpose,' but not to regard an all-embracing theme as basic to Poe's conception or aesthetic intention....."[27]

In a recent article entitled "Post-Modernism and American Literary History" in *The Sewanee Review,*[28] David H. Hirsch maintains that "The new theories did not greatly advance our understanding of literature in particular or of the ways in which we arrive at an understanding of written utterances in general" (42). Hirsch maintains that New Critics have not really eliminated the reader, and that interpretation is a "back-and-forth process" taking place between the reader and the Poem" (41). The Reader-Response critic Stanley Fish himself seeks out image patterns, ironies, and paradoxes, just as the New Critics have instructed him to do, but, instead of attributing "meanings" to an author or a text, he attributes meanings to the mind in the act of reading.[29] Since image patterns, irony, paradoxes, the unity of the text, are all in the mind of the reader, not in the text itself, this ultimately leades him to claim illegically that the text does not exist at all. Diametrically opposed to the American reader–response theory is the intentionalist theory as propounded by E.D. Hirsch Jr. that every text has a single fixed meaning and that this fixed meaning is the "author's intention." Maintaining that "Deconstructionist ideology, that bizarre fusion of Heidegger's pagan spiritualism with Marx's dialectical materialism, is beginning to fall apart," David Hirsch says that it is ungenerous not to acknowledge the New critics' "contribution to the many democratic and expansive tendencies that broke out in American literature and culture during the seventies and eighties" (60).

In a review essay in *The Times Literary Supplement*,[30] Malcolm Bradbury expresses concern that "the New Theorists are making it clear that we live in an age of the Death of the Author, when the autonomous creative subject has been rendered problematic, when the text is the centerless center, when Portraits of the Artist have been replaced by Anxieties of Discourse" (8). He maintains that "The writer is a self–critic, as the critic is a writer; but the imaginative exploration of life and subjectivity, of fictionality and its purposes, is sensationally different when one is 'creating' from when one is 'criticizing.' That is why we benefit from the power of those aesthetic introspections and insights that come from writers themselves, and it is of these that, today, we have a significant shortage" (8). Bradbury emphatically concludes that "It is time that, passing beyond Deconstruction, we began to conceive of some creative reconstruction" (9).

In the present study, an attempt is made at a "reconstruction" of Poe in the context of the flood of recent interpretations. Wherever certain aspects of the "interpretations" (by now becoming worn out) seem helpful for a proper understanding of Poe's meaning, they have been acknowledged. In this study of the craft of Poe's tales, both the thematic and formal concerns of the author are assessed to arrive at a satisfactory meaning of both the author and the text.

NOTES

1. Quoted in A. E. Murch, *The Development of the Detective Novel* (Londo: Peter Owen Limited, 1958)83.
2. John H. Ostrom, ed. *The Letters of Edgar Allan Poe* (New York:Gordian Press, Inc., 1966), II:329. Hereafter referred to as Letters.
3. Ibid., I:5-58.
4. Ibid., II:328.
5. Quoted in George E. Woodberry, *The life of Edgan Allan Poe* (New York: Biblo and Tannen, 1965), II: 39.
6. Arthur H. Quinn, *Edgar Allan Poe: A Critical Biography* (New York: Appleton-Century-Crofts, Inc, 1941) 289.
7. Richard Wilbur, ed. *The Poems of Poe* (New York: Dell Publishing Co., Inc. 1959) 20.
8. W. H. Auden, ed. *Edgar Allan Poe: Selected Prose and Poetry* (New York: Rinehart & Co., Inc, 1950) 50.
9. Stephen Leroy Mooney, *Poe's Grand Design: A study of Theme and Unity in the Tales*. Diss. Universtiy of Tennessee, 1960: 53.
10. G. R. Thompson, *Poe's Fiction: Fomantic Irony in the Gothic Tales* (Madiso: The University of Wisconsin Press, 1973).

11. Daniel Hoffman, *Poe Poe Poe Poe Poe Poe* (Garden City, N.Y.: Doubleday and Company, Inc.,1972).
12. Stuart Levine, *Edgar Poe: Seer and Craftsman* (Deland:Everett/ Edwards, Inc., 1972).
13. David Ketterrer, *The Rationale of Decveption in Poe* (Baton Rouge: Lousisiana State University Press, 1979).
14. David Halliburton, *Edgar Allan Poe: A Phenomenological View* (Princeton: Princeton University Press, 1973).
15. Leon Howard, *Literature and the American Tradition* (Garden City, N.Y.: Doubleday Day and Co., Inc., 1960).
16. Robert D. Jacobs, *Poe: Journalist & Critc* (Baton Rouge: Lousisiana State University Press, 1969).
17. N. Bryllion fagin, *The Histrionic Mr. Poe* (Baltimore: The Johns Hopkins University Press, 1949).
18. Joseph W. Woodkrutch, *Edgar Allan Poe: a Study in Genius* (New York: Alfred A. Knopf. 1926).
19. Marie Bonaparte, *Edgar Poe: Sa Vice-Son ocuvre: Etude Analytique* (Paris: Denoel and Steele, 1933). New edition: Paris: Presses Universitaires de France, 1958.
20. Foger Forciaz, "Psychonanlysis and Edgar Allan Poe: A Fritique of the Bonaparte Thesis," *Critical Essays on Edgar Allan Poe*, ed. Eric W. Carlson (Boston: G. K. Hall & Co., 1987).
21. Claudia C. Morrison, *Freud and the Critic: the Early Use of Depth Psychlogy in Literary Criticism* (Chapel Hill: The University of North Carolina Press, 1968).
22. See jacques Lacan, "Le Seminaire Sur 'La Lettre Volee," in Ecrits 1 (Paris: Editions du Seuil, 1966, 1971); Jacques Derrida, "Le facteur de la verite," *Poetique* 21 (1975).
23. See John Rowe, "Writing and Truth in Poe's *Narrative of Arthur Gordon Pym* "Glyph 2 (Baltimore: Johns Hopkins University Press, 1977): 102-21; Joseph N. Riddel, "The 'Crypt' of Edgar Poe", *Boundary* 27, No. 3 (1979): 117-44; J. Gerald Kennedy, *Poe, Death, and Life of Writing* (New Haven: Yale University Press, 1987); and Michael J. S. Williams, *A world of Words: Lanquage and Displacement in the Fiction of Edgar Allan Poe* (Durham: Duke University Press, 1988).
24. Joseph N. Riddel, "The 'Crypt' of Edgar Allan Poe," 136.
25. Quoted in J. Gerald Kennedy, 192.

25A. Micheal J. S. Williams, *A World of Words: Language and Displacement in the Fiction of Edgar Alla Poe* (Durhan: Duke University Press, 1988).

26. Joan Dayan, *Fables of Mind: An Inquiry into Poe's Fiction* (New York: Oxford University Press, 1987).
27. Burton R. Pollin, ed. *Edgar Allan Poe: The Imaqinary Voyages: Thhe Narrative of Arthur Gordon Pym, The unparalleled Adventure of one Hans Pfaall.The Journal of Julius Rodman* (Boston: Twayne Publishers, 1981) xvi.
28. David H. Hirsch, "Postmodernism and American Literary History," *The Wewanee Review*, XCIX, i (Winter 1991): 40-60.
29. Also see J. Timothy Bagwell, *American Formalism and the Problem of Interpretation* (Houston, Texas: Rice University Press, 1986). Bagwell proposes "a *semantic* understanding of the notion ofthe intentional fallacy and the formalism it aims at; in othher words, I will attempt to defend the notion of what Hirsch calls "semantic autonomy" by showing how it is not the contradiction in terms it seems to be." (3)
30. Malcolm bradbury, "The Bridgeable Gap: Bringing together the Creative Writer and the Critical theorist in an Authorless World," The Times Literary Supplement, No. 4633, January, 17, 1992: 7-9.

2
THE FICTIONAL PRINCIPLE

Let me only add the in this Art, as in the others, there is, and will be always, whatever has been done already, something new to discover, something new to express, some- thing new to describe.

Walter Besant
The Art of Fiction (1884)

The rhetorician's rule–if they *are* rules, teach him not only to name his tools, but to use his tools, the capacity of his toolc, thoir oxtont, thoir limit; and from an examination of the nature of the tools (an examination forced on him by their constant presence), force him, also, into scrutiny and comprehension of the material on which the tools are employed, and thus, finally, suggest and give birth to new materials for new tools.

Edgar Allan Poe,
"Marginalia"

The successful application of any art is a delightful spectacle, but the theory too is interesting; and though there is a great deal of the latter without the former I suspect there has never been a genuine success that has not had a latent core of conviction.

Henry James,
The Art of Fiction

> Objectivity is also increased by constant reference to theory. A judgment can be clarified and expressed only in concepts, and concepts assume distinctness only in an assumed system.
>
> Rene Welleck,
> *A History of Modern Criticism.*

According to William Charvat, in the quarter century preceding Poe the critics had almost no guidance in the field of fiction. In fact, American criticism of fiction began after 1815. Earlier fiction was not either noticed or only attacked or moral grounds by reputable critical journals.[1] Robert D. Jacobs says that Poe based his standards "partly on tradition and partly on rules that he invented for himself."[2] Poe's review of Hawthorne's *Twice–Told Tales* (1842) was indeed the first American statement of the principle of preconceived effect, which, according to Margaret Alterton,[3] derived ultimately from A. W. Schlegel through *Blackwood's Magazine.*

Washington Irving was the first tentatively to define the tale in a letter written in 1824: There is a constant activity of thought and a nicety of execution required in writings of this kind, more than the world appears to imagine in these shorter writings every page must have its merit...woe to him if he makes an awkward sentence or writes a stupid page.[4] Even though Irving recognizes the need for workmanship and attention to detail, he does not mention unity of effect which is the main principle of Poe's tale-writing. In fact, in his letter of June 21, 1841 to Irving, Poe emphasizes the need for "the brief, the terse, the condensed" tale for popular reading.[5]

In a review of *National Tales* published in Bryant's *New York Review* in 1825 the critic said that tales, as distinct from novels, would require talents of a peculiar, though lesser, kind. They do not call for as much development of character and fullness of description and dialogue, but they do require vivacity of narration, and more point and polish of style. While the tale is a miniature, the novel is a full–length picture.

Plot is important in both, though in each it calls for a different execution.[6]

On a survey of the American literary situation in the nineteenth century, Charvat concludes that Poe derived his principle of preconceived effect neither from A.W. Schlegel through *Blackwood's* (as Margaret Alterton says), nor from Irving or any other contemporary writer but from his own original development of the form.[7] In his review of Nathaniel Hawthorne's *Twice–Told Tales* (1842) Poe describes the prose tale as "the short prose narrative, requiring from a half–hour to one or two hours in its perusal."[8] Before the end of the nineteenth century this short prose narrative was usually known as a "tale." Writers of earlier times, like Giovanni Boccaccio and Geoffrey Chaucer too called it so, realizing the rich possibilities of the form in their own writings. Subsequently, British and European writers took up the form and extended it. In the United States, Washington Irving continued the tradition. But it was only Edgar allan Poe who developed this form of prose composition with a distinctive theory applicable to writings beyond his own times. Later, the form came to be known as "short story."

John Gardner and Lennis Dunlap, among others, have shown the distinctions between several short forms like the sketch, the fable, the tale, and the short story.[9] They do not consider the "tale" and the "short story" as being the same literary composition. Northrop Frye says that just as prose romance is different from the novel, the tale form used by Poe is different from the short story. According to him, the romance is distinguished by "subjective intensity"; it does not deal with "real people" in the framework of a stable society but "stylized figures which expand into psychological archetypes."[10] Edmund Clarence Stedman class Poe a "romancer."[11] Poe's contemporary Henry W. Longfellow too called him a "romance-writer."12 It may be profitable to observe, in the course of an analysis of Poe's tales, whether his characters are stylized figures as in a romance or individuals as in a short story.

Despite the fact that reality does not enter the reader's mind while perusing the tale, the tale as such need not entirely be unrealistic. The psychological truth that it represents brings it close to nature and to actuality. It is in this sense that the tale form employed by the nineteenth–century writers comes close to the modern short story. In fact, T.O. Mabbott feels that Poe "thought a tale *ought to be* what we now usually call a short story."[13] Rip Van Winkle may be a character in a romantic tale; but he does remind us of certain indisputable psychological truths. What the tale–writer does is to give the characters in the story sufficient "human interest and resemblance", as Coleridge says. He does not actually compare that human interest with the world of the actual. The world of the tale becomes credible when the writer skilfully manipulates character, setting, and plot.

The short story exploits the principle of rising tension toward a climax, culminating in an effective denouement. Thus the plot of the short story, unlike that of the tale, is unified. Even by Poe's time the loose sort of story-telling gave way to a single incident or episode. Its interest having been centred on acting, it would consist of stirring incidents and pungent style.[14]

In the light of these affinities or divergences between the tale and the short story, it may be interesting to observe what Poe himself has to say about the short prose narrative which has made him so famous across the continents.

Origins of the Fictional Principle:

According to Poe, the end of the tale is the creation of a central unitary impression. As early as 1836, he mentioned "what is rightly termed by Schlegel, 'the *unity or totality of interest*'".[15] The attainment of such a single impression depends largely on the themes and methods of composition that the author chooses. Poe as a writer of the tale was very scrupulous in the choice of his themes and methods of narration. Michael Allen and Robert D. Jacobs have argued that a wide reading of the popular magazines and authors of his time, American, British, and German, helped him in his choices.[16] While admitting in his letter of April 30, 1835 to Thomas W. White that the subject of "Berenice" is "by far too horrible," Poe refers to the taste of the reading public for morbidity:

> The history of all Magazines shows plainly that those which have attained celebrity were indebted for it to articles *similar in nature–to Berenice*–although I grant you, far superior in style and execution. I say similar in *nature*.[7]

While in some respects Poe was catering to the needs of his readers, in other respects he was trying to correct the notions of the public about serious literature. In his letter to James Russell Lowell, the co-editor of *The Pioneer*, he refers to "a certain coincidence of opinion & of taste" between himself and Russell. The prospectus of *The Pioneer* says:

> The object of the subscribers in establishing *The Pioneer* is to furnish the intelligent and reflecting portion of the Reading Public with a rational substitute for the enormous quantity of thrice–diluted trash, in the shape of namby–pamby love tales and sketches, which is monthly poured out to them by many of our popular magazines....[18]

Poe's mission as an editor and writer had been to shape the taste of his readers. His reviews of contemporary writers do show his concern to provide "a rational substitute for the enormous quantity of thrice–diluted trash."

Blackwood's Edinburgh Magazine was one of Poe's sources in regard to the subject matter and the technique. His interest in the *Magazine* was obviously more than superficial. In the postscript to his letter of September 11, 1839 to Joseph Evans Snodgrass he says: "I have made a profitable engagement with Blackwood's Mag....[19] Certain themes of terror like the supernatural, life–in–death, Galvanic Battery, beauty with disease, and premature burial, found in the British periodical, had been fully exploited by him in his compositions. In his review of Hawthorne's *Twice–Told Tales* (1842), Poe praises.

> ...those *tales of effect,* many fine examples of which were found in the earlier numbers of "Blackwood." The impressions produced were wrought in a legitimate sphere of action, and constituted a legitimate although sometimes an exaggerated interest (VII, 33).

"How to Write a Blackwood Article" (1838) describes, though in a burlesque tone, the very methods that Poe copied from the British periodical. As a magazinist he had to satisfy the taste of the contemporary reading public which was found of the German and the British horror writing. Margaret Alterton suggests that besides the thematic materials, Poe got his main critical principle of unity of effect from A.W. Schlegel whom he had known probably through *Blackwood's*. However, scholars like James Southall Wilson and Prescott are of the opinion that Poe might have read A. W. Schlegel's *Lectures* translated by John Black in 1815, included in "Bohn's Standard Library."[20] Poe's interest in Schlegel's ideas on drama is a result of his book-reviewing and attempts at play-writing.[21] Floyd Stovall says that Poe abandoned Schlegel's phrase, "Unity of Interest" for the sake of Coleridge's "Unity of Effect" or "Unity of Impression."[22] However, in his review of *Longfellow's Ballads and Other Poems,* Poe himself attributes the term "unity or totality of interest" to Schlegel (VI, 129). As Stovall contends, Poe could have met with the same term in Coleridge too whom he refers to in his *Letter to B–*(1831), his earliest work of criticism, being the Preface to his 1831 *Poems*.

Poe's ultimate aim is to create in the consciousness of the reader what James Southall Wilson would call "a definite psychological state,"[23] subordinating every other consideration to that end. In the words of Poe,

> ...for that undeniably may be considered great (of whatever seeming littleness in itself) which is capable of inducing intense emotion in the minds or hearts of those who are themselves undeniably great (VII, 284).

Thus the unified effect that Poe aims to produce is one of intense emotion. While Schlegel applies the concept of unity of effect to drama, Poe applies it to the poem and to the tale as well. Whereas Schlegel applies it to the psychology of the audience, Poe applies it to the psychology of the single reader. In this context, Schlegel's words make interesting reading:

> The object proposed [the object of the drama] is to produce an impression on an assembled multitude, to rivet their attention, and to excite their interest and sympathy.[24]

Underlying Poe's theory of the intensity and unity of effect is the idea of communication with the reader or reviewer.

> ...true originality...is that which, in bringing out the half–formed, the reluctant, or the unexpressed fancies of mankind, or in exciting the more delicate pulses of the heart's passion, or in giving birth to some universal sentiment or instinct in embryo, thus combines with the pleasurable effect of *apparent* novelty, a real egoistic delight.. [The reader] is filled with an intrinsic and extrinsic delight. He feels and intensely enjoys it as really novel, is absolutely original with the writer–*and* himself. They two, he fancies, have, alone of all men, thought thus. They two have, together, created this thing. Henceforward there is a bond of sympathy which irradiates every subsequent page of the book (VII, 23).

The "intrinsic" and "extrinsic" delight of the reader thus contributes to the attuning of his sensibility with the writer's.[25]

The psychological process of producing an effect on the reader's mind by carefully controlling his responses is achieved by means of suspense. This is done steadily through the sequential parts and functional parts of the work of art. By making one part lead logically to the other and evoking the reader's sense of curiosity, the writer succeeds in keeping up the sequence of narration for unflagging attention. The reader should be made to ask, as E. M. Forster puts it, " 'and then– and then–' "[26] This is what M. H. Abrams calls "an anxious uncertainty about what is going to happen, especially to those characters with whom we have established bonds of sympathy."[27] Poe's theory of the compositional method conforms not only to the traditional mode of suspense but to a more recent theory presented by Eric S. Rabkin. According to him, suspense is involved not only in the plot of a narrative, but in its thematic development, character development, and style as well. As he puts it, "the diachronic structure which is the plot is but one of the diachronic structures which cooperate to create the entire fabric of a narrative."[28] Thus even though Poe has not elaborated a theory of suspense, through his narrative strategy based on logical connection of incidents he anticipates a modern theory like Rabkin's.

Effect, on which Poe lays so much emphasis, is not an absolute. What comes as an intense effect on one's reader's sensibility may leave another disappointed. The intensity of effect depends upon the degree of emotional and intellectual maturity of the reader, in addition to the attitude with which he approaches a work of art. Poe's tales are broadly divided into four categories: 1) the Gothic; 2) the Grotesque/Comic; 3) the Ratiocinative; 4) the Visionary and the Beautiful. These categories have different types of effect on different types of readers and all the categories may not have the same "intensity" of effect. In addition, the tales of a specific category may not have the same intensity of effect on all the readers. The effect of the tale of ratiocination (based on intellectual curiosity with an initial emotional build-up) loses its grip on the reader once the solution is arrived at. The grotesque tale tickles the reader's wry sense of humor and his critical attitude toward social foibles. However, the reader does not identify himself with the character, or get emotionally involved in the situation. On the other hand, he laughs with the characters as well as at them, always maintaining a certain distance. The sketches under the category of "the Visionary and the Beautiful," though, strictly speaking, not tales proper, evoke a poetic atmosphere.

Whether Poe's concept of the "Unity of Effect" is taken from Coleridge or from Schlegel, what he intends to achieve as a tale–writer is not Romantic vagueness but Classical clarity.

In "The Philosophy of Composition" he has categorically stated that a work of art is the result of careful construction, but not of inspiration.[29] However, writing in an age of Romanticism, he could not help coming under the influence of the British Romantics in that he adopts concepts like the death of a beautiful woman in his poems and tales. Killis Campbell has described the extent of Poe's reading in the British Romantics."[30] Sometimes Poe would venture into what Coleridge calls "the twilight realms of consciousness, and ...a deep interest in modes of inmost being."[31] However, in spite of such excursions into the penumbral zones of experience, Poe is Classical too. As Rene Wellek says, Coleridge himself "carries enough of the Aristotelian and empirical tradition to make the idealistic elements palatable."[32] Poe takes Coloridge's distinction of Poetry Vs science and makes it Poety Vs fiction, so that truth (in Coloridge, of science) becomes "truth in prose fiction."[33] Poe's choice of the Romantic themes or concepts was governed by the exigencies of the times. While thus catering to contemporary taste, he could retain the essential Classical spirit of his writing. Poe's acquaintance with Classical lore has been acknowledge.[34] His empirical attitude was reinforced by his interest in contemporary science and scientific theories.[35] Speaking about the American literary situation in general, William Charvat says, "Classicism was in the blood of our criticism, for Romantic fiction was never greeted with whole–souled and universal unthusiasm."[36] Charvat has shown that the most popular periodicals in America during Poe's youth were the *Edinburgh Review, the Quarterly Review,* and Campbell's *New Monthly Magazine*, all of which were edited by Scots in the critical and philosophical tradition of the Common–sense School. Theirs was the most significant philosophical tradition between the time of the Revolution and the time Poe began to write reviews.[37] Robert D. Jacobs argues that the influence of the Scottish Common–sense School on Poe, though covert, is nevertheless there.[38]

Critics like Edward H. Davidson, Richard Wilbur, Patrick F. Quinn, Sheldon W. Liebman, Daniel Hoffman, and Stuart Levine have taken the symbolist and poetic approaches to the work of Poe. The fact that there are certain themes and technical terms common to Poe's theory of poetry and of the tale is taken to mean the Poe's tales are primarily geared toward the poetic effect of Beauty.[39] However, Poe makes this distinction between the tale and the poem: whereas Beauty is the province of the poem, the tale should aim at truth.[40] As he affirms in "The Poetic Principle," Beauty should predominate over Passion and Truth in a poem:

> ...but the true artist will always contrive to tone them down ["the incitements of Passion, the precepts of Duty, or even the lessons of Truth"] in proper subjection to that Beauty which is the atmosphere and real essence of the Poem (VI, 13).

In addition, Poe differentiates the short prose narrative from the short poem:

> The writer of the prose tale, in short, may bring to his theme a vast variety of modes or inflections of thought or expression (the ratiocinative for example, the sarcastic, or the humorous), which are not only antagonistic to the nature of the poem, but absolutely forbidden by one of its most peculiar and indispensable adjuncts; we allude, of course, to rhythm (VII, 32).

The basis of Poe's preference for the tale over the poem is the former's susceptibility to deal with "a vast variety of modes or inflections of thought or expression," which is not possible in the poem. Subjects suitable for tales of effect, terror or passion, cannot be treated in the poem wherein only Beauty can be properly represented. The province of the tale is Truth. When Poe describes the tale of ratiocination as the form embodying Truth, he does not mean poetic truth but "truth in prose friction." According to J. Lasley Dameron, "Poe's treatment of truth seems bath profoundly abstract and teasingly complex, and yet in line with the Coherence theory of truth of own day."[40-A]

Poe's theory of fiction adopts the basic principles of dramatic writing. In the opinion of Margaret Alterton, his "brief article" is "allied to a dramatic composition, and depends for its effect on the same rules that govern the drama."[41] It is possible that Poe applied the principles of dramatic art, expounded by Schlegel, to his own theory of fiction. Burton R. Polliu discusses his many uses Schlegel. But Poe's understanding of the principles of drama might have been born of his interest in the contemporary theaters in New York. It is well known that he always had friends on the stage. His journalist friend William E. Burton (of *Burton's Magazine*) was a fine comedian. Arthur H. Quinn says that Poe, as Editor of *The Broadway Journal,* had access to the theaters and used to attend them frequently. When Mrs. Mowatt presented *Fashion* in New York in 1840, Poe is said to have attended every performance, and even to have made suggestions. Also he had known a Shakespearean actor named Murdoch, who wrote for *The Broadway journal.*[43] This sense of the theater and a keen interest in the techniques of dramatic writing is evident in Poe's creative writing and criticism.[44]

The range of material of the short prose narrative being limited, the fundamental unity of design is normally provided by a single situation in the life of the main character. This, in addition to the concepts of the unity of effect and reader–response, establishes the affinity of the tale with the drama. While there should be a chain of mutually dependent incidents, even a single situation may sometimes produce the necessary effect. The main characters are prominent in their relation to each other and to the environment. Dialogue, a vividly pictured scene, concentration on a single issue, and isolation of a limited number of characters, are the constituents of drama. In the tales of Poe all these elements are amply present.

The controlling idea of the unity of effect, Poe's main preoccupation since 1836, continued right up to the end of his literary career. It is for this reason that he looked down upon the longer forms of composition. He tried his hand at sustained narration only twice in his career, first in *The Narrative of Arthur Gordon Pym* published in two instalments in the *Southern Literary Messenger* for January and February

1837 and separately as a "finished" book in 1838 and second, in *The Journal of Julius Rodman,* published in *Burton's Gentleman's Magazine* from January through June 1840. Of *Julius Rodman,* a fragment, Poe thought so little that he did not attempt to print it separately or to collect it among his tales. In this narrative, Poe did try to build up a character in Julius Rodman, having established his emotional nature, but he did not fully carry out his intention. Despite the fact that *Pym* was a more sustained effort, it had failed as a narrative, and Poe himself called it "a very silly book."[45] In 1837, Poe moved from Virginia to New York in search of literary reputation. In fact, he left the *Southern Literary Messenger* of was ousted by White for drunkenness and thought New York city as a publication centre, to be more art for a job. During the months he stayed in New York, he decided, on Harper's advice, to write a long story. Even though *Pym* was reprinted several times in England, it was a failure. In the words of Arthur H. Quinn, "The only significant result of his experiments in the long story was to prove to him that his ability lay in the writing of shorter fiction."[46] These experiments might have confirmed Poe in his conviction that the unitary impression could be better produced by the shorter composition. Such an impression cannot be produced by the novel not only because of the profusion of the material involved but also because the book cannot be read at a single sitting. Other interests inevitably break in upon the mind between intervals of reading. Hence Poe asserts in his review of Hawthorne's *Twice–Told Tales:*

> The tale proper, in my opinion, is unquestionably the fairest field for the exercise of the loftiest talent, which can be afforded by the wide domains of mere prose (VII, 29).

He is unequivocal in maintaining that unity of effect "is indispensable in the 'brief article,' and not so in the common novel" (VII, 280). Whereas the tale as a whole is admired for the unity of effect, even the disconnected passages of a novel may sometimes be admired. Poe dismisses the novel because "it cannot be read at one sitting," thus depriving itself of the "immense force derivable from totality." And "simple cessation in reading would, of itself, be sufficient to destroy the true unity" (VII, 31). As Poe says in "The Philosophy of Composition," "If any literary work is too long to be read at one sitting, we must be content to dispense with the immensely important effect derivable from unity of impression; for, if two sittings be required, the affairs of the world interfere, and everything like totality is at once destroyed". Horatio E. Smith has argued that Poe applied these norms to the longer narrative also.[47] Poe underrates Dickens' *Barnaby Rudge* on account of the looseness of its structure. Bulwer's *Night and Morning,* in his view, is defective because of its strained effect of unity. Burton R. Pollin tells us that Poe faced a dilemma in his preference for the tale "since the majority of the books sent him for reviewing were novels"[47-A]. The December 1835 number of the *Southern Literary Messenger*, the first issue to be edited by Poe, seems to have marked Poe's preference for the tale to the novel. In his review of Lady Dacre's *Tales of the Peerage and Peasantry*, Poe praises her artistry in achieving "unity of effect":

> An every day writer would have ended a story of continued sorrow and suffering with a bright gleam of unalloyed happiness, and sunshine—thus destroying, at a single blow, that indispensable unity which has been rightly called the unity of effect, and throwing down, as it were, in a paragraph what, perhaps, an entire volume has been laboring to establish.

While Poe's argument concerning the need for brevity of the literary composition is somewhat convincing, one cannot help wondering whether longer fiction is worth the reader's perusal. Certain types of longer fiction are so engaging and the reader is so much involved in the experience of the fictional world that it is simply impossible for him to escape the spell caste on him. Even a temporary "cessation" of reading does not lessen the intensity of effect but keeps the reader's attention psychologically uninterrupted. Poe admits that mere length may not deter the work of art from producing the desired impression:

> Common-sense, in the time to come, may possibly insist upon measuring a work of art rather by the object it fulfills, by the impression it makes, than by the time it took to fulfill the object, or by the extent of "sustained effort" which became necessary to produce the impression.[48]

Having thus preferred the shorter prose narrative to both the poem and the novel, Poe aims to make the impression visual too. His reviews abound in artistic terminology and his own creative writing employs devices like chiaroscure. In his review of Hawthorne's *Twice-Told Tales,* referring to originality in a work of art, he insists upon "novelty" of combination, involving a variety of incidents. It is like the painter achieving his effects with varying combinations of colors. Poe has also said that in the tale proper, the writer should exclude all irrelevant elements and achieve a more direct conveyance of mood and of narrative idea. Poe stresses the identity of the general principal governing painting and literature. As he puts it, "the principal rules of the plastic arts, founded as they surely are in a true perception of the beautiful, will apply in their fullest force to every species of literary composition." Henry James too, in "The Art of Fiction," establishes an analogy between painting and literature: "the analogy between the art of the painter and the art of the novelist is, so far as I am able to see, complete. Their inspiration is the same, their process (allowing for the different quality of the vehicle) is the same, their success is the same."[49] In a recent study of "Poe and His Illustrators," "Burton R. Pollin says that Poe's insistence on detail in his criticism of fiction and his presenting of striking details like the hiss of the pendulum, the fainting of Pym on the brink of the precipice, and the sinister waving of draperies in "Ligeia" would be significant from the point of view of painting.[50] In fact, Poe's interest in the painting devices can be traced to the origins of his creative writing itself. He used to display considerable talent for drawing when he was at the University of Virginia and in his later years he was personally acquainted with contemporary artists like S.S.

Osgood and R. M. Sully. In addition, he used to write art–criticism for *The Broadway Journal*.[51]

It is generally said that Poe's philosophy of the cosmic unity greatly influenced his literary theory. Margaret Alterton says that his study of philosophy enabled him to enlarge and strengthen his power of thinking, and consequently his comprehension of the Principle of Unity.[52] Poe's fictional principle parallels his philosophical theory of the Unity of the Universe, developed in *Eureka*. Just as the atoms in the Universe tend toward a single Unity so also the atoms of a fictional work constitute its organic structure. Poe speaks of the Divine Adaptation in the organization of the Cosmos and aptly compares it with the adaptation of the elements of a fictional work and maintains that the Divine Plot is perfect, whereas human construction is less than perfect.[53] The question arises whether Poe's philosophical thinking came first and shaped his aesthetic principle—the principle of unity–or the converse. In fact, Poe's philosophical position crystallized much toward the end of his career, in 1848, when *Eureka* was published, whereas his ideal of unity in art had been an important aspect of his theory much earlier. Despite the fact that in "The Conversation of Eiros and Charmion" (1839), "The Colloquy of Monos and Una" (1841), and "Mesmeric Revelation" (1844) Poe tried to discuss certain cosmic issues, it was only in *Eureka* that his philosophical principle of the Unity of the Universe took shape. Whether it was the philosophy or the aesthetics that came first, the structure of the Universe and the structure of an ideal fictional composition are, in Poe's view, identical. This parallelism has led some critics to read Poe's tales in the light of *Eureka*.

Aspects of a Theory of the Tale

The year 1831 marked the creation of Poe's first short stories.[54] While his connection with the *Southern Literary Messenger* was still in an uncertain state, Poe entered into correspondence with other authors, discussing principles of composition. What he gained by way of this correspondence added to his readings in the British and the European theorists.

The principle of Unity, originating sometime in 1836, became the governing principle of his critical theory by 1846 when "The Philosophy of Composition" was published.

According to Poe, the literary artist's principles of composition are governed by his imaginative power. Hence he admires Dickens' *Curiosity shop* for its "vigorous and glorious imagination."[55] Subject matter is the clay with which the creative artist works, by means of his imaginative power, to shape the work:

> In the hands of the *true* artist the theme, or "work," is but a mass of clay, of which anything (within the compass of the mass and quality of the clay) may be fashioned at will, or according to the skill of the workman (VII, 226).

In addition to the choice of the subject-matter and the general handling of the material, Poe prescribes perseverance in the construction of a work of art. Hence he blames John Neal for his impatience as a craftsman:

> His art is great and of a high character—but it is massive and undetailed. He seems to be either deficient in a sense of completeness, or unstable in temperament; so that he becomes wearied with his work before getting it done (VII, 265).

Another mark of greatness in a work of art, in Poe's opinion, is originality and novelty. He speaks of the necessity of literary originality at great length in his review of Hawthorne's *Twice-Told Tales*. The essence of what Poe says about originality in writing is best summed up in the following passage :

> They ["those who have a right to be called critical"] regard as original in letters, only such combinations of thought, of incident, and so forth, as are in fact, absolutely novel. It is clear, however, not only it is the novelty of *effect* alone which is worth consideration, but that also this effect is *best* wrought, for the end of all fictitious composition, pleasure, by shunning rather

> than by seeking the absolute novelty of combination. Originality, thus understood, tasks and startles the intellect, and so brings into undue action the faculties to which in the lighter literature, we least appeal (VII, 22–23).

Even though there is nothing really "original" about Poe's plea for originality, it is significant the he too, like many an eminent writer, emphasizes the novelty of combination. Thus in his view, novelty and originality are not so much of the materials used for a literary construction as the way they are "combined." In his own creative writing, Poe's originality consists in the way his materials, borrowed largely from contemporary sources, are combined to produce works that have captivated generations of readers.

Basic to an understanding of Poe's fictional principle is his review of Hawthorne's *Twice–told Tales* (1842). In that review, he says that an ideal artist, having first chosen a certain unique or single *effect,* "invents such incidents–he then combines such events as may best aid him in establishing this preconceived effect" (VII, 31). Thus, according to Poe, the ideal artist proceeds from a preconceived design. In this sense his concept parallels the eighteenth–century concept of the universe planned by God. It is mechanistic like the Newtonian cosmology.

G.R. Thompson, making a distinction between Poe's concept of the late and Hawthorne's says:

> The modes of both Poe and Hawthorne may be clarified by an examination of Poe's somewhat closed–minded inclination in favor of his own style of narrative–what he considered the "tale proper'–and the politics of literary culture in which his definitions took shape. By contrast, the concept of the "romantic sketch" as practised by Hawthorne demonstrates the artistry of Hawthorne's narrative praxis of "authorial presence," so radically misjudged by Poe.[56]

Poe appreciates Robert R. Bird's "Sheppard Lee" because "Its incidents are well conceived, and related with force, brevity, and a species of *directness* which is invaluable in certain cases of narration–while in others it should be avoided." (VII, 88-89). Only a certain logical relation of incidents and directness of narration would contribute to the effect that the author intends to produce. However, Poe is cautious enough to realize that

> A mere succession of incidents, even the most spirited, will no more constitute a plot, than a multiplication of zeros, even the infinite, will result in the production of a unit... ...a plot, properly understood, is perfect only inasmuch as we shall find ourselves unable to detach from it or disarrange any single incident involved, without destruction to the mass.[57]

It is not a "mere succession" of incidents but a logical sequence that should make up a plot. In saying that in a good plot no part can be displaced "without destruction to the mass," Poe has stressed the Aristotelian requirement:

> ...the plot, being an imitation of an action, must imitate one action and that a whole, the structural union of the parts being such that, if any one of them is displaced or removed, the whole will be disjointed and disturbed.
>
> *(Butcher's Translation)*

This Aristotelian conviction is strengthened by Poe's view in "A Chapter of Suggestions" that "*Plot* is very imperfectly understood, and has never been rightly defined. Many persons regard it as mere complexity of incident." (VIII, 329). According to William Charvat, Poe makes a definite contribution to technique in his emphasis on close–knit plot construction.[58] In his review of Francis Marryatt's "Joseph Rushbrook," Poe speaks of one incident "begetting" another (VII, 82). Referring to Cooper's "Wyandotte," he says: "The tale is a mere succession of events, scarcely any one of which has any necessary dependence on another" (VII, 7). Thus Poe questions the Irvingesque tale of loosely linked incidents and insists upon a basic dramatic structure. He is interested primarily in "that connecting chain which unites into one proper whole the varied events" of the narrative. Thus by visualizing the connecting chain, Poe would like to get to the heart of the narrative, i.e., its "thought" or theme:

> ...mere incidents whether serious or comic, whether occurring (i.e., dramatized) or described–*mere incidents* are not books. Neither are they the basis of books—of which the idiosyncracy is thought in contradistinction from *deed.* A book without action cannot be; but a book is only such, to the extent of its thought, independently of its deed.

The emphasis on "thought" is central to Poe's preference for the Enlightenment spirit in writing.

Poe's insistence on the architectonic structure of the plot is in consonance with his anti–Romantic stance as a theorist. In his review of Charles Dickens' *Barnaby Rudge*, he finds fault with the novelist for violating the unities of time and place.[59] John Paul Pritchard says: "The information from the *Poetics*... came to Poe piecemeal, but aided him immeasurably in the gradual formulation of his demand for unity."[60] In insisting upon a proper beginning, development, and conclusion, Poe has obviously the Aristotelian precept in mind. Aristotle tells us that plot, character, thought, and diction are the four qualitative "parts" common to tragedy and epic. These four ingredients are treated in the *Poetics* not as co-ordinate topics, but hierarchically in a causal sequence of form–matter or end–means relationships in which "plot is the most inclusive or architectonic." Explaining Aristotle's position, R. S. Crane has observed that "Plots will differ in structure according as one or another of the causal ingredients is employed as the synthesizing principle. There are, thus, plots of action, plots of character, and plots of thought."[61] Poe's theory of the plot too may be said to point toward such division.

Poe insists that character and incident be subservient to the dominant plot–structure. But he is aware that sometimes a good story can be written without plot. Reviewing Cooper's *Wyandotte*, he says:

> Plot, however, is at best an artificial effect, requiring, like music, not only a natural bias, but long cultivation of taste for its full appreciation; some of the finest narratives in the world–"Gil–Blas" and "Robinson Crusoe," for example–have been written without its employment;... (VII, 7-8).

If the unit in poetry is the word, in fiction it is the event. This event constitutes the action which in turn defines character. The plot, inclusive of all these elements, is a complex whole. Not only did Aristotle influence Poe but the later theorists too emphasized this aspect of fiction. Differentiating between story and plot, E. M. Forster says that plot arises from causal connection.[62] This causal connection might arise out of what walter O'Grady calls the interior situation and the exterior situation of the character.[63] According to him, plot is nothing but the flow "between the interrelated parts."[64] While it is difficult to find in Poe the kind of "interior situation" presented in Henry James on account of the limited character–development, what Walter O'Grady says might well be relevant for Poe since he draws a distinction between incident and event, even though he does not elaborate on that. An incident is obviously something presented in external terms whereas an event suggests an "interior situation."[65] In the opinion of Marvin Mudrick,

> Most great fiction generates interest through those of its events which establish a community of complex individual lives; through the events which dramatize the collisions between these lives, it achieves intensity.[66]

Thus events in a work of fiction contribute to the complexity of character and this complexity in turn determines action and plot. According to Aristotle, plot is the imitation of action, it is the arrangement of incidents. And fiction is the representation in language of an action that is not real but probable. In the course of the perusal of a tale, the reader gets involved in the consequences of an action for a certain character or for several characters. In his emphasis on plot at the expense of character, Poe is nearer Aristotle. Even though he maintains that in the short prose narrative no development of character is possible, he does not altogether ignore character as such. In fact, in the best fiction, plot and character are correlative. In modern fiction, the individual takes precedence over everything else. Poe is modern in the sense that in his tales he is concerned with the study of the individual that is at odds with society and with himself.

Poe says, in "The Philosophy of Composition," that the literary artist should consider whether the effect "can be wrought by incident or tonne---whether by ordinary incidents and peculiar tone, or the converse, or by peculiarity both of incident and tone..." (VI, 32). Unity of effect can thus be achieved by the combination of incident and tone in different ways. And the predominance of either may determine the structure of a work of art. If the incidents are to predominate, they should logically cohere. Thus unity of effect is achieved through unity of plot. If the tone is to predominate, it must be single and unified. Disharmony of tone in a literary composition, as cacophony in music, produces nothing but a confused effect.[67]

Deniel Haffman calls "The Philosophy of Composition" "an intricate mechanism for the production of the effects of passion."[68] However, Stephen Railton is more communising when he moves, with schlegel and the other theorists of Romantaism, the definition of a successful work of art into the subjective realm: " 'Unity' is not a formal concept (dependent on such external qualities as time and place and action), but a psychological one, with its source in the mind of the responding of audience."[69]

In "How to Write a Blackwood Article," Poe speaks (although in a burlesque manner) of different tones such as "the tone didactic," "the tone enthusiastic," "the tone natural," "the tone elevated, diffusive, and interjectional," "the tone transcendental," and "the tone heterogeneous." Mr. Blackwood tells psyche Zenobia: "Having determined upon your subject, you must next consider the tone, or manner, of your narration" (IV, 204).

By means of one of the many attitudes that the writer can assume, he produces an emotional effect on the reader.

Tone in a literary composition, the manner of narration, as Poe puts it, is the author's attitude toward his subject–matter. It is related to feeling and involves conscious emotional commitment on the part of the author. As I. A. Richards says, the author "chooses or arranges his words differently as his audience varies, in automatic or deliberate recognition of his relation to them."[70] Tone implies the author's relation to both his subject–matter and the audience. Feeling being very much a part of the texture of the story, the reader is likely to relate it to the subject rather than to himself. The author, however, might deliberately alternate his attention between the reader and the subject–matter. Tonal variations, as Wayne C. Booth tells us, may enable the reader to understand some aspects of the implied author. The major qualities of the implied author, however, depend also on the hard facts of action and character in the tale.[71] The form and content relationship is stressed by Mark Schorer when he says,

> ...technique is the means by which the writer's experience, which is his subject matter, compels him to attend to it; technique is the only means he has of discovering, exploring, developing his subject, of conveying its meaning, and finally of evaluation it.[72]

Even though Poe appears to be overemphasizing the technical aspects of a fictional composition, he discovers a variety of themes through a variety of techniques.

According to Poe, a skillful writer, Poe says, should develop his idea logically through character and incident, having established it at the initial sentence itself. The feelings evoked in the opening paragraph may sometimes proceed in a set pattern and evoke a mixed reaction on the part of the reader since different actions may have different emotional values. In addition, the varying responses of the character may contribute to the variability of the mood. The author is successful in his airns if the emotions he evokes are identified with specific objects or events. Through what T. S. Eliot would call the "objective correlative," the evocation of feelings brings the reader close to the emotional content of the tale. Thus by means of the mood in a fictional composition the author renders in more or less subtle manner his feelings about the subject. Authorial voice in fiction as a device to control character and incident and the reader's response has been employed by writers since Fielding. In his review of Captain Marryat's "Joseph Rushbrook," Poe syas:

> The commenting force can never by safely discarded. It is far better to have a dearth of incident, with skillful observations upon it, than the utmost variety of event, without (VII, 83).

The reviewer questions Marryat's narration for the absence of the "binding power" which, according to him, "gives a species of unity (unity of the writer's individual thought) to the most random narration" (VII, 83). This "binding power" is what the twentieth-century theorists of fiction like Percy Lubbock and Wayne C. Booth would call "authorial comment." It is also, in the words of Booth, "Molding Beliefs" or "Manipulating Mood."[73] Mood becomes "tone" when the author projects his attitude from the subject–matter to the audience. When he shares his character's mood, and when that mood is reflected in the environment, tone becomes identical with *atmosphere*.[74] William Charvat confirms that during the decade following 1835, Poe's chief contribution to technique was the development of atmosphere and close–knit plot construction. In the preceding period there was hardly a mention of either, though there was a general demand for unity and workmanship.[75] Thus as a theorist of fiction, Poe, beginning with the Aristotelian concept of plot, attempted to evolve new methods of presentation.

The events of a tale should be manipulated logically toward an effective climax so as to keep the emotional involvement of the reader unflagging. Hence Poe finds fault with John Neal for his failure in this regard:

> ...but his [John Neal's] conclusions are sure to be

> hurried and indistinct; so that the reader, perceiving a falling-off where he expects a climax, is pained, and closing the book with dissatisfaction, is in no mood to give the author credit for the vivid sensations which have been aroused *during the progress* of perusal. Of all literary foibles, the most fatal, perhaps, is that of defective climax (VII, 265).

If the climax is not skillfully managed, the emotional tension of the reader slackens. In fact, climax in a story is the focal point of interest. All other aspects of the narrative should be logically related to it.

In "The Philosophy of Composition," Poe refers to Charles Dickens' letter to himself in which the Englishman speaks of Godwin's building *Caleb Williams* "backwards," and suggests "a somewhat similar process" of constructing a tale.[77] The tale–writer, according to Poe, should constantly have the denouement in view while elaborating the incidents and tone in the narrative :

> It is only with the *denouement* constantly in view that we can give a plot its indispensable air of consequence, or causation, by making the incidents, and especially the tone at all points tend to the development of the intention (VI, 320).

The term denouement in a fictional or dramatic composition signifies a very brief disentanglement of the knots of the plot following the climax. Sometimes the time between the climax and the denouement is short. As a result, the narrative concludes with a surprise ending. While in some tales there may be gradual preparation for the conclusion by means of atmospheric build-up, in some the conclusion may come unexpectedly on account of a sudden change in the character or events. It is the latter type of tale that O'Henry has popularized.

Referring to character, Poe draws a distinction between a fictional construct and a living human being. He questions the interpretation of Shakespeare's characters:

> to account for their actions–to reconcile [Shakespeare's] inconsistencies–not as if they were the coinage of a human brain, but as if they had been actual existences upon earth. We talk of Hamlet the man, instead of Hamlet the *dramatic persona*–of Hamlet that God, in place of Hamlet that Shakespeare created.

In his conception of character, Poe strikes a balance between the individuated personalities and sociological or historical types. Poe admires Dickens for a "faithful depicting of what is called still–life, and particularly of *character* in humble condition."

Characterization, in Poe's opinion, is possible in a tale to a very limited extent. There cannot be a variety of characters just as there cannot be profusion of incidents. As Poe states, "In the tale proper... there is no space for development of character...." (VII, 209). While development of character is not possible in a tale due to spatial limitations, a psychological crisis in the life of the character may be effectively described. Having minimized the importance of character development in the tale proper, Poe lays great stress on the logical development of incidents. But, as Henry James asks, "What is character but the determination of incident? What is incident but the illustration of character?"[77] Poe takes great pains to portray character in a Gothic tale like "Ligeia." Incident in such tales is only a logical consequence of character.

Theory and Practice

Poe is confident of his abilities in realizing in practice the critical concepts enunciated in his reviews and critical essays. He says in his review of *Barnaby Rudge,*

> ...theory and practice are in so much *one* that the former implies or includes the latter. A theory is only good as such, in proportion to its reducibility to practice. If the practice fails, it is because the theory is imperfect (VII, 40).

However, the actual practice of a creative writer may be significant, whatever the imperfections of his theory. Generally, critics agree with Poe and maintain that his theory and practice are inseparable. For instance, Hardin Craig admires Poe for his "compliance with such high principles."[78] Norman Foerster is of the same opinion :

> An artist may, of course, be deficient in the critical faculty ("Poets are by no means, necessarily, judges of poetry," says Poe); but when he possesses the critical faculty, his theory and practice will tend to coincide.[79]

While the critical faculty of a writer enables him to enunciate principles of writing, it is debatable whether his theory and practice actually "coincide." The Creative imagination is so elusive that it is not always possible for the writer to control it in a rigid theoretical framework. Even if he succeeds in partly ordering it, sometimes he may just remain a spectator to the magnificent course the creative urge takes, going beyond his own conscious control. Nevertheless, a writer's critical principles often help him check the subjectivity of his writings. Referring to Schlegel's idea of subjectivity and objectivity of criticism, Rene Wellek says,

> Objectivity is also increased by constant reference to theory. A judgment can be clarified and expressed only in concepts, and concepts assume distinctness only in an assumed system. Critical reflection is thus a constant experimentation to discover theoretical statements.[80]

There is no doubt that Poe's position as editor and reviewer immensely helped him in organizing his critical principles.

In his letter to Beverley Tucker, Poe complains: "Generally, people praise extravagantly those [tales] of which I am ashamed and pass in silence what I fancy to be praiseworthy.[81] Every writer has certain intentions in his writings, sometimes explicitly stated and sometimes just implied. W. K. Wimsatt and Monroe C. Beardsley discuss intention as revealed in the "internal evidence" (the work itself) and in the "external evidence (letters, prefaces, etc.) According to them,

> the meaning of a work resides within the work; no judgment of intention has relevancy unless corroborated by the work itself, in which case, it is supererogatory. It is therefore circular and misleading to speak of judging the work with respect to its success in carrying out the author's intention.[82]

However, it is difficult to reject "intention" altogether as Wimsatt and Beardsley do. While inspiration may be responsible for the idea of a work of art, the actual composition involves conscious control and intention on the part of the artist. Also the writer as a conscious artist will constantly have to evaluate his own achievement implicitly or explicitly in an attempt to advance in his writing. Cleanth Brooks rules out critical evaluation of a work of literature in the light of intention. As he puts it, "the reduction of a work of literature to its causes does not constitute literary criticism."[83] While avoiding a mere "reduction" of a work of literature to its "causes," the critic can explore the range of the writer's creative imagination that might possibly go even beyond the "causes" in the actual achievement. F. R. Leavis, however, is more convincing when he maintains that

> Intentions are nothing in art except as realized, and the tests of realization will remain what they were. They are applied in the operation of the critic's sensibility; they are a matter of his sense, derived from his literary experience...[84]

According to J. E. Spingarn, "the poet's aim must be judged at the moment of the creative act, that is to say, by the art of the poem itself."[85] Kenneth Burke too says that certain principles are implicit in every composition: "Whether or not authors do formulate the principles of choice by which they are guided, such principles are necessarily implicit in the choice they make."[86] These principles are logically prior to the composition of the work. The critic "should aim to formulate the principles of composition implicit" in the work—from which the poem should be "logically deducible."[87] This substantiates Poe's view that the theory is not easily separable from its practice. The diversity of his tale-writing adds to the richness of his theory. From his practice itself it is possible to formulate significant critical principles.

While some of poe's tales are plain illustrations of his theory, a few have strictly individual traits without falling under any of the categories. These tales contain within them the principles by which they should be judged. No external evidence in available. Also in the case of the grotesque/comic tales and the tales of adventure, the practice is significant while there is no elaborate theory as that of the Gothic or the Ratiocinative tale. Thus the critic will have to "formulate the principles of composition" implicit in the work itself. In addition, even where Poe has an explicit theory of the tale, his actual practice may be at variance with it. Although he takes pains to define the various kinds of effect and modes of composition, he does not say much about the various technical devices that he employs in his tales for achieving these diverse effects. For instance, he does not elaborate on the telling methods. In his actual practice he employs certain patent short–story devices like atmosphere, suspense, suggestion, and dialogue that contribute to the intensity of effect. These elements too do not find elaboration in his theory. Thus just as the writer may fail to put into practice his own principles, so also he may unconsciously achieve certain objectives which he never "intended" to do. As T. S. Eliot says, "the poet's theories should arise out of his practice rather than his practice out of his theories."[88] Hence a close analysis of a large number of Poe's tales may bring out the multiplicity of his fictional principle.

Whether the twentieth–century theorists of fiction like Percy Lubbock, Wayne C. Booth, and Mark Schorer acknowledge Poe or not, one can find elaborated in their studies several fictional aspects dealt with by Poe in the nineteenth century. Percy Lubbock's emphasis on character, point of view, atmosphere, pictorial mode, etc. can be seen in Poe's criticism of fiction too. Wayne C. Booth's elaboration of the strategy of controlling the responses of the reader brings to mind Poe's attempts to produce an "effect" on the reader's consciousness by means of the several technical devices. In spite of the fact that he is concerned with the short prose narrative, Poe does employ the devices of the point of view and authorial comment. Mark Schorer sounds familiar to a student of Poe's fictional principle when he says that technique discovers the theme. Poe insists upon tone as a means to establish the technique, saying that through it the author's theme comes out.

In *A Rhetoric of Irony* Wayne C. Booth describes irony as a technique by which an author consciously or unconsciously controls the reader's responses. He first discusses the workings of what he calls "stable irony," irony with a clear rhetorical intent. He also deals with intended instabilities–ironies that resist interpretation and finally lead to the "infinite absolute negativities" that have obsessed criticism since the Romantic period. According to him,

> The most obvious use of stylistic clues in stable irony is found in parody, the mocking imitation by one author of another author's style... Though parody is not ordinarily thought of as "irony," it is ironic in our definition: the surface meaning must be rejected, and another, incongruous, and "higher" meaning must be found by reconstruction.[89]

In the sense that Booth calls parody "irony," Poe exploits the device both in his comic and Gothic tales. In the comic tales such as "The Psyche Zendria and Lionizing," he parodies contemporary writers and modes for comic purposes. But in the Gothic tales, he employs the device of irony for serious purposes. Thus the effect of a tale of terror like "The Cask of Amontillado" is heightened by the narrator's ironic stance. Joseph J. Moldenhauer tells us that Poe vacillates between formalist and affective poetics.[90] While trying to prove that the "effect" of a work depends upon its constituent elements, Poe also maintains that the reader has access to ineffable qualities inhering in the work—an affective process. In fact, this apparent paradox viewed in the context of the twentieth–century critical jargon, constitutes the uniqueness of Poe as theorist and practitioner of tale–writing. The distinctions between the formalistic and the affective are after all a twentieth–century development.

The contemporary developments in critical theory have caused immense confusion in the minds of critics. According to the *Encyclopedia of Philosophy,* "the word 'intention' is ambiguous in the way...that the word 'belief' is ambiguous, for ...the word may refer either to a state or episode (in this case intending) or to the intentional object of such a state or episode– that is, to that which is intended."[91] The debate concerning "authorial intention" originated in this ambiguity. W. K. Wimsatt and Monroe C. Beardsley in their debate over "intentional fallacy" draw a distinction between the author's intention as "episode" and the literary "object." For E. D. Hirsch, intention *is* the literary object. Wimsatt and Beardsley maintain that the plan of an author *is* not adequate for measuring the success of the work. According to Stanley Fish, both the Wimsatt and Beardsley school and the Hirsch school are wrong, since neither the text *nor* the author exists independently of the act of interpretation.

In "Genesis: A Fallacy Revisited," Wimsatt's emphasis shifts from the problem of evaluation to that of interpretation:

> It seemed to me then, and it still seems, that Mr. beardsley and I succeeded in formulating a clear, reasonable, and viable statement of the thesis that the intention of literary artist qua intention is neither a valid ground for arguing the *presence of a quality or a meaning* in a given instance of his literary work nor a valid criterion for judging the value of that work.[92]

In fact, Wimsatt admits that the intention of the author may guide or even coincide with the interpretation of the poem.

E.D. Hirsch defends the author by challenging the distinction between what an author means and what the text means. According to him,

> *Meaning* is that which is represented by a text: it is what the author meant by his use of a particular sign sequence; it is what the signs represent.

> *Significance,* on the other hand, names a relationship between that meaning and a person, or conception, or indeed anything imaginable.[93]

When the authorial intention is at variance with the text, the problem is with the "significance," not the "meaning," which is stable.

Stanley Fish considers the reader as author. For him, intention and the text "itself" have actual status in respect of the reader's experience. As he puts it, "the form of the reader's experience, formal units, and the structure of intention are one, that they come into view simultaneously, and that therefore the questions of priority and independence do not arise."[94] Author, reader, and text depend upon the prevailing conventions of interpretation. Malcolm Bradbury sums up the current critical confusion when he says that "we live in the age of the Death of the Author, when the autonomous creative subject has been rendered problematic, when the text is the centerless center, when Portraits of the Artist have been replaced by Anxieties of Discourse."[95] And he is emphatic that "we benefit from the power of those aesthetic introspections and insights that come from writers themselves."[96]

Thus in spite of the confusing din of the recent critical theory, the text and its author still seem to constitute the right voice for a proper comprehension of meaning. And the meaning of Poe's fictional whiting is multiple, not strictly conforming to any single critical principle on account of its variety and diversity. A close reading of the tales in the various categories will no doubt be a fruitful intellectual exercise. In the course of such a study, a majority of the tales as well as the longer narratives are analyzed in the light of not only Poe's critical pronouncements but also the Poe criticism past and present with the conviction that whatever the changing critical fashions, the author and the text continue to be relevant to literary history.

NOTES

1. William Charvat, *The Origins of American Critical Thought 1810-1825* (1936; rpt. New York: A.S. Barnes and Company, 1961) 135-136.
2. Robert D. Jacobs, *Poe: Journalist & Critic* (Baton Rouge: Louisiana State University Press, 1969) 160.
3. Margaret Alterton, "Origins of Poe}s critical Theory," *University of Iowa Studies*, II, No. 3 (April, 1925).
4. Pierre Irving, *Life and Letters of Washington Irving* (New York, 1862), II, 226.
5. *Letters*, I, 162.
6. See William Charvat, 162.
7. *Ibid.*, 160.
8. Edmund Clarence Stedman and George E. Woodberry, eds. *The Works of Edgar Allan Poe* (London: Lawrence & Bu;llen, 1895), VII, 31. Hereafter referred to as *Works*. Page references are given in parantheses after each quotation from the text.
9. John Gardner and Lennis Dunlap, eds. The forms of Fiction (New York: Random House, 1962) 23-37.
10. Northrop Frye, Anatomy of Criticism: Four Essays (Princeton: Princeton University Press, 1957) 305.
11. "Introduction," *Works*, I, 91 & 93.
12. See *Letters*, I, 159.
13. T. O. Mabbott, "Introduction," ed. *Collected Works of Edgar Allan Poe* (Cambridge, Mass: The belknap Press of Harvard University Press, 1978), II, xxvi.
14. See William Peden, "The Recent American Short Story," *The Sewanee Review,* LXXXII, iv (Fall, 1974); 712-729. Peden tells us how in the twentieth century the American short story shows a still greater divergence from the "old-fashioned conflict-through-complications-to-climax kind of magazine story."
15. See Poe's review of Mrs. Sigourney's *Zinzendorf and Other Poems, Southern Literary Messenger*, January, 1836.
16. See Michael Allen, *Poe and the British Magazine Tradition* (New York: Oxford University Press, 1969) and Robert D. Jacobs, *Poe: Journalist & Critic*. According to Burton R. Pollin, there is much doubt that Poe read the German tales in German-only in English translation-but the number of tales translated then was *not* large. Somchow Poe could *never* tackle the translated sentences properly. See Burton R. Pollin's review of Michael Allan's book in *Nineteenth–Century Fiction*, 12/1970, 25: 371-75

17. *Letters*, I, 57-58.
18. See Frank Luther Mott, *A History of American Magazines* (Cambridge, Mass: Harvard University press, 1938-39), I, 735-736
19. *Letters,* I, 116.
20. See James S. Wilson, "Poe's Philosophy of Composition," *The North American Review,* CCXXIII (1927), 683. Poe's earliest referrence to Schlegel occurs in a review of the poems of Mrs. Sigourney, Miss Gould, and Mrs. Ellet, published in January, 1836.
21. The unfinished but promising *Politian* was all that Poe could achieve in this direction.
22. See Floyd Stovall, "Poe's Debt to Coleridge," *University of Texas Studies in English*, X (1930) 92.
23. James S. Wilson, *op. cit.,* 678. See also Walter Blair, "Poe's Conception of Incident and Tone in the Tale," *Modern Philology,* XLI (May, 1944) 228-240. Blair maintains that Poe "saw a work as the stimulus to a response on the part of the reader. Understandably, therefore, his primary concern was with so molding the work as to assure its havisng the desired effect."
24. A. E. Schlegel, *Lectures on Dramatic Art and Literature*, trans. John Black (London: G. Bell and Sons, Ltd., 1914) 37.
25. This happens because, all art is, as David C. Stineback says, "a deliberate technique in service to something beyond itself: the bridge of comprehension between the human world of the author and the human world of the reader." David C. Stineback, "On the limits of Fiction," *The Midwest Quaraterly,* XIV, iv (Summer, 1973) 347. See also Brewsterr Ghiselin, "Imagination, Communication, and the Cultural Order," *Western Humanities Review*, XXX, ii (Spring, 1976) 135-143.
26. E. M. Forster, *Aspects of the Novel* (1927); rpt. Harmondsworth: Penguin Books. Ltd., 1962) 94. According to Forster, what keeps a plot engaging is the element of mystery or the detective element: "the element of surprise or mystery--the detective element as it is sometimes rather emptily called--is of great importance in a plot." (95).
27. M. H. Abrams, *A Glossary of Literary Terms* (New York: Holt, Rinehart & Winston, 1962) 70.
28. Eric W. Rabkin, *Narrative Suspense* (Ann Arbor: The University of Michigan Press, 1973) 60.
29. *Letters,* II, 329.

30. Killis Campbell, *The Mind of Poe and Other Studies* (Cambridge, Mass: Harvard University Press, 1933) 101.

31. S. T. Coleridge, *Biographia Literaria* (1906; rpt. London: Everyman's Library, 1967) 268.

32. Rene Wellek, *A History of Modern Criticism* (London: Jonathan Cape, 1955), II, 187.

33. See Poe's "Letter to B--" and Floyd Stovall, "Poe's Debt to Cobridge," *University of Texas Studies in English*, X (1930): 70-127.

34. See Hervey Allen, *Israfel: The Life and Times of Edgar Allan Poe,* I, 72, 83, 98-99, 112-113, 149, 155-156, & 162; George E. Woodberry, *Edgar Allan Poe* (New York: Biblo and Tannen, 1965), I, 24, 36; Margaret Alterton and Hardin Craig, eds. *Edgar Allan Poe: Representative Selections* (New York: American Book Company, 1935) xxi-xxii, xxiii-xxiv; Katherine Norman, "Poe's Knowledge of Lathin," *American Literature*, VI (March, 1934) 72-77; John Paul Pritchard, "Horace and Edgar Allan Poe," *The Classical Weekly,* XXVI (1933) 129-133; John Paul Pritchard, "Aristotle's *Poetics* and certain american Literary Critics," *The Classical Weekly,* XXVII (1934) 81-85.

35. See Norman A. Graebner, Gilbert C. Fite, and Philip L. White, *A History of the American People* (New York: McGraw-Hill Book Company, 1970). "By the 1830s and 1840s, a new scientific spirit prevailed throughout the United States. Many people believed they saw a definite conriection between democracy and science." (449). Poe's emphasis on the cause and effect relationship makes D. H. Lawrence complain that poe is "rather a scientist than an artist." D. H. Lawrence, *Studies in Classic American Literature* (New York: The Viking Press, 1961) 65.

36. William Charvat, 144.

37. Herbert W. Schneider, *A Hostory of american Philosophy* (New York, 1946) 246.

38. Robert D. Jacobs, 21.

39. See Stuart Levine, *Edgar Poe: Seer and Craftsman* (Deland: Everett/Edwards, inc., 1972); Sheldon W. Liebman, "Poe's Tales and His Theory of the Poetic Experience," *Studies in Short Fiction,* VII, iv (Fall, 1970): 582-96.

40. See *Works,* VI, 32.

40A. J. Lasley Damaron, "Poe's concept of Truth," *The Mississtippi Quarterly*, XLIII, i (Lintor 1989-90): 20.

41. Margaret Alterton, "Origins of Poe's Critical Theory," *University of Iowa Studies*, II, No.3 (April, 1925): 470.

42. See Burton R. Pollin, ed. *Collected Writings of Edgar Allam Poe,* Vol. II, *Brevities.*

43. Letter to the author from T.O. Mabbott, January 25, 1965.

44. See N. Bryllion Fagin, *The Histrionic Mr. Poe* (Baltimore. The Johns Hopkins Press, 1949).

45. Arthur H. Quinn, *Edgar Allan Poe: A Critical Biography* (New York: Appleton-Century-Crofts, Inc., 1941) 470.

46. *Ibid.*, 294.

47. Horatio E. Smith, "Poe's Extension of His Thheory of the Tale," *Mordern Philology*, XVI (August, 1918): 195-203. The idea of the viability of the shorter poetic from is expressed by Poe in "The Poetic Principle." Coleridge too says: "A poem of any length neither can be, nor ought to be, all poetry." (*Shakespearean Criticism*, ed. T. M. Raysor, London, 1930, I, 226). Poe, obviously, adopted this idea from Coleridge and applied it conveniently to the prose from of the narrative too. In spite of that similarity, a prose tale need not be poetic in theme and technique. Poe, always aware of the "wide domains" afforded by prose, contracts it with the poetic form. Giacomo Leopardi, an Italian critic, said, anticipating Poe, that "the labors of poetry desire by their very nature to be short." (Quoted in Rene Welek, 275). Rene Welek says: "Like Poe, Schopenhauer thinks that there is inevitably something insipid and boring in long works such as *Paradise Lost* or the *Aeneid.*" (Rene Welek, 311).

47A. Burton R. Pollin, *Discoveries in Poe* (Notre Dame : University of Notre Dame Poe) 128.

48. Review of Hawthorne's "Tales," *Works*, VII, 27. Poe expresses the same idea in "The Poetic Principle." (See *Works*, VI, 5).

49. *Selected Literary Criticism: Henry James,* ed. Morrib Shepira (New York: McGraw-Hill Company, 1964) 50-51.

50. Burton R. Pollin, "Edgar Allan Poe and His Illustrators," *American Book Collector*, II, ii (March-April, 1981): 3.

51. For some interesting observations on Poe's art in respect of the popular school of painting of his day, see Thomas Holly Chivers's *Life of Poe* (New York, 1952) 86-87.

52. Margaret Altertorn, *Origins of Poe's Critical Theory*, 32.

53. *Works*, IX, 115.

54. Arthur H. Quinn, 191-192.

55. See *Works*, VII, 278-281.

56. G.R. Thompson, "Literary Politics and the 'Legistriate Sphere':

Poe, Hawthorne, and the 'Tale Proper,' *Nineteenth-Century Literatwe* Vol 49, No. 2 (September 1994): 171.

57. *Works*, VI, pp. 210-211. See also *Works*, X, 116-117.

58. William Charvat, 162.

59. In a "Prospective Notice" in the *Saturday Evening Post*, May 1, 1841, Poe anticipated the plot of Dickens's *Barnaby rudge*; he reviewed the book at length, recalling his earlier analysis, in *Graham's*, February 1842. In his letter of February 3, 1842, to Frederick W. Thomas, Poe says: "Did you read my review of 'Barnaby Rudge' in the Feb. No.?" You see that I was right throughtout in my predictions about the plot. Was it not you who said you believed I would find myself mistaken?" (*Letters*, I, 193). Again in his letter of February 24, 1845 to Rufus W. Griswold he says, referring to his own style of criticism, "of my serious manner Barnaby Rudge is a good specimen." (*Letters*, I, p. 280).

60. John Paul Pritchard, *Return to the Fountains: Some Classical Sources of American Criticism* (New York: Octagon Books, Inc., 1966) 35.

61. R. S. Crane, "The Concept of Plot and the Plot of *Tom Jones*," *Critics and Criticism* (Chicago: University of Chicago press, 1952) 67.

62. E. M. Forster, *Aspects of the Novel*, 103.

63. Walter O'Grady, "On Plot in Modern Fiction: Hardy, James, and Conrad," *Modern Fiction Studies*, XI, No. 2. (Summer, 1965), 108. "The exterior situation may have been created by the interior situation of the character or characters, and conversely, the interior situation may have been created by the exterior situation."

64. *Ibid*., 109.

65. Walter O'Grady says: "An incident may be caused by a combination of an event and an exterior situation, or it may happen to a character and be caused by fate or circumstance." (Walter O'Grady 109). Marvin Mudrick says that "in the work of fiction, a character lives in and is an aspect of events; and events have their own internal cause, duration, and consequence." ("Character and Event in Fiction," *Critical Approaches to Fiction*, ed. Shiv K. Kumar and Keith Mckean (New York: McGraw-Hill Book Co., 1968) 108.

66. *Critical Approaches to Fiction*, ed. Shiv K. Kumar and Keith McKean, 109.

67. In spite of so much insistence on the mathematical construction of the tale, Poe seems to be aware of the fact that the ultimate

effect of a work of art on the reader is not only emotional but intuitional, as opposed to the merely intellectual. In this regard it will be interesting to see what Henri Bergson says: "It must be noted that fiction, when it has the power to move us, resembles an incipient hallucination: it can thwart our judgment and reason, which are the strictly intellectual faculties." (Henri Bergson, *The Two Sources of Morality and Religion*, trans. by R. A. Audra and C. Brereton (New York, 1935) 99.

68. Daniel Haffman, *Poe Poe Poe Poe Poe Poe Poe* (1972; rpt. Garden City, N. Y.: Anchor Press, 1973) 91.
69. Stephen Ralton, *Authorship and Audience: Literary Performance in the audience Renaisance* (Prrinceton, NJ: Princeton University Press, 1991) 138.
70. I. A. Richards, *Practical Criticism: A Story of Literary Judgment* (London: Routledge & Kegan Paul Ltd., 1929) 182. Walter Blair finds ambiguity in Poe's use of the term "tone" and says that he uses the word in the sense of style. See Walter Blair, "Poe's Conception of Incident and Tone in the Tale," *Modern Philology,* XLI (May, 1944): 231n.
71. Wayne C. Booth, *The Rhetoric of Fiction* (Chicago: University of Chicago press, 1961) 74. See also Fred B. Millett, *Reading Fiction* (New York, 1950): "This tone, the general feeling which suffuses and surrounds the work, arises ultimately out of the writer's attitude toward his subject...*The subject derives its meaning from the view of life which the author has taken*" 11.
72. Mark Schorer, "Technique as Discovery," *Hudson Review*, I, No. 1 (Spring, 1948) 67.
73. Wayne C. Booth, *The Rhetoric of Fiction*, 177-82, 200-205.
74. See Robert Stanton, *The Short Story and the Reader* (New York: Henry, Holt and Company, 1960) 33.
75. William Charval 182-183.
76. In his letter of March 6, 1842 to poe during his visit to Philadelphia, Charles Dickens said when the former sent him a copy of his "Tales" and the analysis of "Barnaby Rudge": "Apropos of the 'construction' of 'Caleb Williams', do you know that Godwin wrote it *backwards*--the last volume first,--" (Quoted in George E. Woodberry, *Edgar Allan Poe,* I, 327.
77. *Selected Literary Criticism: Henry James*, ed. Morris Shapira (New York: McGraw-hill Company, 1965) 58.
78. "Introduction" to *Edgar Allan Poe: Representative Selections,* ed. Margaret Alterton and Hardin Craig (New York: American Book Company, 1935) lxxix.

79. Norman Foerster, *American Criticism* (New York: Houghton Mifflin Company, 1928) 5.
80. Rene Wellek, *A History of Modern Criticism: The romantic Age* Vol. II (New Haven, 1955) 56.
81. *Letters*, I, 78.
82. W.K. Wimpatt & Monroc C. Beardsley, *The Verbal Icon: Studies in the Meaning of Poetry*. Kentucky: University of Kentucky Press, 1954.
83. Cleanth Brooks, "The Formalist Cristics," *Kenyon Review*, XIII (1951): 78.
84. F.R. Leavis, *The Common Pursuit* (1952; rpt. Harmondsworth: Penguin Books, 1963) 225.
85. J.E. Spingarn, *Criticism in America* (New York, 1924) 24-25.
86. Kenneth Burke, "The Principle of Composition," *Poetry*, XCIX, No. 1 (October, 1961) 50.
87. *Ibid.*, 51.
88. T.S. Eliot, "From Poe to Valery," in *To Criticize the Critic and other Writings* (London: Faber and Faber, 1965) 42.
89. Wayne C. Booth, *A Rhetoric of Irony* (Chicago: The University of Chicago Press, 1974) 71-72.
90. Joseph J. Moldenhauer, "Murder as a Fine Art: Basic Connections Between Poe's Aesthetics, Psychology and Moral Vision," *PMLA,* Vol. 83, No. 2 (May 1968), 284-297. See also Catherine Rainwater, "Poe's Landscape Tales and the 'Picturesque' Tradition," *Southern Literary Journal,* 16, ii (Spring 1984), 30-43.
91. Encyclopedia of Philosophy, Vol. 4 (1967) 198.
92. W.K. Wimsatt, "Genesis: A Fallacy Revisited," *The Disciplines of Criticism,* ed. Peter Demitz, Thomas Greene, and Lowry Nelson, Jr. (New Haven: Yale University Press, 1968) 195.
93. E.D. Hirsch, *Validity in Interpretation* (New Haven: Yale University Press, 1967) 8.
94. Stanley Fish, *Is There a Taxt in This Class?* (Cambridge: Harvard University Press, 1980) 165.
95. Malcolm Bradbury, "The Bridgeable Gap: Bringing Together the Creative Writer and the Critical Theorist in an Authorless World," *The Times Literary Supplement,* No. 4633 (January 17, 1992) 8.
96. *Ibid.*

3

"TERROR OF THE SOUL": POE'S GOTHIC TALES

"If in many of my productions terror has been the thesis, I maintain that terror is not of Germany, but of the soul,..."

Preface to *Tales of the Grotesque and Arabesque, 1840*

"the fearful colored into the horrible"

Letter to *Thomas W. White,* April 30, 1835

"I do not consider any one sof my stories better than another. There is a vast variety of kinds and, in degree of value, these, kinds vary... but each tales is equally good of its kind."

Letter to *P.P. Cooke, August 9, 1846*

The Major Gothic Tales

In 1840, Edgar Allan Poe published a collection of serious and comic tales entitled *Tales of the Grotesque and Arabesque*. Since then critics have considered the nature of the two types of tales, conjecturing Poe's possible meaning of the terms, "Grotesque" and "Arabesque". Arthur H. Quinn's 1941 distinction of the terms still seems to be valid. According to him, Poe "eluded a definition of the terms...but generally speaking, the Arabesques are the product of powerful imagination and the Grotesques have a burlesque or satirical quality."[1] L. Moffitt Cecil maintains that the term "Arabesque" signifies "Eastern" or "Near Eastern" from Arabia. However, he does not take into account the fact that the German Romanticists had transmuted the Oriental tale and the term "arabesque" into the Gothic.[2] G.R. Thompson says that the meanings of the two terms were to undergo some radical shifts between 1750 and 1830, and that the apparent antithesis between the two styles was to blur into a paradoxical fusion. In his opinion, "This paradox of meaning is underscored by the usual twentieth-century application of arabesque to Poe's serious Gothic tales..."[3] In Rebert D. Jacbos' view "arabesque" is a surface decoration, painted or in low relief, in which fantastic figures are intertwined with flowers, leavers, leaves, branches and scroll work. The entire design is called an "arabesque", while the term "grotesque" deriving from the *grotto* or excavations in which such decorations are found on ancient ruins (cf, grotto), applies chiefly to the figures. In other words, the two terms represent different aspects of a unified design, which was probably what Poe intended in his arrangement of the tales in his book, leaving the reader to understand that individual tales suggested the grotesque, while others, not monstrous, exhibited the beauty of the design itself.[4] As for the twentieth-century application of arabesque to Poe's serious Gothic tales, it should be noted that the Gothic is something higher than the merely ludicrous, whereas the Grotesque, in spite of the presence of the horrible, is ultimately comic in effect. In this sense, the arabesque, the product of "powerful imagination," as A.H. Quinn defines it, is identical with the Gothic. It is interesting to note that in "Ligeia", Poe comes close to explaining the term "Arabesque". Lady Rowena's bridal chamber is described as having a ceiling of "gloomy-looking oak... excessively lofty, vaulted," having been fretted with the "wildest" specimens of a "semi-Gothic, semi-Druidical device." There is a huge gold censer hung from the center of the ceiling "by a single chain of gold... Saracenic (Scapital) in pattern, and with many perforations so contrived that there writhed in and out of them as if endued with a serpent vitality, a continued succession of parti-colored fires" (I, 193). The word "Saracenic" is evidently the "Arabesque" and it describes the typical Gothic atmosphere of the bridal chamber. The effect of the setting on the narrator, as Poe proceeds in that tale, is one of terror, typical of the Gotic tales. But, the husband is both narator and perpetrator of the horrifying effect on Rowena.

In 1853, John Ruskin defined grotesque as the art of a disturbed imagination and declared it to be an essential feature of the Gothic.[5] Recent critics like Wolfgang Kayser have identified the Gothic with the Grotesque.[6] The twentieth-century view of the Grotesque as being a combination ofthe ludicrous and the sinister, different from Poe's own meaning ofthe term, sounds unconvincing in ascribing ludicrousness to the Gothic.

The sublime terrors caused by great catastrophes and intense passions may be akin to the tragic emotions of pity and fear. It is in this sense that Poe's Gothicism appeals to us. The Schauer-Romantiks advanced the theory of the beauty of the Medusa, a leprous beauty tainted with pain, corruption, and death. Poe's own conception of the beautiful, as he explains it is "The Poetic Principle", differs from the repulsively horrible. Even passion in ruled out in a poem which represents the Beautiful (VI, 13). In his review of Nathaniel Hawthorne's *Twice-Told Tales*, Poe categorically states that

> ... the author who aims at the purely beautiful in a prose tale is laboring at a great disadvantage. For Beaty can be better treated in the poem. Not so with terror, or passion, or horror, or a multitude of such other points (VII, 32).

In the light of such statements made by Poe, it is difficult to see the element of Beauty in his Gothic tales which constitute a sizable part of his writing. Thus Stuart Levine is not convincing when he arges that Poe's fiction is poetic, associating the idea with the Beauty of horror.[7] Joseph H. Garrison too misses the spirit of Poe's Gothic writing when he argues that horror in Poe is compatible with Beauty.[8] The horrible, on accout of the repulsiveness associated with it, goes against the very sense of the Beautiful as Poe conceived it. The presence of the intensely emotional negates the idea of the Beautiful. Thus in the words of Alexander Smith, a romantic theorist.

> In common discourse, if I mistake not, we apply the word *emotion* more exclusively to mental affections of a more violent kind, or at least very high degrees of mental affection in general. Except in philosophical writings, the percenption of the *beautiful* is not designated as a state of emotion. A man who is tranquilly admiring a soft and pleasing landscape, is not, in common language, said to be in a state of emotion; neither are curiosity, cheerfulness, elation, reckoned emotions. A man is said to be under emotions, who is strongly agitated with grief, anger, fear.[9]

The Gothic tale is noted for the intensity of the emotion experienced by the character as well as the reader. The way a mounting emotion is built up by means of incident and atmosphere leaves no scope for any tranquil enjoyment of the Beautiful.

Before attempting a close study of Poe's Gothic tales to see how far his own idea of "the terror of the soul" is exemplified, it may be profitable to observe how scholars have defined the "Gothic". A broader conception of the Gothic enables us to place Poe in the tradition of horror fiction.

The Gothic novel came into existence in the later part of the eighteenth century as a reaction against the prevailing realistic and sentimental fiction. The works of Horace Walpole, Mrs. Ann Radcliffe. "Monk" Lewis,[10] Maturin, and Mary Shelley exemplified the form. The reaction against the eighteenth-century fiction, according to Lowry Nelson, could be ascribed to the flourishing of the "graveyard enthusiasts" and to the "new passion for the awesome in secular nature, the 'sublime' as distinct from the 'beautiful'."[11] According to scholars like J.M.S. Tompkins, Montague Summers, and D.P. Varma,[12] Gothic is of three types—historical Gothic, terror Gothic, and horror Gothic or "Schauer-Romantik." Oral Sumner Coad defines the Gothic as "that kind of literature which, originating in Walpole's *Castle of Otranto*, seeks to create an atmosphere of mystery and terror by the use of supernatural or apparently supernatural machinery, or of pronounced physical or mental horror."[13] James K. Keech attempts to define the term as "a response, or effect, of fear characterized by foreboding and intensity rather than a set of traditional stock devices."[14] But D.P. Varma not only enumerates the devices but alsomakes a broader statement on the Gothic response in saying that "The tale of terror appeals to some deep-rooted human instinct; an irresistible, inexplicable impulse drives us towards the macabre."[15] However, Varma stretches is point too far when he asserts that the Gothic novels "are characterized by an awestruck apprehension of Divine immanence penetrating diurnal reality."[16] The Gothic spirit is certainly somethig more than the repulsively horrible; but one wonders whether it implies the Divine.

Referring to the work of the Gothic novelists like Mrs. Radcliffe and Maturin, Herbert Read says:

> Burke himself, preoccupied with the sublime at the time these (Gothic) novels were being written, would have held that the Gothic flame is capable of tempering the soul to a purity beyond the range of our dingy realism.[17]

Thus the proper spirit of the Gothic may not be Ruskin's "grotesqueness" or the tendency to delight in the fantastic and the morbid, but the Gothic flame that is "capable of tempering the sould to a purity beyond the range of our dingy realism." The awe-inspiring nature of the Gothic spirit raises it to a level higher than the merely ludicrous. Poe says in his Preface to *Tales of the Grotesque and Arabesque* that the terror of his tales is "not of Germany, but of the soul."[18] This statement hs been taken by the psychological critics as a warrant for reading Poe's personal psychology into his tales. It would, however, be more appropriate to say that he meant here not the Gothicism of his own soul, but that he was referring to his aim of exploring certain states of the human psyche for deliberate artistic purposes. In denying German influence,

Poe meant that he avoided "pseudo-horror" in the works of second-rate German writers. His contempt for Germanism is further evident from his reference to "Germanism & such twaddle" in a letter of November 11, 1839 to Joseph Evans Snodgrass.[19] As Robert D. Jacobs argues, Poe did not mean to deny German influence altogether and was aware of Sir Walter Scott's essay, "On the Supernatural in Fictitious Composition."[20] However, what Poe obviously meant was "Psychological terror," which he deduced "only from its legitimate sources," that is, human nature. Having been thrust into a world of nightmarish experience, the reader of the Gothic story finds himself confronted with elemental evil. This foreboding and intensity of the Gothic fiction is achieved by means of its ominous atmosphere and mood created by the physical settings and the corresponding mental states of the character.

Normally, critics associate the terrible and the horrible with the Gothic, using the two terms as being synonymous. However, the terms denote the two aspects of the Gothic, the horrible representing an extreme state. The novels of Mrs. Ann Radcliffe cause terror while those of "Monk" Lewis cause sheer horror. As D.P. Varma says, "the difference between Terror and Horror is the difference between awful apprehension and sickening realization: between the smell of death and stumbling against a corpse."[21] In the opinion of G.R. Thompson, terror suggests "frenzy" and horror is "perception of something incredibly evil or repellent."[22] The "awful apprehension" that D.P. Varma finds in the Gothic terror is not the apprehension of the "Divine," as he puts it. In fact, is "Frenzy," the apprehension of the unknown, a purely psychological experience.

This psychological aspect of the Gothic greatly appealed to the major American writers. Irvin Malin says that images like the haunted castle and the voyage into the forest in the writings of Horace Walpole, "Monk" Lewis, and Mrs. Ann Radcliffe are regarded in the works of the American Gothicists as "'objective correlatives' of the psyche."[23] Charles Brockden Brown was the first American Gothic writer to achieve this transformation. Dispensing ith medieval castles and superstition, Brown Americanized the Gothic, choosing as his themes American characters and environment. With Brown and his successors fear is more a psychological experience related to the character than something presented only as an objective phenomenon as it is with Mrs. Radcliffe. After Brown, Hawthorne, Poe, and Melville fully exploited the Gothic and brought fiction to new heights. The then prevailing Romanticism at home and abroad, with its mystery, wonder, aspiration, and yearning for the unknown, contributed much to the growth of the Gothic spirit in their work. This sense of mystery and wonder is blended with an attempt on the part of the writer at analyzing the human heart. In addition, the Puritan inheritanceand Southern climate[24] have provided a congenial ground for the flowering of the Gothic spirit. The following analyses of Poe's major and minor Gothic tales bring out these strains in his writing.

The Tales of Atmosphere

Thomas O. Mabbott calls the earliest of Poe's tales, "Metzengerstein" (1832), "a masterpiece, though a minor one."[25] Edd Winfield Parks says that the tale "started as an imitation of the Gothic romances but...gathered such momentum that it became a powerful allegory, with evil leading to its own self-destruction."[26] According to A.H. Quinn, the tale is "a powerful story of evil passions in a young man's soul."[27] T.O. Mabbott tells us that Poe regarded the tale as Germanic and that the subtitle of the second publication (*Southern Literary Messenger*, January 1836) calls it "A tale in imitation of the German." But Mabbott adds that as part of the Holy Roman Empire, Hungary was considered Germanic, and indeed, the population was of mixed ethnic origin.[28]

"Metzengerstein" has a chronicle-like beginning. The first-person author-narrator reports on certain historical incidents and comments on them and tries to achieve for his account authenticity and credibility. At the very outset the narrator sets up a psychological milieu for the story: he speaks of "horror and fatality" and "the doctrine of the Metempsychosis," thus preparing the reader for the incidents to follow. The technique of mood-building, that is employed in this early tale finds its perfection in maturer tales like "The Fall of the House of Usher" and "Ligeia."

Even though the narrator in "Metzengerstein" is for all practical prposes the author himself, the central intelligence, the character of the baron is presented to us from a distance. We are not admitted into the inner workings of his mind. The narrator presents the incidents from the point of view of an observer. The reasons for Poe's choice of the narrative device are three-fold. First, the narrator merely plays the role of a *raconteur* who is reporting certain historical events and claims authenticity for his narration. Secondly, the incidents of the story have been interpreted in the light of the Hungarian superstition and fulfil the prophecy about the families of Berlifitzing and Metzengerstein. Hence it is only natural that the narrator views his material through the eyes of the Hungarian people; and the interpretation of the incidents is the interpretation that the people place upon them. And lastly, the distance with which the character of the baron is presented is also justified on aesthetic grounds. The distance intensifies the sense of mystery and superstitious awe that surround the character and behaviour of the baron. The ancient prophecy about Metzengerstein and Berlifitzing is introduced in the second paragraph with a deliberate purpose—the conclusion of the tale is to come as a fulfillment of the prophecy. And the reader is given an inkling of the course that the tale will take.

The Gothic setting in which the hero is placed reveals him as isolated and suffering from some imaginary malady. The character is buried in reveries and this increases his sense of loneliness and fear. This perticular state of mind and the setting provide the context for the baron's fantasies. "It was with difficulty that he reconciled his dreamy and incoherent feelings with the certainty of being awake" (I, 301). The hubbub going on outside the palace and the strange commotion that is taking place in the moving tapestries of the apartment, and the simultaneous turmoil in the character's mind are rendered with great vividness. This suspenseful description of the setting in tune with the character's state of mind contributes to the atmosphere of the tale. The paragraphs dealing with the pictured horse coming to life are highly suggestive. The baron is evidently in the grip of some strange fascination precipitated by the movements of the demon horse. The appearance of the demon horse, metamorphosed out of the tapestry, seizes the baron with horror and fascination. It is, in fact, a turning point in his psychology. Henceforward the baron is like a man walking under a strange spell which at once horrifies and transfixes him with a peculiar attraction. He now seems to be one mechanically obeying the dictates of some phantom. His perverse attachment to his charger is at once dictated by fear and attraction. It is a strange state of mind that Poe calls *perverseness*, a state in which the subject is prompted by contradictory motives of which he has no full comprehension: "Through its promptings we act, for the reason that we shall not." Thus the demon horse is the baron's nemesis that leads him on to his predestined end through the agency of his own will. It might be a projection of the subject's psychology, but it also takes on an objective character. As in the "Oval Portrait", her Poe's achievement consists in the objectification of the subjective states of the character.

The conclusion is both a purgation for the protagonist and a fulfillment of the ancient prophecy. Thus the opening of the story comes full circle and justifies itself.

In "Ms. Found in a Bottle" (1833), Poe adopts the kind of journal-writing method that he is to try more elaborately in *The Narrative of Authur Gordon Pym* and *The Journal of Julius Rodman*:

> I shall from time to time continue this journal. It is true that I may not find an opportunity of transmitting it to the world, but I will not fail to make the endeavor. At the last moment I will enclose the MS in a bottle, and cast it within the sea (II, 230-231).

This specific strategy, like the chronicle mthod employed

in "Metzengerstein", enables the writer to achieve greater immediacy and to present the incidents in the very act of their happening.

While agreeing with Beverley Tucker's criticism of "Ms. Found in a Bottle", Poe refers in his letter of December 1, 1835, to the "*mere physique*" of the horrible" which prevails in the tale and says that he would not be "guilty of a similar absurdity *now*." In this connection he contrasts the mere physical sensations of the tale, "one among the first I ever wrote," with the more refined aspects of "Morella".[29] What Poe calls "absurdity," referring to "Ms. Found in a Bottle," constitutes the fantasy in the tale. The reader, faced with a series of incredible events, finds himself transported into a world of make-belief. According to Joseph. T. Shipley's *Dictionary of World Literature*, "Fantasy includes in the action, characters, or setting, things that are impossible under ordinary conditions or in the normal course of human events. In the case of no other genre is the willing suspension of disbelief so requisite."[30] In the opinion of Herbert Read, "A fantasy is more than a conceit, implying a sustained invention in the realm of fancy."[31] And Carl Jung in *Psychological Types use* "phantasy" as a synonym of "reverie." The atmosphere that Poe creates in "Ms. Found in a Bottle" is such as to require our willing suspension of disbelief in order to experience the events.

At the very outset of the story we have the background of belief and attitude of the character, his mental composition and the milieu in which he appears. The narrator says that he is a person of strong scientific predilections and not liable to superstitious belief. Thus the narrative is directed strictly along pre-designed lines:

> I have thought proper to premise thus much, lest the incedible tale I have to tell should be considered rather the raving of a crude imagination than the positive experience of a mind to which the reveries of fancy have been a dead letter and a nullity (II, 223).

The succeeding happenings of the tale serve to intensify

the contrast that is hinted at in the opening paragraph – the professed rationality and sanity of the narrator and his fool-proofness to the *ignes fatui* of superstition and the kind of supernatural experiences that he is subjected to. It is typical of Poe to open some of his tales in this mnner to establish the credibility of events. The narrator of Charles Brockden Brown's *Wieland* tells the reader:

> How will your wonder, and that of your companions, be excited by my story! Every sentiment will yield to your amazement.. Listen to my narrative, and then say what it is that has made me deserve to be placed on this dreadful eminence, if, indeed, every faculty be not suspended in wonder that I am still alive and am able to relate it.[32]

Thus in Brown too, as in Poe, there is an attempt to rivet the reader's attention to the course of the events. The narrator of "Ms Found in a Bottle", however, is unlike the narrator of "Ligeia" in that he is more rational and the events narrated are not emanations of his disturbed mind.

The strange happenings of the narrator's voyage, like the behavior of the captain and the seamen of the second ship and the very structure of the ship with its extremely porous condition, force him to acknowledge the presence of a supernatural order of which he has a presentiment, and of the operation of some ungoverned chance. The atmosphere of the sea and the appalling nature of the simoom force on him this sense of supernatural order. Poe's mastery of the painter's art is illustrated in the description of the situation when "Eternal Night continued to envelop us, all unrelieved by the phosphoric sea-brilliancy to which we had been accustomed in the tropics" (II, 227). This blending of light and shade ("chiaroscuro") intensifies the terror in the hearts of the forlorn sailors. In addition, the descriptions of the approaching simoom and the setting sun are the masterly strokes of an artist:

> It (the sun) gave out no light, properly so called, but a dull and sullen glow without reflection, as if all

> its rays were polarized. Just before sinking within the turgid sea, its central fires suddenly went out, as if hurriedly extinguished by some unaccountable power. It was a dim, silver-like rim, alone, as it rushed down the unfathomable ocean (II, 226).

Thus a remarkable feature of this early tale is that Poe achieves his effect by visual means. Not only does the chiaroscuro have an impact on the mind of the character but also it makes the scene vivid for the reader. And it serves to intensify the impression of terror, building up the mood for the kind of experiences the character has to undergo.

The atmospheric effects in this tale are not, however, as vividly felt and as much fraught with psychological meaning as in some of Poe's maturer tales like "The Fall of the House of Usher" and "Ligeia". The few Gothic images (like the "Eternal Night") that are introduced in the tale do not acquire any deep psychologial value as in "The Fall of the House of Usher." The second ship and its crew take on an unreal aspect of the denizens of a ghostly world. The unnatural distension of the ship, its porousness, etc. become associated with a rottenness and worm-eaten condition that is spectral. On the whole, the picture of the Spanish ship seems to suggest a meaning beyond itself; but about the nature of this meaning the author gives us no inkling. It is not also explained why the ship and her crew have attained to that condition and why the narrator himself should be destroyed along with it. The incident of the Spanish ship together with the narrator's experiences, thus, fails to acquire any symbolic significance. The whole happening at sea looks rather like an unfortunate accident than as a revelation of some inner meaning. It has no basis in the psychology of the character. Poe might be telling us here a horrid tale for its own sake without investing it with any deep psychological significance. While agreeing with Floyd Stovall concerning the parallels between Poe's tale and Coleridge's "The Rhyme of the Ancient Mariner," T.O. Mabbott asserts that "Ice and albatross in Antarctic region semitropical seas."[33] Thus in some of the Gothic tales like

"Ms found in a Bottle," Poe achieves a subtle combination of fact and fantasy. However, the Coleridgean element in the present tale is not properly developed; the element of sheer horror distorts the "strangeness" that is so remarkable in Coleridge's poem. The paradoxical combination of the Coleridgean atmosphere and the verisimilitude contributes to the dramatic immediacy of narration:

> In the meantime, the wind is still in our poop, and as we carry a crowd of canvass, the ship is at times lifted bodily from out the sea! Oh, horror upon horror!—the ice opens suddenly to the right, and to the left, and we are whirling dizzile, in immense concentric circles, round and round the borders of a gigantic amphitheater, the summit of whose walls is lost in the darkness and the distance. But little time will be left me to ponder upon my destiny! The circles rapidly grow small – we are plunging madly within the group of the whirlpool–and amid a roaring, and bellowing, and thundering of ocean and tempest, the ship is quivering–oh God! and–going down! (II, 235-36).

The vividness of description and the intensity of effect of the conclusion at once remind the reader of the hair-raising experiences related in "A Descent into the Maelstrom" and the head-long plunge of Pym's canoe in *The Narrative of Arthur Gordon Pym*. Thus in the present tale Poe has tried the method that he is to employ more successfully in his later works.

George E. Woodberry says that "A Descent into the Maelstrom" (1841) "is to be classed with the "Ms Found in a Bottle," and is the best of its kind."[34] According to T.O. Mabbott, it is "one of the most popular of Poe's tales."[35] The tale is an elaborately worked out fantasy. By a stretch of the imagination Poe pictures with vividness of detail the experience of a descent into the gigantic whirlpool. This experience might have been somewhat improbable in the ordinary course of things; but the author describes it as an actual occurrence and succeeds in rendering it fully convincing.

The opening of the tale presents a situation different from those in the other atmospheric tales. And the story is narrated by the central character, the fisherman, to the narrator, retrospectively on the very site of the occurrence of the incident. The maelstrom is given a local habitation and reality in maritime Norway. The double-narrator device increases the credibility of the experience described. Before the experience itself is rendered, the narrator feels with the intensity of a sensation the dizzy precipice of the black rock and the fury of the maelstrom that he observes below. The success of the tale is in the fact that the reader fully identifies himself with the narrator and feels that he too, like the narrator, is in the awful and relentless presence of the gyrating maelstrom. Both image and detail support this impression which is realized for us through the sensations of the narrator himself. As the narrator reaches the brink of the precipice with his companion, he is so deeply excited by the perilous position of the crag that

> ...I fell at full length upon the ground, clung to the shrubs around me, and dared not even glance upward at the sky—while I struggled in vain to divest myself of the idea that the very foundations of the mountain were in danger from the fury of the winds (II, 238).

As the narrator, together with the fisherman, ascends the summit of the crag, the sea "bursts" upon him: "I became aware of a loud and gradually increasing sound, like the moaning of a vast herd of buffaloes upon an American prairie...". (II, 240). Poe's descriptive skill for rendering graphic effects is amazing:

> Here the vast bed of the waters, seamed and scarred into a thousand conflicting channels, burst suddenly into frenzied convulsion – heaving, boiling, hissing–gyrating in gigantic and innumerable vortices, and all whirling and plunging on to the eastward with a rapidity which water never elsewhere assumes, except in precipitous descents (II, 240).

The "swaying and sweltering motion" and "the appalling

voice, half shriek roar" of the whirlpool presents the terrifying presence of some living monster:

> The mountain trembled to its very base, and the rock rocked. I threw myself upon my face, and clung to the scant herbage in an excess of nervous agitation (II, 241).

Thus by means of these striking details, Poe succeeds in conveying the presence of the maelstrom in terms of a keenly felt sensation. The character's agitated state of mind and the sweltering waters around are masterfully fused. Unlike in tales such as "The Fall of the House of Usher" and "Ligeia," the fantasy here is based on Poe's reading of factual accounts regarding maelstroms.[36]

Having rendered the impression of the maelstrom with such a piling up of detail in the manner of Brockden Brown or Daniel Defoe, Poe proceeds to describe the experience of the descent itself. He establishes an elaborate chain of realistic events (such as the unexpected hurricane and the stopping of the fisherman's watch) leading to the catastrophe. The experience of the maelstrom comes to the character as well as to the reader as a vivid sensation of "awe and horror and admiration." The wonder that the character experiences at his perilous situation and his admiration of the beauty of the funnel-like whirlpool that he enjoys while he is violently gyrating, are similar to the feelings of the narrator of Brown's *Edgar Huntly:* "My surprise was so abrupt, and my sensations so tumultuous, that I forgot for a moment the perilous nature of my situation."[37] Like the narrator of Poe's tale, the narrator of Brown's novel enjoys the "sublimity and grandeur" of the scene. Poe's description of the rotating black funnel of a whirlpool is so exquisite that it comes upon the reader as a picture. He is able to achieve this effect by means of realistic detail and economy of language.

In his letter of July 12, 1841 to Joseph Evans Snodgrass, Poe says about "A Descent into the Maelstrom:"

> It was finished in a hurry, and therefore its conclusion is imperfect. Upon the whole it is neither

> good nor has it been ½ so popular as "The Murders in the Rue Morgue."[38]

Whatever Poe's dissatisfaction with the conclusion of the tale, in his letter of July 2, 1844 to James Russell Lowell, he includes both "A Descent into the Maelstrom" and "The Murders in the Rue Morgue" in the category of his "best tales" of the order of "Ligeia", "The Fall of the House of Usher," and "The Gold Bug."[39] However, compared with some of the "best tales," "A Descent into the Maelstrom" has neither the element of mystery nor psychological complexity. It is realistically fantastic and as such is more convincing than "Ms Found in a Bottle". But within its own limited terms the tale is perfectly consistent and successful in what it aims at. Poe's dissatisfaction with its conclusion is difficult to understand. His comparison of the tale with "The Murders in the Rue Morgue" may be incidental in terms of the popularity of the two tales. What is common between the two is the ratiocinative element. Despite the use of epithets relating to the Gothic, there is in this tale more of the rational control avoiding morbidity of character. The morbidity, if any, in the old man is more convincingly presented as being circumstantial. The old man, who relates the actual experience of the whirlpool is, like the narrator of "The Pit and the Pendulum", a rational being before and after the supposed reasoning of the morbid narrators of "Berenice" and "Ligeia". The peripheral narrator, unlike the narrators of tales like "The Fall of the House of Usher", is more rational, coming close to the omniscient author. On the whole, the drama of effect in "A Descent into the Maelstrom" is a product of the tension between the Gothic and the Ratiocinative. The story celebrates the triumph of reason in overcoming disaster, even as "The Fall of the House of Usher" laments the tragedy of the failure of reason.

There is a wide divergence of critical opinion regarding "The Masque of the Red Death" (1842) ranging from clinical diagnosis to mystical impressionism, as listed by Josepn P. Roppolo.[40] In the opinion of T.O. Mabbott, the tale is "unsurpassed", perhaps unequalled, among Poe's very short stories."[41] In theme, tone and movement, the tale closely parallels "Shadow." The two tales have identical themes and follow the same broad outlines. In both the tales the initial situation is that a group of people trying to escape a pestilence and shutting themselves in a closed vault, and the central incident relates to the appalling visitation of the mysterious figure of death. The visitation occurs in the midst of a revel in which the men are engaged in a feverishly desperate bid to shut themselves from the fear of death. In the desciption of the setting, too, the tales follow a nearly identical decor and aim at the same effect of terror. In their general moral intent, too, the tales are identical: both the "Shadow" and the "Red Death" are dramatizations of death. There are, of course, differences of detail and treatment. Apart from a more effective handling of the conclusion than in "Shadow", "The Masque of the Red Death" develops on more elaborate scale elements such as tone, atmosphere and symbolism.[42] The narrative achieves a definite harmony of the character's mood with the Gothic setting. The varying colors of the rooms and the chimes of the clock cause agitation in the minds of the masqueraders at intervals of time. The setting represents a symbolic construct of life itself: the seven chambers represent the seven ages of man and the clock is the traditional warning signal of the diminishing human life. The surrealistic masquerading figures symbolize human folly and vanity desperately struggling to escape the inevitability of death. In the last chamber, the red window throws on the revellers a light that symbolizes the "Red Death" symptomized by blood. Thus atmosphere of the tale is achieved by means of color symbolism and the chiming of the clock that control the very movements of the masqueraders.

However, the crucial issue in the tale seems to be whether it possesses a strict narrative structure, whether it can, in short, be called a tale or whether it is simply a kind of mythic parable, built rather on the poetic elements of tone and suggestion. For instance, Joseph Patrick Roppolo doubts whether the piece can be called a short story or a tale even by the freest definition. He says:

> Instead, "The Masque of the Red Death" combines elements of the parable and of the myth. Not as explict or as pointedly allegorical always as the parable, "The Masque of the Red Death" nevertheless can be (and has been) read as a parable of the inevitability and the universality of death; but it deals also with the feats of a hero or demigod–Prospero–and with Poe's concepts of universal principles, and it has the mystery and the remoteness of myth. What Poe has created, then, is a kind of mythic parable, brief and poetic, of the human condition, of man's fate, and of the fate of the universe.[43]

There is no doubt about the mythic-parabolic character of the narrative; no doubt also that it depends to a large extent on the elements of tone and suggestion. But Roppolo's objection to its title as a tale – that "it is deficient in plot and in characterization"–is open to question.

As for the plot, it would be wrong to say that the tale has none, for, in its structure and movement the tale follows the general pattern of most of Poe's tales in that it centers round a single dramatic incident toward which all other events lead us inevitably and with premeditated design. The opening itself creates a strong impression of the devastation caused by Red Death:

> The Red Death has long devastated the country. No pestilence had ever been fatal, or so hideous. Blood was its avatar and its seal – the redness and the horror of blood. There were sharp pains, and sudden dizziness, and then profuse bleeding at the pores, with dissolution. The scarlet stains upon the body, and especially upon the face, of the victim were the pest ban, which shut him out from the aid and from the sympathy of his fellow-men. And the whole seizure, progress, and termination of the disease were the incidents of half an hour (I, 249).

Poe's skill consists in keeping up the emotional tension right up to the point of the climax when Prospero and his companions are brought to their doom by the masked figure.

Tales like "The Masque of the Red Death" do not record reversals or take surprising turns. Poe's aim in plot-construction generally is unity of effect rather than complexity, with tone and atmosphere contributing to a climactic incident. Thus his tales are monolithic structures. In this sense "The Masque of the Red Death" has as much plot as "Ligeia" or "The Fall of the House of Usher". And its movement is dramatic in the sense that it takes us through ominous hints and suggestive details to an expectation of the inevitable doom, and the visitation of the masked death is itself a terrifying incident. Thus the climax completes and fulfills the central design of the narrative. The further objection that the tale is deficient in characterization may be partly true. Unlike "Ligeia" or "William Wilson" where the focus is on the psychology of character and where the incidents emanate from the complex and mysterious constitution of the character's mind, "The Masque of the Red Death" and "Shadow" develop the incident in purely external terms. The experiences of Prince Prospero and his companions may represent a general human condition,[44] but they do not reflect any inner predicament.

Thus "The Masque of the Red Death" has a firm narrative structure. The symbolic elements are more fully developed in this tale than in "Shadow". And Poe bestows a good deal of care on building up tone and atmosphere. Character in this tale, as in the other atmospheric tales, is very much a part of the environment and is shaped by it. Just as in "Ms Found in a Bottle" the effect is achieved largely through the manipulation of light and shade, in "The Masque of the Red Death" it is done through the color symbolism. On the whole, Poe succeeds in creating fantasy in the tale. But here too, as in some other tales, he is able to create part of the drama by juxtaposing fact and fantasy. This is evident from T.O. Mabbott's testimony that the plot of the tale "involves the supernatural, but the chief incidents are historical, referring to the epidemic of cholera at Paris in 1832."[45] Kermit Vanderbilt seems to stretch the meaning of the tale too far when he interprets it in the light of Poe's aesthetic theory in 1842. Vanderbilt says that Prospero is "an exact portrait of Poe's artist–hero and "The Masque of the Red Death" becomes a fable of nature and art. Placed in a larger context, the tale allowed Poe to dramatize the tensions of the 'Romantic' artist in America, and helped him to discover the way which led through "The Domain of Arnheim" into the cosmic regions of Eureka."[46] The beauty of "The Domain of Arnheim" and other sketches is idyllic whereas the setting of "The Masque of the Red Death" is urban Gothic. The arrangement of colors with its visual effect is dramatic rather than poetic.

The story of "The Pit and the Pendulum" (1843) opens with an account of a victim of the Spanish inquisition. The opening paragraph reveals the narrator describing the scene of the trial in which he was sentenced by the black-robed judges. An impression of the entire scene is suggested to the reader through the blurred vision of the man as he gradually loses consciousness. The "dreamy indeterminate hum" of the Inquisitorial voices striking the narrator a short time as "the burr of a mill-wheel" and the voice of the black-robed judges issuing the decrees against him (gradually fading away out of his hearing), are the experiences of one getting into a deep sleep. The picture of the black-robed judges on his mind is intensified by that of the "waving of the sable draperies which enwrapped the walls of the apartment," thus producing an atmospheric effect on the reader. The seven tall candles momentarily appearing to be seven angels who may save him from the torture only turn out to be spectral in the end. These experiences immediately merge into one pitch-blackness and he loses consciousness.

The narrator gathers from his memory all that he had experienced in the torture-chamber following the trial:

> These shadows of memory tell, indistinctly, of tall figures that lifted and bore me in silence down–down–still down–till a hideous dizziness oppressed me at the mere idea of the interminableness of the descent (I, 311).

Here is an account by the narrator of the faint memory of how he was carried into the cell in a semi-conscious state. Having been in the cell he comes to his senses and recollects the whole series of events:

> And now a full memory of the trial, of the judges, of the sable draperies, of the sentence, of the sickness, of the swoon. Then entire forgetfulness of all that followed; of all that a later day and much earnestness of endeavor have enabled me vaguely to recall (I, 312).

The narration of the events of the tale is not reliable since it is done by one frequently falling into a state of semi-consciousness. Nevertheless, Poe's skillful rendition of the dusky region between waking and sleeping (through the consciousness of the character) produces surrealistic effect. The narrator's frequent stumbling on the brink of the abyss intensifies the sense of expectation. When the victim escapes the fatal accident of the pit, he is faced with the relentless torture of the descending pendulum and by the rats that surround him. The description of the gradually descending pendulum with its hideous motion and the narrator's experiences of it are fraught with suspense. The final experiences of the chamber diminishing in its dimensions to squeeze the victim, and of the descending heated iron complete the tension of the narrative, only to be suddenly relieved by the prisoner's rescue by the French. Here Poe's masterful handling of suspense contributes much to the effect of the tale. Suspense is the reader's emotional reaction to the information deliberately withheld by the author. In "The Pit and the Pendulum," suspense comprises terrible mental turtures experienced by the character. His bafflement serves to heighten the reader's expectation too. The setting of the Spanish Inquisition is suitable in attitude and method to build up the suspense of the narrative. The subtlety and intensity of purpose of the inquisitors provide the author the best atmosphere and a means to his study in suspense. The series of narrow escapes for the character heightens the intensity of the ultimate effect of the tale.

The author achieves emotional intensity for his narrative by playing upon the reader's senses and building up the tone of narration. The first impression is of the sense of hearing: "the voices seemed merged in one dreamy indeterminate hum." Also the hissing noise of the descending pendulum unnerves the victim. From the sense of sound we come to that of sight:

> I saw the lips of the black-robed judges. They appeared to me white, whiter than the sheet upon which I trace these words, and thin even to grotesqueness; thin with the intensity of their expression of firmness, – of immovable resolution, of stern contempt of human torture. I saw that the decrees of what to me was Fate were still issuing from those lips. I saw them writhe with a deadly locution. I saw them fashion the syllables of my name; and I shuddered because no sound succeeded. I saw, too, for a few moments of delirious horror, the soft and nearly imperceptible waving of the sable draperies which enwrapped the walls of the apartment. And then my vision fell upon the seven tall candles upon the table. At first they wore the aspect of charity, and seemed white slender angels who would save me... (I, 309-310).

Toward the end of the tale, the reader, like the narrator, experiences the terrible sight of the "glittering steel" of the Pendulum and the dazzling luster of the heated iron. Such is the power of Poe's description that juxtaposes white and black, light and shade, producing a visual effect on the reader. The impression created by the senses of hearing and sight is strengthened by that of bodily feeling. The feeling of deadly nausea in the opening scene benumbs every fibre of the narrator's frame. Subsequently, in the damp cell, "the peculiar smell of decayed fungus" and the "odour of the sharp steel" increase the feeling of dread. In the final scene the "vapor of heated iron" producing a "suffocating odor" completes the emotional effect that these various sense impressions produce on the reader.

A major device employed by Poe in this tale is the romantic metaphor of the dungeon causing what Victor Brombert calls "dialectical tensions between oppression and the dream of freedom, between fatality and revolt, between the finite and infinity."[47] The device adds to the overall emotional effect of the tale. The central idea of the tale, according to T.O. Mabbott, is that "the fear of the unknown exceeds the fear of anything known."[48] In this respect, the experiences of the character in facing imminent death followed by a series of hairbreadth escapes are similar to those of the protagonist in "A Descent into the Maelstrom".

In "The Pit and the Pendulum" Poe does not tell us the exact nature of the narrator's crime for which he is being tortured in the pit (presumably heresy). In Kafka's *The Penal Colony* too the condemned men do not know their sentences; nor are they informed of the nature of their crimes. In *The Trial*, the hero Joseph K. is accused, but does not know the nature of his crime. Thus the protagonists in Kafka lead a life of nonexistence similar to that of Poe's hero. Whereas in Kafka's *The Penal Colony* the effect is serious with the machine inscribing on the body of a prisoner the commandment he has unwittingly transgressed, killing him and throwing his body into a trench, in Poe's tale it is somewhat melodramatic. The description of the descending pendulum and the closing metal walls of the torture chamber give the impression that Poe is aiming at making the reader's flesh creep rather than creating an experience with a serious meaning. Schopenhauer compares the world with a penal colony. In comparison with Kafka's, Poe's tale merely evokes physical horror by means of an ingenious manipulation of atmosphere.

According to George E. Woodbery, "The Fall of the House of Usher" (1839) is unsurpassed for "unity of design."[49] In the opinion of T.O. Mabbott, the tale "is probably the most popular of Poe's earlier tales of wonder."[50] It is in the first person–peripheral–narration, the point of view being that of a non-central character, an intimate friend of Roderick Usher, the neurasthenic dilettante. Despite occasional authorial intrusions, it is mainly through the consciousness of the narrator that we have an account of the characters and incidents in the story. The narrator of the present tale, like that of "The Assignation", is an outsider with his own individual consciousness and sanity of outlook corresponding to that of the reader. However, his limited and confused understanding of the course of events makes his point of view largely unreliable. At times the story is rendered from Usher's own point of view, the narrator remaining just a transmitter.

The tale is one of the most famous of Poe's atmospheric tales in successfully synchronizing the character's mood and the setting. One of Poe's requirements in the craft of tale–writing is fully exemplified here: the beginning should foreshadow the entire course of events of the story. The keynote of the story is struck at once in the opening paragraph, describing the narrator's arrival at the Usher mansion and the environment he finds himself in:

> During the whole of a dull, dark, and soundless day in the autumn of the year, when the clouds hung oppressively low in the heavens, I had been passing alone, on horseback, through a singularly dreary tract of country; and at length found myself, as the shades of evening drew on, within view of the melancholy House of Usher. I know not how it was--but, with the first glimpse of the building, a sense of insufferable gloom pervaded my spirit (I, 131).

Every word here contributes toward an effective manipulation of the reader's mood. The "dull, dark, and soundless day," with the clouds hanging "oppressively low in the heavens" on the "singularly dreary tract of country" and "the melancholy House of Usher" create "a sense of insufferable gloom" not only in the narrator's mind, but in the reader's as well. This is how Poe at once establishes the tone and atmosphere of the narrative in the opening paragraph. His success lies in sustaining the atmosphere throughout the course of the tale. Instead of the authorial comment, the commentary spoken by a character in the story, according to Wayne C.Booth, is more suitable for mood-building. Booth counters the objection raised by Caroline Gordon and Allen Tate that the story has "not one instance of dramatized detail,"[51] and says, "For Poe's special kind of morbid horror, a psychological detail, as conveyed by an emotionally charged adjective, is more effective than mere sensual description in any form."[52]

The narrative opening in this tale is different from those of the other tales. Tales like "Metzengerstein" and "Berenice" have reflective openings—the author himself gives a philosophical statement, which is to be developed in the story, more or less as its theme. In the present tale, however, with its emotional beginning, we are at once given the physical setting and the narrator's reaction to it. The very first sight of the mansion causes "shadowy fancies" in the narrator's mind. The "black and lurid tarn" and the inverted image of the house within its depth produce a "strange fancy" in his mind. The narrator is stupefied on observing the whole mansion and its immediate vicinity, "an atmosphere which had no affinity with the air of heaven, but which had reeken up from the decayed trees, the gray wall, and the silent tarn: a pestilent and mystic vapor, dull, sluggish, faintly discernible, and leaden-hued" (I, 134). Thus the very environment has a profound emotional effect on the narrator and prepares the reader to receive the events to follow. Ian Walker's study of the atmosphere as producing Usher's madness is interesting.[53]

Poe develops a consistent symbolic association between the mansion and the Ushers with their abnormal mental condition. Richard Wilbur says, "The Fall of the House of Usher" is, in allegorical fact, the physical body of Roderick Usher, and its dim interior *is*, in fact, Roderick Usher's visionary mind."[54] However, what gives so much dramatic significance to character and event in the tale is not a consistently developed allegory, but symbolic overtones. Complaining to Rufus W. Griswold that "The Haunted Palace" was plagiarized by Longfellow, Poe says: "...by the Haunted Palace I mean to imply a mind haunted by phantoms–a disordered brain."[55]

"The Haunted Palace" of the quoted verse corresponds to "The Fall of the House of Usher" and its tragic destiny. Initially, the narrator himself becomes aware of the "indication of extensive decay" in the mansion; and he is struck by "a wild inconsistency between its still perfect adaptation of parts and the crumbling condition of the individual stones" (I, 135). He also notices a "barely perceptible fissure" running all the way down the wall fo the mansion. This suggests the broken mental condition of the tenants and their portentous doom. And the house becomes a looming animated presence symbolizing the tragic destiny of its occupants. To Usher himself the mansion is a sentient being. He sees sentience in its gray stones and in the order of their collocation.[56] Hence he speaks of the house as a "silent yet importunate and terrible influence which for centuries had molded the destinies of this family." Thus the point of view of the narrator becomes the Usher's own point of view. The symbolic connection between the house and its inmates is brought to full realization when, at the end of the tale, the crumbling of the house coincides with the crumbling of the inmates. The long fissure that is noticed by the narrator at first rapidly widens into a breach and the house comes down into a heap of stones.

> While I gazed, this fissure rapidly widened—there came a fierce breath of the whirlwind—the entire orb of the satellite burst at once upon my sight—my brain reeled as I saw the mighty walls rushing asunder—there was a long tumultuous shouting sound like the voice of a thousand waters—and the deep and dark tarn at my feet closed sullenly and silently over the fragments of the "House of Usher" (I, 155-56).

The symbolism in the tale contributes to the heightening of the emotional atmosphere. The emotion is built up by means of recurring images like "the dark and intricate passages," "the ebon blackness of the floors," "the somber tapestries," and the "dark tapestries."

In addition to the tonal unity, Poe insists upon the unity of the plot in a tale—an interlinking of the incidents of the narrative, the denouement having been always kept in view. There should be a natural and quick succession of incidents. The incidents in "The Fall of the House of Usher" are remarkably well–knit, and lead to an impressive climax when Usher is brought down to his death by the revived Madeline. And this is instantly followed by the narrator's fleeing away and the house itself collapsing into "the black and lurid tarn." Thus from a slow and steady movement of the narrative with its atmospheric build-up, we come to a sudden conclusion.

The incident of the sudden appearance and disappearance of the sickly Madeline through a remote portion of the apartment heightens the already existing confusion on the part of the narrator. His confusion is worse confounded when he looks at Usher's painting of "a ghostly picture" presenting "the interior of an immensely long and rectangular vault or tunnel" at "an exceeding depth below the surface of the earth." In addition to his confusion at the strange course of events, the narrator admits his fundamental failure to comprehend the mind of his friend. The narrator, who initially appears to be a very rational being, finds himself ultimately in a situation no better than Usher's. Darrel Abel says that the narrator, "a common–sense witness," accepts "imaginatively the supernatural explanation."[57] In fact, the narrator gets highly confused and flees. Imagination and reason fail him. Thus on the fateful stormy night the two friends observe, with their hearts beating intensely, the sky with clouds exceedingly dense, with no glimpse of the moon or stars, or any flash of the lightning. They also notice with dismay that

> ...the under surface of the huge masses of agitated vapor, as well as terrestrial objects immediately around us, were glowing in the unnatural light of a faintly luminous and distinctly visible gaseous exhalation which hung about and enshrouded the mansion (I, 150).

The "unnatural light" and the "gaseous exhalation" are

perhaps the result of some strange illumination coming from the infernal regions, suggesting the impending doom. All this corresponds to the hallucinations developed by both the narrator and Roderick Usher.

In addition to the atmospheric effects, certain structural aspects of the tale are interesting. As the narrator looks puzzled, Usher plays the verses of "The Haunted Palace" on his guitar. In the words of one of these rhapsodies, the narrator fancies that he perceived "a full consciousnes, on the part of Usher, of the tottering of his lofty reason upon her throne" (I, 142). Usher reads books dealing with strange ideas concerning the matter-spirit relationship, the doubles, and demons. the reading of the weird romance "Mad Trist" quickens the pace of the events toward the inevitable catastrophe. Certain incidents of the Launcelot story coincide with the happenings of Madeline's breaking through the coffin. This coincidence is, in its deeper significance, not merely a fortuitous happening, but an exact correlative to the structure of feeling within the mind of the subject. It is a coincidence of inner fear and outer happening, and it is fully anticipated by Usher. The breaking of the hermit's door, the death–cry of the dragon, and the clangor of the shield are interpreted by Usher as corresponding to Madeline's rending of her coffin, the grating of the iron hinges, and her struggles within the coppered archway of the vault. And in the certitude of his inner fear, Usher clearly visualizes the approach of Madeline as the anticipated approach of doom. As a climactic happening, Madeline bears her brother "to the floor a corpse, and a victim to the terrors he had anticipated" (I, 155). T.O. Mabbott says that Usher is sure that Madeline is alive because she is still alive and that "he avoids her actual burial by a temporary entombment."[58] Another way of looking at the situation is that Madeline's premature burial by Usher causes a sense of guilt in him, a guilt that is deeply rooted in the family of the Ushers. But it is difficult to agree with the view of J.O. Bailey that "Madeline is a vampire."[59] D.H. Lawrence sees incest in the relationship between Usher and his twin sister.[60] Such a view does not stand the test of critical scrutiny.

There is certainly a terrible feeling of guilt on the part of Usher. However, the guilt is something more deeply rooted in the family itself than in the personal relationship between the twins. On the whole, the tale is an impressive study of the protagonist's complex state of mind. Referring to Nathaniel Hawthorne, Frederick Crews says that he "rested his whole achievement on the premise that the only important truth is that which has been repressed."[61] The story of Roderick Usher is significant for such psychological truth.

The peripheral narrator of the tale is the eyewitness recorder of fantastic events like the narrator of Washington Irving's "Adventure of the Mysterious Picture.[62] However, these are nervous characters, embodying a combination of objective fact and suggestion—a combination of what they subjectively observe and their own ways of observing it. Joseph Warren Beach ranks Conrad's *Heart of Darkness* with Poe's story in respect to the "limited point of view."[63] But Marlow in Conrad's tale is more knowledgeable and reliable than Poe's narrator whose knowledge of human nature is limited and who is somewhat confused. Marlow is a wiser man when he leaves Kurtz, whereas Poe's narrator is utterly puzzled. Marlow, like Captain Delano in Melville's *Benito Cereno*, observes the protagonist from a greater distance and is able to present character and event with greater intellectual detachment. However, Kurtz in Conrad's tale and Benito Cereno in Melville's present a striking resemblance to Roderick Usher. All the three protagonists are afflicted by some strange malady, a deep-rooted sense of evil. Their hearts are engulfed in dreadful darkness and the study of their situation is a journey into the darkness of the human heart. The essential drama of "The Fall of the House of Usher" arises from the narrator's efforts to adhere to logic and to a common sense world and the ultimate shattering of reason into fragments.

The Tales of Character

In his letter of August 9, 1846 to P.P. Cooke, Poe says, referring to the "vast variety of kinds" of his tales: "The loftiest kind is that of the highest imagination—and, for this reason only, "Ligeia" may be called my *best* tale."[64] Thus in his tales of the order of "Ligeia" (1838) Poe attempts to embody "the highest imagination" by means of character and event. The tale lends itself to a clean division into two parts: the first part marking the first phase and the second part marking the second, in the spiritual life of Ligeia. The first part contains more of character-portrayal (of Ligeia) and less of incidents. The care that the author bestows on descriptive detail contributes to a vivid projection of the image of Ligeia with the superhuman appeal of her character. The theme of reincarnation casually dealt with in "Metzengertein" is rendered more effectively in "Ligeia" and "Morella."

The narrative opens with a description of Ligeia's character, since Ligeia herself is the story. In this respect the opening of this tale is different from the openings of tales like "The Fall of the House of Usher", "The Masque of the Red Death", and "Berenice." The elaborate character-portrayal in the opening pages of "Ligeia" makes the incidents in the story psychologically probable. In fact, in no other of his tales does Poe bestow so much attention on the depiction of a single character.

Critics have interpreted the character largely in poetic terms. For instance, Arthur H. Quinn says that Poe "took a poetic conception from "Al Aaraaf," Ligeia, the soul of beauty, and developed it in a prose story."[65] George E. Woodberry also expresses the same opinion when he says that Poe "incarnated the motions of the breeze and the musical voices of nature in the form of a woman...of no human quality... She is...the air-woven divinity in which he believed."[66] Such theories as these, interpreting the character of Ligeia in purely symbolic terms, as the embodiment of Poe's poetic principle, seem to miss the real focus of the tale. The portrayal of Ligeia's character is no doubt largely in poetic terms—Ligeia corresponds to Poe's Helen and his Ligeia of "Al Aaraaf." These women represent Poe's conception of supernal beauty and they are of a highly refined poetic sensibility. The language in which Ligeia's character is rendered is also highly imaginative so as to qualify the tale as a prose poem. But here we must make some important reservations. "Ligeia" is not a prose poem in the sense that it is a symbolic rendering of some poetic principle or that it is even about that principle. To all intents and purposes, Poe here is not trying to embody some conception of the Poetic Muse but he is telling a tale with a well-defined, though extraordinary and fantastic motive and he renders this in a supremely effective way. Viewed in the light of this a dramatic characterization of Ligeia is required. It is necessary for establishing the motive. And Poe's success lies in relating every detail of the portrayal directly to the motivation of the character, in rendering it highly functional. Thus, Ligeia's character, however poetic and visionary in conception, establishes a relevance to the main concern of the tale. Ligeia has supernal beauty in which strangeness is an essential component and with an extraordinary brilliance of eyes which both delight and appall the narrator: these together with her glossy raven-black tresses only establish her highly passionate nature. There is a greater significance in her eyes—they seem to speak for that "gigantic volition" which is the central motivation of her character. The eyes grow in intensity of look and brilliance as Ligeia's illness grows on her: "The wild eyes blazed with glorious effulgence." At another place, the narrator observes a certain meteoric quality in them, an intensity such as he felt in the glances of unusually aged people. Ligeia's eyes thus exert an almost hypnotic fascination on the narrator. But it is the woman's inordinate longing and her supernatural volition that are reflected in her eyes. In the very unearthliness of her aspect the narrator recognizes the "principle of her longing," that expresses her highly passionate nature. Poe says in "The Poetic Principle" that in a poem Beauty should predominate over all other elements like Passion and Truth:

> ...but the true artist will always contrive to tone them down ["the incitements of Passion, the precepts of Duty, or even the lessons of Truth"] in proper subjection to that *Beauty* which is the atmosphere and the real essence of the poem (VI, 13).

In "Ligeia", Passion is not in "proper subjection" to Beauty, but rather, predominates over it: "The outwardly calm, the ever-placid Ligeia, was the most violently a prey to the tumultuous vultures of stern passion" (I, 187). Thus Ligeia's character is more passionate than beautiful and less poetic than is generally supposed. Hence a conception which might have seemed poetic in the beginning becomes dramatic as the narrative proceeds.

Ligeia's illness is a turning point in the course of the events. Her death comes as the climax of a life of inordinate passion and a long struggle of the spirit, as a natural consequence of the way the subject is constituted. The intense struggles of the dying lady with the Shadow, "... in the intensity of her wild desire for life—for life—*but* for life" (I, 189), described with vividness, make the scene alive as much to the reader as to the narrator. At this point of the narrative the verse quotation[67] is introduced. These verses, read by the narrator to Ligeia on her death bed, embody the theme of the Conqueror Worm coming with writhing motion into the scene of a "motley drama" and making the mortals its prey, while the angels stand by as spectators. The poem is presented in the form of a drama[68] a kind of symbolic rendering (in the form of a pantomime) of the tragic condition of the character herself. The drama of the Conqueror Worm foreshadows the drama of Ligeia's death as "Mad Trist" leads to Roderick Usher's death. The hysterical outburst of Ligeia and her death soon after the narrator completes the reading of the verse contributes to the heightening of the climax of the first part of the story:

> O God! O Divine Father! shall these things be undeviatingly so? shall this conqueror be not once conquered? Are we not part and parcel in Thee? Who–who knoweth the mysteries of the will with its vigor? "Man doth not yield him to the angels, *nor unto death utterly*, save only through the weakness of his feeble will" (I, 191).

The words of the motto have been repeated here by the dying heroine and thus the central motivation of the tale—Ligeia's will to live—is reiterated.

At this point of our study it might be worthwhile to examine the significance of the epigraph:

> And the will therein lieth, which dieth not. Who knoweth the mysteries of the will, with its vigor? For God is but a great will pervading all things by nature of its intentness. Man doth not yield himself to the angels, nor unto death utterly, save only through the weakness of his feeble will.

Repeated as a refrain, it serves a vital structural function in reinforcing the central motivation of the tale. Broadly speaking, "Ligeia" is about this theme of the Mighty Will. This theme not only motivates Ligeia's character, but it is fully elaborated and developed by the subsequent events in the tale. The final triumph and fulfillment of the motif comes at the climax of the tale with the actual materialization of the dead Ligeia as a living presence within the body of her rival, Lady Rowena.

Poe's epigraph (the Glanvill passage) has been the subject of much critical attention. The question has been asked whether the epigraph originated with Glanvill or with the narrator and whether the narrator fully understands its import. It has been suggested that he does not penetrate the meaning of the Glanvill idea whereas Ligeia does and "makes the idea work." T.O. Mabbott says that this passage was never found in Glanvill. Therefore, it was made by Poe.[69] James Schroeter's theory is that Poe maintains "a separation between it and the narrator...because the narrator's surprise, on which the effect of the story depends, would otherwise have been impossible."[70] However, this suggested separation between the Glanvill idea and the narrator flies in the face of the facts. The fact of the case Is that the narrator is reminded of Glanvill's lines while he gazes intensely at Ligeia's eyes (I, 191). Subsequently, he hears the same words of the quotation from the lips of the dying lady. There is not the least suggestion anywhere that Ligeia remained opaque to the narrator. On the other hand, the narrator has recognized even from the beginning the Ligeia embodies the indomitable will to live that the Glanvill quotation speaks of:

> ...I at length recognized the principle of her longing, with so wildly earnest a desire, for the life, which was now fleeing so rapidly away. It is this wild longing; it is this eager vehemence of desire for life—*but* for life, that I have no power to portray, no utterance capable of expressing (I, 190).

The narrator's surprise at the changed aspect of Lady Rowena, which Schroeter thinks is vital to the effect of the story, is not caused by his misunderstanding of the Glanvill motto, but by his sudden realization that Ligeia has made the idea work by actually materializing her will in the body of Lady Rowena. As Roy Basler contends, the idea does originate with the narrator and is his *idee fixe*.[71] To the narrator himself, the Glanvill passage is of considerable significance in that it makes him alive to the intensity of Ligeia's longing in the strength of her volition: it provides him with a clue to her strange character. It is also as much a knowledge shared by Ligeia herself and it becomes her *idee fixe*. It is equally the *idee fixe* of the tale itself, as it provides its central motivation and receives elaboration by its events. It would be no exaggeration to claim that the entire story is built around the dominant motif of the epigraph which is integrated into the very structure of the tale. Also the epigraph narrows down the distance between the author and the narrator and the point of view becomes the author's.

The incidents in the second part of the tale follow up as a sequel to the first phase and exemplify the central theme of the will. As in the first part the author prepares for the culmination in Ligeia's death through character—delineation so in the second part he creates the atmosphere for the kind of experience that the narrator is to undergo. The dwelling in which the narrator settles down with his second bride Lady Rowena is an abbey "in one of the wildest and least frequented portions of fair England." Many details of description contribute to the establishment of the character's state of mind and the atmosphere of the tale. The grotesque hangings and tapestries of the walls and the phantasmagoric aspect of the bridal chamber with its ceiling of "gloomy-looking oak," "excessively lofty, vaulted, and elaborately fretted with the wildest and the most grotesque specimens of a semi-Gothic, semi-Druidical device...", (I, 193) are reflected through the troubled consciousness of the narrator. They impress themselves upon his sensibility in a manner that gives the feeling of utter isolation and abandonment, investing his surroundings with "a hideous and uneasy animation." But this external setting is only a reflection of the narrator's state of mind. T.O. Mabbott says that the pentagonal shape of the bridal chamber is intended for magical effect and that the character's experience is not hallucinatory.[72] The external setting of the chamber produces a visual effect, serving a basic dramatic purpose to present character and incident. Having been preoccupied with his reveries about the departed Ligeia, the narrator has been fiercely moody in his temper, excited by the effects of opium. This harmony of the external setting with the character's distempered mind makes the second phase of the tale atmospheric in its effect. Phrases like "the slight sounds," "the unusual motions among the tapestries," "the gentle variations of the figures upon the wall," describing Rowena's experiences, heighten the suspense of the narration. The incident of the "three or four large drops of a brilliant and ruby colored fluid" falling into the goblet is suggestive. Vincent Buranelli takes the drops to be poison.[73] But T.O. Mabbott is of the opinion that "they are rather a primary corporeal form attained by Ligeia's spirit; and in themselves the elixir of life."[74] The narrator hears or thinks that he has heard some noise. Such a psychological experience is similar to Clither's in Brockden Brown's *Edgar Huntly*: "I heard a noise from without, or imagined that I heard it."[75]

In the climactic part of the tale, the sight of Lady Rowena's revivification and the low sobs repeatedly startle the narrator from his reveries. The final incident of the enshrouded corpse slowly rising from the bed and advancing into the middle of the apartment paralyzes the narrator. But this is not yet the height of this climax of horror. The narrator jumps to his feet in the grip of this unspeakable horror and grabs at the shroud. Instantly, the apparition let fall her ghastly cerements and reveals herself in the image of Ligeia:

> ...there streamed forth into the rushing atmosphere of the chamber huge masses of long and dishevelled hair; *it was blacker than the raven wings of the midnight!* And now slowly opened *the eye* of the figure that stood before me. "Here then, at least," I shrieked aloud, "can I never—can I never be mistaken—these are the full, and the black, and the wild eyes—of my lost love—of the Lady—of the LADY LIGEIA" (I, 202).

As Poe himself explains in his letter to P.P. Cooke, this revelation comes on the narrator as "a sudden half-consciousness."[76] Throughout the scene the narrator has not been alive to the nature of the presence that he and Lady Rowena experienced. In spite of his obsession with the image of Ligeia, he has not suspected that Ligeia would impress her will in this fashion. But now the realization of this is entirely unexpected for him.

Though thus, the final incident is rendered with psychological realism, the end of the tale is left rather ambiguous. What are the narrator's reactions to the revelation of Ligeia through the corpse of Lady Rowena? Before the revelation itself, the narrator is chilled with terror caused by the apparition. But after the lovely and fantastic image of Ligeia reveals itself from the shroud, is the terror transformed for the narrator into an ecstatic vision? The indication would seem to be that it is, that the narrator is delighted and thrilled by the revelation. After publishing "Ligeia", Poe sent it to P.P. Cooke inquiring whether the conclusion of the story was intelligible. Cooke replied, "I of course 'took' your 'idea' throughout...your intent is to tell a tale of the 'mighty will' contending with and finally vanquishing Death." He was "shocked by a violation of the ghostly properties...and wondered how the Lady Ligeia—a wandering essence—could, in quickening *the body of the Lady Rowena*...become suddenly the visible, bodily, Ligeia." Cooke wished the narrator had only become gradually aware that the "blue Saxon eye...grew daily darker...a mind of grander powers...occupied the quickened body."[77] In his reply of September 21, 1839 Poe said that because he had already written "Morella", he was "forced to be content with a sudden half-consciousness, on the part of the narrator, that Ligeia stood before him."[78] But while this is so, the reader himself is left in an uneasy state of indecision whether to react to the conclusion as that of a horror tale or as a final culminating vision of a delightful fantasy. The overall impression of the scene would no doubt rule out the latter alternative. There is undoubtedly something supernatural and terrifying in the idea of the spirit of the dead tenanting the person of the living. The fact that Ligeia's will asserts itself after death and possesses the person of Lady Rowena would naturally suggest the evil act of a vampire. Joseph Andriano maintains that the female demons that seem omnipresent in male Gothic fiction are often, though not always, signs of anima, the feminine aspect of the male.[79] T.O. Mabbott asserts, "The heroine is not an orthodox vampire. Her resemblance to a dybbuk is undeniable, but is probably fortuitous, since it is not easy to say how Poe could have met with legends current in Jewish folklore of Poland and Russia."[80] D.H. Lawrence is convincing when he says,

> It is the spirit of Ligeia, leagued with the spirit of the husband, that...lusts in the slow destruction of Rowena. The two vampires, dead wife and living husband.[81]

The entire development of the second part of the tale would justify the impression of a horror tale. But "Ligeia" is different from "Berenice" and "Morella" in respect to the narrator's attitude toward the woman who "possesses." The narrators in these latter tales are not in love with the women. They even hate them and are repelled by them. In the case of Morella, the woman's vampirism is an act of vengeance; but it is not so in the case of Ligeia. Ligeia is depicted as being angelic and lovely and she is throughout the subject of the narrator's absorbing, though obsessive, visions. But the circumstances in which she reveals herself in spirit to her lover are of the most terrifying kind. Ligeia's death at the end of the first part of the tale takes on a sublime tragic aspect, but her reappearance in the second is associated with horror. There is thus a seeming disharmony between the image of Ligeia that is presented in the first part and the later circumstances of her "resurrection—a disharmony that only produces a confused response to the ultimate "effect" of the tale. Did Poe in his effort to render the Morella-theme more sublime and invest it with a poetic significance fall between the two stools of the poetic significance fall between the two stools of the poetic and the Gothic modes?

In his letter of September 21, 1839 to P.P. Cooke, Poe seems to be uncertain about the conclusion:

> The *gradual* perception of the fact that Ligeia lives again in the person of Rowena is a far loftier and more thrilling idea than the one I have embodied.[82]

He feels so because "It was necessary, since 'Morella' was written, to modify 'Ligeia'." Poe thus admits that while in view of a more gradual ending in "Morella", here he had to be content "with a sudden half-consciousness on the part of the narrator, that Ligeia stood before him."

> ...I should have intimated that the *will* did not perfect its intention—there should have been a relapse—a final one—and Ligeia (which had only succeeded in so much as to convey an idea of the truth to the narrator) should be at length entombed as Rowena—the bodily alternations having gradually faded away.[83]

It is doubtful whether a conclusion in the manner suggested by Poe would have been more effective; at any rate it would not have strengthened the case of the self-assertion of the will. As it is, the felt presence of Ligeia and her possessing the body of Lady Rowena are presented as objective phenomena—Ligeia's disturbing presence is the shared experience of both the narrator and Rowena—not merely a hallucination, the product of an abnormal, fevered brain. Several critics have said that the tale is one of remorse and hallucination.[84] In fact, Ligeia's resurrection is meant to be taken as an objective occurrence in which the theme of the will is carried out to the plotted end. It is also doubtful whether a more gradual perception would have made Idea of the tale any "loftier." As it is, we can claim that the surprise ending is, if different from that of "Morella," equally effective and even more natural in terms of the facts of the tale.

"Morella" (1835), written three years before "Ligeia", contains thematic and technical features that find elaboration in the latter tale. Poe's high opinion about "Morella" is evident when he said, in his letter of December 1, 1835 to Judge Beverley Tucker, "It was my best,"[85] and elsewhere viewed it in relation to "Ligiea."[86] Both the tales depict the exertion of the will of the dead upon the living. In "Ligeia," the force of the will is directed against the rival Lady Rowena and in the present tale Morella lives again in the person of her own daughter. Again, whereas in "Morella" the narrator has a more definite knowledge of the fact of the dead wife living again, in "Ligeia" the realization comes at the end of the story only as a "sudden half-consciousness." Technically too *Morella* has some resemblances to "Ligeia." The opening of the tale gives us no philosophical statement but starts with a portrayal of Morella's character as in the case of "Ligeia". The narrator sketches Morella's intellectual and psychological background and his own relations with her. In "Morella," as in "Ligeia," the character-portrayal (even though not as elaborate as in "Ligeia,") brings out the powerful nature of the heroine and her vengeful attitude toward the narrator. However, the attitude of Ligeia toward the narrator is not one of vegeance but of passion for reunion.

The character of Morella is fully Gothic both in detail and general outline. The mysterious propensity of the woman, her erudite learning, her superhuman predilections, her very beauty and the music of her voice "tainted with terror," her unearthly aspect which falls like a shadow upon the spirit of the protagonist—all these traits not only alienate the woman from the protagonist, but inspire in him an unknown fear.

Certain details like the following significantly suggest the unfortunate turn that the character is to take:

> And then, hour after hour, would I linger by her side, and dwell upon the music of her voice—until, at length, its melody was tainted with terror, and there fell a shadow upon my soul, and I grew pale, and shuddered inwardly at those too unearthly tones. And thus joy suddenly faded into terror, and the most beautiful became the most hideous, as Hinnom became Gehenna (I, 175).

The woman is of uncommon sensitivity and of a high-strung nature. She is a fragile spirit, falling victim to a strange disease that consumes her and gives her a wasted, almost ghostly look.

In his letter of December 1, 1835 to Beverley Tucker, Poe contrasts the "mere *physique* of the horrible" in "Ms. Found in a Bottle" with the finer sensibility in "Morella" and calls the latter "my best." He adds, "I do not think that I would be guilty of a similar absurdity now."[87] While "Morella" may be more refined than "Ms Found in a Bottle" it cannot be called a "poetic" tale on account of the predominance of the element of passion.

The story of "Morella" deals with the idea of metempsychosis like "Metzengerstein", "A Tale of the Ragged Mountains", "The Black Cat," and "Ligeia."[88] It turns on two significant incidents. The fist is that of Morella's death. Her dying words reveal to the narrator her deep hatred for him and the strength of her desire to continue after death if only to take revenge on him:

> "I am dying, yet shall I live."
>
> "Morella!"
>
> "The days have never been when thou couldst love me – but her whom in life thou didst abhor, in death thou shalt adore."
>
> "Morella!"
>
> "I repeat that I am dying. But within me is a pledge of that affection—ah, how little!—which thou didst

feel for me Morella. And when my spirit departs shall this child live—thy child and mine, Morella's" (I, 177).

In fulfillment of this Morella relives in the person of her daughter, and the significance of her portentous words at the time of her death is fully revealed in the baptism scene. Right from the beginning the narrator notices a growing resemblance in the child to her dead mother. Finally, though he has always dreaded the very mention of Morella's name he unconsciously repeats these syllables at the baptismal font and hears the shocking response of Morella's spirit that inhabits the child:

> What fiend spoke from the recesses of my soul, when, amid these dim aisles, and in the silence of the night, I whispered within the ears of the holy man the syllables—Morella? What more than fiend convulsed the features of my child, and overspread them with hues of death, as, starting at that scarcely audible sound, she turned her glassy eyes from the earth to heaven, and, falling postrate on the black slabs of our ancestral vault, responded—"I am here!" (I, 180).

The conclusion of this tale, however, is not as effective as that of "Ligeia" and "The Fall of the House of Usher." Poe himself says that the present tale has a more "gradual" ending than "Ligeia."[89]

A noteworthy feature of "Morella" is that the incidents emerge from the character (of Morella) and illustrate her motivation. As Henry James says, "What is character but the determination of incident? What is incident but the illustration of character?"[90] Thus "Morella", however limited in perspective, as a tale of character achieves its effect without any external Gothic decor and atmosphere. But Poe's treatment of a similar material in "Ligeia" demonstrates greater mastery of such technical resources as suspense, suggestion, tone, and atmosphere. Nevertheless, his experiences with "Morella" might have made possible a more impressive achievement in "Ligeia".

Replying to a comment made by Thomas W. White, Poe says in his letter of April 30, 1835 that "Berenice" (1835) "approaches the very verge of bad taste—but I will not sin quite so egregiously again."[91] Of course, the tale concludes on a note of such gruesome horror that it may not be palatable to men of taste. As Poe himself says, "Berenice" was the result of his having on a bet selected a subject fit only for burlesque (being "too horrible") and "treated it seriously."[92] Constance Rourke says: "In the midst of the burlesque in *Tales of the Folio Club* he (Poe) reached an antithetical horror in "Berenice!"[93] "Berenice", however, cannot be dismissed as a mere "burlesque." Burlesque in Poe, as in many other writers like Herman Melville, is but an intellectual preparation for serious writing. Poe has successfully demonstrated that he is capable of treating the same subject for both serious and comic purposes.

Whatever the reaction of critics like Constance Rourke to the "antithetical horror" of "Berenice," T.O. Mabbott calls it "one of Poe's best known storiesl"[94] From the point of view of technique, the tale is certainly one of Poe's best in achieving concentration of effect. From the initial paragraph, the author works to set the tone of the narrative. The tale opens with the narrator's reflection on the misery and the evil that emerge out of the good and the beautiful.

> How is it that from beatuy I have derived a type of unloveliness? from the convenant of peace a simile of sorrow? But as, in ethics, evil is a consequence of good, so, in fact, out of joy is sorrow born. Either the memory of past bliss is the anguish of today, or the agonies which are have their origin in the ecstasies *which might have been.* (I, 157).

Poe's major concern as an artist is the portrayal, through incident and character, of this ambiguity of beauty and ugliness. This ambiguous state of character may facilitate a sudden and dramatic change caused by the course of events, as it happens in "Berenice." The transmutation of Berenice's moral and physical being under the influence of a fatal disease causes a dramatic change in the protagonist's behavior, thus giving a new direction to the course of the narrative.

The already exsting symptom of disease in his mind and body—the predispostion to disease—comes to the surface and assumes a dominant hold on him. Henceforth he feels like a monomaniac, and develops intense nervous excitability. The nature of the protagonist's monomania is explained; but the explanation is patently in the authorial voice rather than in dramatic terms. The intruding presence of the author is evident from the following passage:

> In the one instance, the dreamer or enthusiast, being interested by an object usually *not* frivolous, imperceptibly loses sight of this object in a wilderness of deductions and suggestions issuing therefrom, until at the conclusion of a day-dream *often replete with luxury*, he finds the *incitamenturn*, or first cause of his musings, entirely vanished and forgotten (I, 161).

Such authorial intrusions are intended more to exhibit Poe's knowledge of the dream states than to strengthen character and incident. As a result, the reader's attention is distracted from the course of events. However, the narrator describes his own psychology as a strange propensity to contemplate and pay intense attention to some frivolous object which utterly possesses him for the moment. The very sight of the emaciated figure of Berenice fills him with morbid horror:

> An icy chill ran through my frame; a sense of insufferable anxiety oppressed me; a consuming curiosity pervaded my soul; and, sinking back upon the chair, I remained for some time breathless and motionless, with my eyes riveted upon her person. (I, 164).

In his peculiar state of mind: the narrator's attention is riveted to the teeth of the changed Berenice he cannot shake himself from the contemplation of the object, "the ghostly *spectrum* of the teeth." The monomania comes over him in full fury and the horrid object takes complete possession of his being like a phantasm.

The incidents that follow are a natural consequence of these happenings. The narrator opens up the grave of the deceased Berenice and digs out her teeth and brings them home in a box. He does this horrible deed in a semi-conscious state in the manner of a somnambulist. Here Poe's use of suggestion conveys frightful horror committed between two periods of consciousness. As the narrator says,

> I found myself sitting in the library, and again sitting there alone. It seemed that I had newly awakened from a confused and exciting dream. I knew that it was now midnight, and I was well aware that, since the setting of the sun, Berenice had been interred. But of that dreary period which intervened I had no positive, at least no definite, comprehension. Yet, its memory was replete with horror – horror more horrible from being vague, and terror more terrible from ambiguity (I, 166).

The point of this strange and acute fear psychology is that the subject is so caught up in the magnetic field of the dreaded object that he cannot shake himself free. It exerts upon him the strange fascination of an obsessive fear that at once repels and attracts. Elsewhere, Poe calls this "perverseness."

On account of the intensity of horror, the tale loses its grip on the reader's sensibilty and ends up in sheer grotesquerie. Piling up of horror upon horror seems to have been done for its own sake without an ultimate purpose on the part of the author. Also the reader's participation in the events of the narrative is adversely affected on account of the confused point of view. Not only is the deranged narrator unreliable but his point of view becomes more confusing on account of the authorial intrustions.

The Dramatic Tales

In his letter of July 2, 1844 to James R. Lowell, Poe refers to "The Black Cat" (1843) as one of his "best tales" of the order of "Ligeia" and "The Fall of the House of Usher."[95] T.O. Mabbott calls the tale "Unsurpassed of its kind," combining several themes that fascinated Poe—reincarnation, perversity, and retribution.[96]

The tale records a number of incidents that follow as a succession of natural causes and effects; and, to use Poe's own words, "one incident begets another" (VII, 82). Thus the tale has a predominantly causal structure unlike tales like "The Fall of the House of Usher," which build their effect on tone and atmosphere. This causal or dramatic structure is not, however, an accident or an arbitrary choice but is related to the primary intention of the tale and marks the stages through which the character changes. The emphasis in the opening paragraph is on the fact of how "a series of mere household events" produced consequences that "have terrified—have tortured—have destroyed" the narrator. In an opening like this, instead of mood–building, what the author does is taking the reader straight into the course of the events. The narrator says that his "immediate purpose is to place before the world, succinctly, without comment," a series of circumstances that have followed in the strict succession of natural causes and effects. Thus the present tale, being different from the atmospheric tales, is, like "The Tell-Tale Heart," more firmly incident-oriented.

In the beginning, the narrator is a perfectly normal and sane individual noted for the docility and humanity of his disposition. He is a person with an extraordinary tenderness of heart—a feeling that becomes manifest by his fond attachment to pets. But the madness and the perverseness of his spirit start only after his initial act of atrocity which he commits in a fit of fury under the influence of alcohol. The cutting of Pluto's eye is itself a sadistic act and might have been symptomatic of an already growing disease. It is evident that it is this first act of damnable atrocity that brings in its train a succession of horrid consequences. The narrator is seized by a sense of horror mingled with remorse; but there also comes upon him the spirit of perverseness "that urged me to continue and finally to consummate the injury I had inflicted upon the unoffending brute" (II, 45). The peculiar nature of this perverseness is that he commits the second act in the full consciousness of its sin and horror:

> ...hung it *because* I knew that in so doing I was committing a sin—a deadly sin that would so jeopardize my immortal soul as to place it, if such a thing were possible, even beyond the reach of the infinite mercy of the Most Merciful and Most Terrible God (II, 46).

This train of events is climaxed by the conflagration of the house and the apparition of the "gigantic *cat*" on the wall. These occurrences suggest a deep psychological significance for the narrator: an act of Retribution. The appartition of the cat may be the symbolic projection of his guilt. The character is henceforward caught in the consequences of his atrocious deeds; he is to be haunted by the phantom of the cat. This may be said to mark the first phase of the narrative, representing the beginning of a crisis in the life of the narrator.

As the first phase leads us up to a point of crisis in the narrative so the second works out its fuller unfoldment. The consequences of the first act must be completed and a sufficient retribution worked out for the character. And the second cat becomes the instrument of this process. All the evidence in the text points to the symbolic role of the second cat. This cat is presented as an antagonist in the inner drama of the narrator. Symbolically, it is the instrument of nemesis. The narrator looks upon it with unutterable loathing and tries to flee from its odious presence "as from the breath of a pestilence." However, the animal dogs his footsteps with a strange pertinacity. It becomes his unwitting tormentor; and he recognizes in it the dread of some evil presence and sees in its white spot a hideous reflection of the Gallows. Under this haunting image of the cat the narrator lives in a nightmare world. The dread of the animal also prompts in him "the darkest and the most evil of thoughts," and inspires in him hatred of all things and of all humankind. Consequently, he falls a victim to ungovernable outbursts of fury. This makes up a second and more acute crisis in the life of the narrator. The incident of the murder of his wife follows as a natural consequence of this crisis and completes it. Yet the process of retribution is not complete. The cat must skillfully play out its role. The bliss of relief that the narrator feels at the supposed departure of the cat is to be short-lived, as evidenced by the dramatic turn of events leading to the narrator's confession. The unexpected reappearance of the animal causes as much surprise to the reader as to the narrator.

Thus the tale falls into two divisions, marking the two phases in the mind of the character. The incidents are artfully knitted together into a causal sequence in the scale of a growing intensity and a clear progress of events is maintained. The character, too, undergoes transformation from phase to phase and registers crisis of development. There is about the narrative a certain psychological convincingness in respect to character-behavior—the character acts in obedience to the dictates of an irresistible inner impulse and is led from one act to another. There is thus a dramatic change from the naturalness of the initial events to the abnormality of the later phase.

"The Tell-Tale Heart" (1843) is a supreme example of Poe's artistry and is often read as a dramatic monologue.[97] Like "The Imp of the Perverse," the tale assumes the presence of a listener. As the story opens, the narrator is seen addressing himself in an uninterrupted speech to a listener who doubts his sanity. He tries to convince the listener that though he is very nervous, his sanity has not been destroyed. He has never been mad, even when he executes the murder of the old man; he has done the deed in an absolutely calculated manner. In the opening paragraph, the narrator attempts a rational explanation of his act and of the motives that had prompted him to it. This listener-context of the narrative is merely a device, theatrical in its import; but the listener does not in any way become specially significant, nor is there much internalization of the experience. The occasion of a narrator addressing himself to a listener gives the tale the external form of a prose monologue. But the presence of the listener is the merest pretext for telling the tale and there is not much of an interaction between him and the speaker. The tale's focus is on the incidents and the narrator's character rather than on the speaker-audience situation. The author might have given it a descriptive opening, but he adopts the present method for the advantage it affords to the narrator of interpreting his motives and actions in a more intimate and direct manner. However, both hypocrisy and honest confession are possible in a situation like this. As a result, the narrator's point of view is unreliable.

Poe does not follow here his usual method of affixing an epigraph to the tale. In tale like "Ligeia," "The Fall of the House of Usher," and "William Wilson," the plot develops around a central motto and illustrates it. The epigraph is thus at once the index and epitome of the tale. These other tales also contain a good deal of reflective, interpretative comment in the light of which the incident is illumined. But "The Tell-Tale Heart" is more pronouncedly action-centered. Unlike "The Fall of the House of Usher" or "Ligeia," it offers us no philosophical interpretation or world-view. On the other hand, it at once plunges into the drama of the incident, providing but the minimum background information and without any authorial intrusions.

Like several other psychological tales of Poe, "The Tell-Tale Heart" presents a type of monomania. The narrator, who is in a sense a Gothic type like the narrator in "Berenice," labors under a single obsession—the evil faseination of the old man's eye. In fact, the tale is founded on the popular superstition regarding the Evil Eye.[98] The eye becomes his sole horror and he executes the treacherous murder of the man in a desperate attempt to free himself from it.

The circumstances leading to the murder are narrated with dramatic immediacy. Right from the opening paragraph, where the narrator tries to assert his sanity, the narrative has a rapid movement that is matched only by the nervous excitement of the protagonist himself. The incidents relating to the narrator's cautious opening of the door on the several pitch-dark nights to focus a ray of light on the eye resulting in intense heart-beating in the old man, have been rendered artistically till finally "With a loud yell, I threw open the lantern and leaped into the room. He shrieked once—only once" (II, 59). As at the initial stages of the action the "Evil Eye" has been the narrator's sole obsession, so at the later stages it is the "Tell-Tale Heart" that keeps pounding away on his fevered brain. Finally, the circumstance of the narrator's self-betrayal, resulting from his bravado, marks the climax of an intensely dramatic sequence of events. As the murder of the old man was to the character the only means of escape from his obsession with the "Evil Eye," the second act of self-exposure presents to him his only means of escape from the "Tell-Tale Heart." As the entire deed has been undertaken by him at the intensest pitch of mental excitement and fever, its accomplishment may be a source of cathartic relief for him from that state of mind.

"The Cask of Amontillado" (1846), "a tale of Italian vengeance," as George W. Woodberry calls it,[99] is perhaps the only one of Poe's Gothic tales that comes closest to being a drama both in structure and spirit. Though it is cast in the overall framework of a narrative, the story makes the largest use of dialogue and builds upon a lively and dynamic character-interaction. With its swift movement, its general scenic presentation, its rare concentration, and its scrupulous economy of detail, the tale has all the essentials of a dramatic presentation. No wonder that it has lent itself to stage-presentation so naturally.[100]

At the opening of the tale there is a brief sketch of the background of relationship between Fortunato and Montresor and the case for the latter's revenge has been stated. But the author does not say anything about the reason for the revenge. Having stated the prima facie case, he hurriedly leads us on to the real drama of the revenge itself. This drama commences with a brief yet vividly painted scene of the carnival, the character of Fortunato, and the occasion of the meeting between him and his victimizer. In a few strokes

Poe draws a vivid portrait of the unsuspecting Fortunato in his motley and his conical cap and bells. Thus the name of the character and his clownish appearance at once establish the dramatic irony. The author also achieves remarkable scenic effects appropriate for the drama in his brief description of the vaults and the family catacombs of the Montresors. This is, however, done with the greatest concentration and economy of detail.

Having thus set the scene, the author proceeds to the presentation of incident strictly in terms of a dramatic dialogue, The handling of the dialogue in this tale is superb and unmatched even in the best of Poe's tales. He fully exploits the possibilities offered by his theme for dramatic irony, keeping the reader in a state of breathless excitement. The contrast between the unsuspecting innocence of the victim and the cold calculation and deliberate plotting of the victimizer reveals character. The author leads the action on to its plotted end with the neatness and precision of a close deliberation. At the very outset, the narrator describes the precise nature of his method:

> A wrong is unredressed when retribution overtakes its redresser. It is equally unredressed when the avenger fails to make himself felt as such to him who has done the wrong (I, 274).

Montresor displays an uncanny perception and exercises a superb control in handling his victim and in leading him to his entombment alive:

> "Amontillado!"
>
> "I have my doubts."
>
> "Amontillado!"
>
> "And I must satisfy them."
>
> "Amontillado!"
>
> "As you are engaged, I am on my way to Luchesi. If any one has a critical turn, it is he. He will tell me—"

"Luchesi cannot tell Amontillado from Sherry."

"And yet some fools will have it that his taste is a match for your own."

"Come, let us go."

"Whither?"

"To your vaults."

"My friend, no; I will not impose your good nature. I perceive you have an engagement. Luchesi—"

"I have no engagement;...come."

"My friend, no. It is not the engagement, but the severe cold with which I perceive you are afflicted. The vaults are insufferably damp. They are encrusted with nitre."

"Let us go, nevertheless. The cold is merely nothing. Amontillado! You have been imposed upon. And as for Luchesi, he cannot distinguish Sherry from Amontillado" (I, 275-76).

The dialogue reminds us of some of the most striking scenes of Shakespeare like the bond-scene in *The Merchant of Venice* between Shylock and Antonio. Also it reveals Montresor's skill in playing upon the mind of Fortunato. Like the "rigid mathematical calculation" that Poe speaks of in "The Philosophy of Composition", the step by step method adopted by Montresor gradually and effectively ensnares the victim in the horrid catacombs.

The repetition of the word "Amontillado" as Fortunato is led to his entombment contributes to the subtle irony in the tale. Charles W. Steele suggests (rather fantastically) that Poe might have had a pun in mind, since the Italian *ammonticchiato* and the Spanish *amontanado* both in sound remotely resemble the name of the wine and both mean "collected in a heap." He adds, "collected in a heap' suits very well the pile of bricks revealed at the climax of the story. Poe was an inveterate punster...already a grim pun on 'mason' is surely recognizable..." Also Dana D. Nelson has dealt with the infamous "drinking and carousing habits" of the Freemasons.[101] The narrator adopts an ironic posture in the telling of the tale. The victim's good nature and nobility of disposition in walking so unsuspectingly into the narrator's trap is contrasted with the cold-blooded calculation with which the narrator leads him into it. As he explains in the initial paragraph, his whole plan is to bring his victim to a shocking realization of his revenge. Hence he conducts the plan with the cool deliberation of a smiling villain. The real excitement of the tale is not so much in a single climactic incident as in the process through which the end is arrived at. The irony that Montresor uses against Fortunato is ultimately directed against himself when in the final incident he finds that his victim rests in peace whereas he himself had been unable to do so for fifty years.

All in all, the tale is a triumph of Poe's dramatic technique. Not only does he give us an exciting portrait of an uncanny mind in the character of Montresor but he succeeds in investing the action of the story with an urgency of movement. And in the handling of the dialogue he exhibits great skill in delineating the subtleties of character-gesture that makes the tale effective.

The Minor Gothic Tales

The minor Gothic tales of Poe do not exemplify the kind of logical continuity and unity of effect that he so much demands in a fictional composition. Nevertheless, they deserve critical attention since they contain some interesting features, reminding us of Hawthorne's sketches. The sketch, as distinguished from the tale, was current in America during the nineteenth–century. Unlike the tale, the sketch was topical and discursive, without being moral or grave. It might be flippant treating its material lightly. Longfellow greatly admired the sketches in Hawthorne's *Twice-Told Tales*. Poe also preferred them to the tales. As John Gardner and Lennis Dunlap say,

> Essentially, the sketch is a description of a person or place; occasionally it is a description of an event.

> In the sketch, narrative is usually subordinated to other elements so that though a sketch may use action, the action calls little attention to itself since it is directed primarily at characterizing the subject of the sketch. In other words, the writer's use of action is mainly to characterize some person or place.[102]

The principle of selection and organization in a sketch is thus characterization, a principle which may not involve an object with the ultimate significance of an abstraction. Thus Hawthorne's "The Gray Champion" or "Little Annie's Ramble" are sketches. While Poe's minor Gothic tales somewhat resemble these sketches of Hawthorne, they are not as interesting and technically successful as Hawthorne's.

In these minor tales Poe seems to fail, for one reason or another, in his central aim of producing a unified impression. "Hop-Frog" and "The Sphinx" are of the sort. "The Oval Portrait" somewhat succeeds in its effect but it has too meager a structure. "The Assignation" is, within its own limits, a successful tale. But it is perhaps a little difficult to classify. In its central effect, the tale is more a romantic mystery than a strictly Gothic type. Yet both in its character and decor it exhibits Gothic traits. Also interesting are "William Wilson" and "The Man of the Crowd," which defy rigid classification. Since these pieces do possess some Gothic lineaments, they are treated as a group, together with "The Assignation," under section II. At the end of the chapter an attempt will be made at summation of the variety of the techniques employed by Poe in the major and minor Gothic tales.

I

George E Woodberry calls "Shadow—A Parable" (1835) "at once the most noble and most artistic expression of Poe's imagination during the first period of his career."[103] T.O. Mabbott asserts that the tale "is one of the finest of all Poe's productions.[104] The tale opens with a rhetorical address by the narrator who is the central character himself. He is speaking to the whole of the living humanity, as it were, from the valley of the Shadows, in ominous accents. But from the second paragraph onwards the tale is given a narrative movement. The narrator proceeds to tell us about the horrifying experiences of seven characters who are shut inside an ancient chamber, in an ancient Greek city, on the eve of a pestilence that had struck the whole of the city (a situation to be developed later more effectively in "The Masque of the Red Death"). The scene is laid in the city of Ptolemais where no shadow is cast by the Sun at noon during the summer solstice. The characters are visited by the frightening vision of a death-like Shadow. Thus the time and occasion are set for an appalling kind of experience. The description of these circumstances as well as of the chamber is done largely in terms of gothic horror tales. Poe employs all the familiar trappings of the Gothic tales: the black draperies, the nervous excitability of the characters, their premonitions of evil, etc. With a few deft touches, he creates the psychological setting for the incident. The presence in the chamber of a dead tenant—Zoilus lying full length in his shroud—inspires a feeling of chill in the hearts of his companions. The dead person of Zoilus is "the genius and the demon of the scene," in the midst of sanguine life. The characters themselves become acutely sensitive to this and to the enveloping presence of death all around them. They drink and revel, but their mirth is "hysterical." Against such a psychological background, the awful shadow of Death seems to rise out of Zoilus' shroud and confront the inmates.

Despite the fact that Poe has called the tale a parable there does not seem to be a distinctive parabolic center of intention in the tale. No moral or allegorical conclusion seems to be suggested by the narrative. Yet a symbolic or allegorical value could be attached to some of the elements of the tale. The characters assembled in the chamber are seven in number; the lamps in the chamber too are seven. Revelers at a banquet around a corpse are all reminded of the universal presence of death. This theme is developed by Burton R. Pollin.[105] The shadow that appears before the inmates may be some sort of a symbolic representation—most obviously of Death. Another proof that the Shadow is a personification is that it speaks to the characters in the unearthly voice of "a multitude of beings" "in the well remembered and familiar accents of many thousand departed friends" (I, 128).

While thus the author attempts the dramatization of a certain psychological experience, he seems to destroy the effect of that when he makes the Shadow declare, "I am SHADOW, and my dwelling is near to the Catacombs of Ptolemais, and hard by those dim plains of Helusion which border upon the foul Charonian canal" (I, 128). What is up to this point a vague and horrifying presence is reduced to an allegorized character and is deprived of its reality. This would appear to be a violation of the dramatic nature of the tale. However, in the opinion of George E. Woodberry, "The elements in this rhapsody of gloom are simple and massive, the accessories in perfect keeping; the...emotion...is just sustained at its initial pitch until the...emergence of the Shadow...."[106] The handling of the situation in "The Masque of the Red Death" shows superior artistry in that the implications of the masked figure, death, are not made explicit but are rendered with great suggestion and dramatic effect. This at once ensures its reality as a presence and invests it with greater psychological suggestion.

The theme of "Shadow" was obviously suggested to Poe by the line of the epigraph, "Yea, though I walk through the valley of the Shadow." The epigraph might even have suggested to him the method of the tale. The tale itself might be viewed as an expansion of the utterance from the Psalm of David echoed in the tone of the narrator at the beginning and of the Shadow at the end of the tale. According to T.O. Mabbott, the style recalls the King James Bible. As he says, "the action takes place in the twilight of Greco-Roman Civilization in Egypt, where even older cultures had flourished and were no more. The scene is appropriately laid in the city of Ptolemais, when the Sun casts no shadow at noon during the summer solstice: what better city could have been chosen for the ever-present Shadow, Death, than that in which the Sun himself casts none?" (Mabbott, Vol. II, 287). The epigraph might have suggested to Poe the promise of a dramatic situation embodying a dweller in the valley of Shadow. But the author mars the dramatic effect by his too obtrusive allegorizing at the end of the tale. Whatever the extent of Poe's success in dramatizing the presence of death in the tale, the idea is continued in "Silence," its companion piece. It says that man clings to the rock of reality, however terrible. "Silence" is particularly significant for its poetic element. Hence the piece will be dealt with in some detail in the chapter on "The Visionary and the Beautiful". Poe is telling us in these two pieces about death as a reality even though "Silence" has not as much of a story line as "Shadow".

"The Sphinx" (1846) is a sketch different from the Gothic or comic pieces. It is a fine study of viewpoint affected by physical distance and mood. The tale starts in a truly Gothic strain; both in character and incident it is given the consistent development of a Gothic romance. But the rather unexpected ratiocinative end is what causes the disappointment.

The narrator is by his disposition a typically Gothic character. The situation in which he is placed is fraught with the ominous fear of death. The monstrous vision of the sphinx that he sees is partly induced by his predisposition to superstitious fear and partly prompted by his horrifying obsession with death at a time when there is all around him the reign of death. The situation here is similar to that in "Shadow" and "the Masque of the Red Death". The development of the plot creates a sense of portentous evil so much so that we are led to expect that something horrible is happening. However, the reader realizes at the end that the narrator has only been tricked by an optical illusion. In "Ms Found in a Bottle" Poe uses the device of optical illusion—the brushed paint on the sail. There is from the beginning, no doubt, a clear contrast between the character of the narrator and that of his friend. The friend, through whose reasoning the illusory nature of the narrator's vision is demonstrated, has, in sharp contrast to the superstitious mind of the narrator, a richly philosophical intellect such that "To the substances of terror he was sufficiently alive, but of its shadows he had no comprehension" (VII, 249). Nevertheless, this contrast only serves to bring into relief the highly impressionable and imaginative mind of the character.

All points thus go to strengthen the reader's initial impression of a world of ominous horror; but the conclusion disappoints us as it belies the initial expectations of the Gothic aroused by the tale. As a result the unity of impression is lost. The narrator's direct address to the reader further complicates the matter. This "slight story," as T.O. Mabbott says, "is based mainly on the old idea that things are not always what they seem, and a realization that our senses may sometimes mislead us even when they function normally."[107] Perhaps expecting any kind of artistic achievement in a tale like this is as deceptive as the Sphinix itself.

"The Oval Portrait" (1842) is framed around a single brief situation of a maiden of rarest beauty who pines away and dies owing to the passionate absorption of her artist husband in his pursuit of perfection in Art. This artist is so much engaged in creating through his Art the very image of life itself that he fails to attend to the living image of beauty in his own wife. He reminds us of the artist in Hawthorne's "Birth Mark" who destroys his wife in his attempts to improve the beauty of the woman by removing the birth mark. The central idea of the tale is that the spirit may take up its residence in a facsimile. This was doctrinal to the Ancient Egyptians, who made statues for the *ka* (what modern Occultists call the astral body), and to modern primitive peoples who are afraid of photography.[108]

Despite the fact that in Poe's tale the character of the painter is sketched in a few vivid, though slight, strokes, the materials used by the writer in shaping his narrative are not adequate for his purpose. He invents an enveloping action which could be a kind of framework. The narrator's discovery of the oval portrait gives a setting for the tale. The tale itself is of the nature of a brief *vignette*—an all too slight word-sketch of an incident. The incident of the narrator and the setting of the chateau not only give the tale its required magnitude, but they also create the mood and atmosphere proper for it. The chateau into which the narrator is admitted in the initial paragraph of the sketch is "one of those piles of commingled gloom and grandeur which have so long frowned upon the Appennines, not less in fact than in the fancy of Mrs Radcliffe" (I, 169). The story of the oval portrait gains considerably in its intensity by being set against the consciousness of the narrator. The incident of the oval portrait is itself in the nature of an ipitaph to the vignette of the young lady.

Thus the structure of the tale may be described as a brief *vignette* mounted on the larger frame of the narrator's experience. In so designing the tale, Poe might have proceeded from the simple intention of presenting an idea, namely, the passion for Art and invented the narrative framework for the purpose of giving proper embodiment of it. As the incident that he devises is by itself so slender, he has to invent the elaborate pretext of a dramatized narrator. However, the Gothic beginning and setting in the ruined castle, with "the bizarre architecture of the chateau," "the commingled gloom and grandeur" add to the effect of the tale.

The Latin epigraph to "Eleonora" (1842), *Sub conservatione formae specificae salve anima* ("The safety of the soul lies in the peservation of a specific form") at once suggests a Ligeia-like motif of the departed sould of the beautiful woman impressing itself upon the living. Both Ligeia and Eleonora may be representations of Poe's conception of Supernal Beauty for all outward appearances. The portrayal of the characters is done largely in poetic terms. However, the character of Ligeia takes on definite Gothic aspects and motivation and the element of passion predominates over the Beautiful. It is not a poetic vision but a character with a strong dramatic orientation. Eleonora is not without a certain resemblance to Ligeia in this respect as well. Not only is she like Ligeia a beautiful woman who dies, but she is also inspired by a strong attachment to life and by a powerful craving to preserve herself after death and to impress her continued presence on her lover. As in "Ligeia" once again, the narrator is involved with two women, and though he is possessed by the image of the first, he takes a second woman and is struck by feelings of penitence for his disloyalty to the first. But here the resemblance ceases.

Both in its tone and treatment "Eleonora" is different from "Ligeia". Whereas in "Ligeia" the dreaded curse of the second wedding is visited upon the narrator, in "Eleonora" its bitterness has not visited upon the protagonist. The visitation of Eleonora is not associated with horror but comes to the narrator as a sweet vision bringing him peace and assurance. Thus "Eleonora" is a tale of reincarnation since the virtuous Eleonora returns as Ermengarde. The motto announced in the epigraph might of course have been the motto of "Ligeia", as also of "Morella; but here though it is fully substantiated by the continuing indications of the presence of Eleonora, the mode of its fulfillment is quite different from that of the other tale. The soul does preserve its specific form in an atmosphere of sweet and ecstatic visions, and it does not take a vampiric possession of the living.

Critical opinion has generally regarded "Eleonora" as some kind of a prose poem and has dwelt at length on its poetic associations. For instance, Hardin Craig and Sam S. Baskett[109] have made out a case for its being a poetic tale. It has been suggested that in this tale Poe has tried to embody his poetic principle—his conception of Supernal Beauty and Love. Baskett has shown in detail how the various points of Poe's essay "The Poetic Principle" are illustrated in it and he suggests close resemblances between the tale and Coleridge's *Kubla Khan*. According to Oswald Doughty, Coleridge's early reviews of Gothic novels reveal his fascination for their description and excitement and his dislike for their lack of realism and degenerate playing on the emotions. Coleridge's first poem in the tradition, *The Raven* (1797) parodies these excesses. Yet in the same year in *The Ancient Mariner* he exploited the tradition. He published his two other great Gothic poems,

Christabel and *Kubla Khan*, in 1816 at Byron's urging.[110] There is, in Poe's tale, the romantic landscape, the theme of the narrator's yearning for Ideal Beauty and Love. There is also the suggested resemblance between "Eleonora" and the romantic maiden of *Kubla Khan*, the damsel with a dulcimer. Even though Baskett obviously overstates his point, the resemblance between Eleonora and the damsel of *Kubla Khan* and the poetic qualities cannot be denied. Phrases like the "Valley of the Many-Colored Grass," repeated like a refrain, and the description of the foliage and the transparent waters of the streams in the valley give a truly poetic touch to some parts of the tale. They echo P.B. Shelley's words "Life, like a dome of many-coloured glass—stains the white radiance of Eternity."

In spite of these poetic elements there is also a firm narrative structure. Burton R. Pollin calls the piece an "arabesque allegory."[111] T.O. Mabbott says it is "perhaps the last of Poe's tales in his extreme arabesque manner."[112] Even though Poe many have intended in the tale an allegory of the poetic principle, he has also given it an unmistakable narrative movement. The characters (of Eleonora and the narrator) are invested with a strong dramatic motive that gives the tale a clear action-content. The career of the narrator falls into two clear phases, and there is an expectation aroused of what will follow. There is also a vividly described setting. The narrative does have certain incidents—those relating to the gradual development of the love between the narrator and Eleonora; and those in the second phase of the narrator's life (after Eleonora's death) in which, while being absorbed in his passion for Ermengarde, he cannot forget Eleonora. Finally, there is a clearly marked *finale* to the story which brings to the narrator satisfaction and repose and resolves his doubts and tensions. Somehow Poe is not quite satisfied with the ending of "Eleonora" since he calls it a tale "which is not ended so well as it might be—a good subject spoiled by hurry in the handling."[113] The final message is of course that of the triumph of Love, "for the Spirit of Love reigneth and ruleth." The narrator's ardor of passion is not only rewarded but sublimiated in the realization of the supremacy of Love. According to T.O. Mabbott, "Eleonora" is "a story of happiness lost and regained, and a favorite of romantic readers."[114] George E. Woodberry says: "In this alone of all his tales is there...the warmth, the vital sense of human love."[115] However, the image of Love is realized not purely in terms of a poetic elaboration of mood or idea. It follows a strictly narrative course of development with some Gothic overtones, particularly in the narrator's passion. In this respect the tale is different from the landscape sketches which are poetic visions. It is difficult to agree with T.O. Mabbott, when he calls "Eleonora" "primarily a fairy tale" and likens it to "The Island of the Fay."[116]

"Hop-Frog" (1849) is apparently a fiasco failing to achieve a proper integration of its various strands—in relating the beginning to the end and the character to the incident, and above all, in establishing a unity of tone. However, the tale is frequently illustrated by artists (including James Enson of Philadelphia) because it so *clearly* presents Poe's views on the artist as suppressed and exploited by the gross powers of the rulers (whether kings or bourgeois publishers or financiers). It is of course a great theme.

From the beginning right up to the point of its climax the story is given the consistent development of a jest. Both character and tone give the promise of a perfectly innocent and light-hearted incident. All indications are toward such light-hearted end. The king is portrayed as a comic figure, large and corpulent, with a protuberant belly, and a keen lover of practical jokes rather than the verbal. The image of him that is given is of a Robelaisian character with the capacity of a Gargantua for laughter. And his companions themselves are a merry band of jokers. Poe's opening comments on the king's disposition for mirth and practical jokes strengthen the impression of him as a perfectly innocent, innocuous lover of jokes without the least malice. Hop-Frog himself is introduced as the king's professional fool and as his most agreeable boon companion—a most lovable jester whom the king laughs *with* as much as he laughs *at*. Shakespeare's fools too are often wise and sensitive as in *King Lear*. The minikin Trippetta also figures as a source of much diversion and pleasure for the company of the king's court.[117] All things thus confirm us in our impression of a happy world of innocent mirth-lovers. The circumstances of the planned masquerade itself comes as the promise of a big joke; and the elaborate preparations for the big *fete* arouse in the king and his courtiers the keen expectation of a climax of fun—an expectation in which the reader too participates. The alert reader at *once* expects disaster for the king and courtiers.

However, as it turns out, the promised jest of Hop-Frog ends in the most horribly wicked and deliberately vengeful burning alive of his masters. This of course comes as a rude shock to the characters of the tale as much as to the reader. The question here is whether a conclusion of this kind is at all justified in terms of the tale. Has the author prepared us for such a climax? Has he convinced us that such a horrid end could naturally follow from such an innocent beginning and above all, has the conduct of Hop-Frog been sufficiently accounted for by the image of the character that has been presented to us? In short, is Hop-Frog's action sufficiently motivated? Does it meet the ends of poetic justice? The king and his jesting companions, we feel, have certainly not merited this cruel treatment. In Poe's eyes the status of the artist demands such revenge. He no doubt gives us a few vague hints of the king's tyranny and the captured Hop-Frog's secret vengeance. There are the incidents of the king striking a defenseless girl and the vaguely suggested smarting of Hop-Frog at the king's conduct (the incident of the sound of grating which might have been the gritting of his teeth by Hop-Frog). But the full significance of these incidents is completely lost on us since the author has not given us any background for this, nor has he given us any inkling into the secret motivations of Hop-Frog's character. The circumstances of the jester's captive condition might of course have inspired in him a secret desire for vengeance. Perhaps he is a type figure and no motive or background details are furnished to us. Hop-Frog might have secretly smarted under the king's tyranny. By this step Poe has missed an opportunity for irony and dramatic suspense, but he has administered a shock on the reader. T.O. Mabbott says: "The reader is expected to sympathize with the murdorous dwarf, but the vengeance is too much for poetic justice. The story is notable mainly as a terrible exposition of the darkness of a human soul.[118] However, the dwarf's conduct may be justified on the ground that art is sacred to Poe.

The reader is likely to be repulsed by the kind of horror presented at the conclusion. However, it is evident from Poe's letter of February 8, 1849, to Annie L. Richmond that Poe himself was aware of the effect of "Hop-Frog": "Only think of *your* Eddy writing a story with such a name as Hop-Frog! You would never guess the subject (which is a terrible one) from the title, I am sure."[119] True, the lot of the artist (author, poet, musician) *is* terrible, he would say he knew it!

In "The Premature Burial" (1844), as in "The Imp of the Perverse," a theory is expounded and a case history given in illustration of it. There are actually a number of case histories. Perhaps the chief merit of the tale is that the theorizing does not predominate over the narrative parts. The interest is focused on the case histories themselves, instead of the expository comment. The best of these histories and the most fully developed is the last one—that of the narrator himself. The narrator at once makes it plain to us that he is going to give us a number of instances of an extraordinary kind of human suffering relating to the twilight region between life and death. This is the experience of premature burial The narrator then proceeds to give a number of what he claims to be factual accounts of premature burial. While the expository part is confined to the opening paragraphs, the narrative soon develops interest in the various case histories that it proceeds to relate. Even though these accounts are disjointed pieces, they are of sufficient interest to carry the reader along. The last piece containing the narrator's own experience is the most fully developed of the accounts and may be regarded as a tale with an independent interest. It is an excellent dream fantasy resulting from the narrator's obsessive fear of being entombed alive and the fact that he has actually provided himself against such a possibility by designing a special coffin and a vault that would enable him to escape the dreadful catastrophe of premature burial if it should ever happen.

The unseen figure holding the narrator by the wrist and trying to arouse him seems to be allegorical. The rather elaborate and well-articulated dialogue that the figure holds with the narrator only serves to drive the allegory home. However, for the rest, Poe's reconstruction of the nightmare is convincing. The circumstances of the narrator's awakening from the nightmare are related with vivid detail. The arrangement of the incidents of this last piece is causal. The narrator first presents the nightmare vision that followed a cataleptic trance and then connects it to the scene and circumstances of this happening. The incidents, alternating between illusion and reality, have a theatrical import. However, the whole experience is really comic, as Poe says at the end and implies also at the futility of avoiding trivial errors.

"The Imp of the Perverse" (1845) follows Poe's habitual method of prefacing the tle with a theory. But in this case the theorizing far outweighs the tale proper, which is a thin substance indeed. The theorizing has been fitted into the framework of a narrative, in which the narrator—a prisoner convicted to death–sentence—gives his account to a listener. The occasion of the narrative is dramatic: the narrator is now in chains, committed to his cell and is going to face the gallows soon. But this narrative framework does not vastly enhance the effectiveness of the tale. The dramatized narrator situation is merely a pretense. Poe is clearly more interested in his thesis than in the narrative which, as it is, happens to be a sort of appendix to the theory for purposes of illustration. Not only is the theory given a disproportionate weightage, but an elaborate theorizing of this kind sounds rather improbable, coming from the mouth of one who is going to meet with his death shortly. In other words, the heavy theoretical discourse limits the scope for the development of the narrative; character and incident become insignificant.

The opening of the piece is merely expository and is not in the voice of a dramatized character.

The narrative part of the piece succeeds in the purpose for which it is intended and becomes effective within its own slender limits. The narrator tells his story as a reply to the listener's enquiries about the cause of his (the narrator's) imprisonment. The account of the murder and of the subsequent self-exposure due to perversity, though rendered with some effect, is thin indeed. The murderer's bravado in repeating the words 'I am safe—I am safe—yes—if I be not fool enough to make open confession,' (II, 40) and his running through the crowded thoroughfares lead to the inevitable denouement. Poe fails in this tale to maintain a proper balance between the theorizing and the narrative parts. In his more successful tales like "Metzengerstein" and "Morella" he is able to subordinate the theorizing to the narrative interest.

While in pieces like "The Premature Burial" and "The Imp of the Perverse," Poe presents and elaborate theory and then illustrates it with the example of a thin story, in "The Case of M. Valdemar" (1845), he dramatizes the theme of mesmerism by means of character and incident. However, the tale is incided in the present chapter only to show that it is not merely a comic piece but a tale with some Gothic lineaments without any significant character, atmosphere of causal structure.

The advertisement in the pamphlet published in 1846 in England described "The Facts in the Case of M. Valdemar" as an "Astounding and Horrifying Narrative Shewing the Extraordinary Power of Mesmerism in Arresting the Progress of Death."[120] However, this is not a tale that, like "The Imp of the Perverse, is intended to illustrate a thesis or an idea. Mesmerism is the theme of the tale and not its thesis. The interest in the mesmeric power is subordinated to the interest of the incident itself, so much so that we attend to the course of the incidents and how they happen rather than to any question about why they happen. The theme of mesmerism, however, helps the author to invest his subject with the necessary credibility; it provides him with a plausible motivating context. The various technical devices are carefully manipulated toward that end. Poe's theoretical excursions are to be viewed as necessary expositions of his themes and as a means to create a dramatic context, and not as independent foci of interest.

A closer examination of the tale reveals that Poe uses mesmerism to achieve his effect by means of verisimilitude, or to use his own coinage "lifelikeliness" or "lifelikeness." His two coinages of the synonym show the importance to him of the concept and the artistic method. In his letter to P.P. Cooke Poe refers to Miss Elizabeth Barrett Barrett's opinion regarding the tale:

> Then there is a tale of his (Poe's)...about mesmerism (The Valdemar Case) throwing us all into most admired disorder or dreadful doubts as to whether it can be true, as the children say of ghost stories. The certain thing in the tale in question is the power of the writer and the faculty he has of making horrible imporbabilities seem near and familiar.[121]

In his letter to Evert A. Duyckinck Poe makes clear his own conception of verisimilitude. Referring to "Valdemar Case", he says:

> In my "Valdemar Case" (which was credited by many) I had not the slightest idea that any person should credit it as anything more than a "Magazine Paper"—but the whole strength is laid out in verisimilitude.[122]

The incident of the arrest of death by the extraordinary power of mesmerism is in itself highly incredible but Poe's art lies in rendering it serious and credible by a skillful marshalling of plausibe details. Arthur H. Quinn says:

> The frame of the story is realistic, the actions of the characters, with the exception of Valdemar, are possible; the result is impossible. But the critical faculties have been dulled by the influence of plausible details, and the story was taken seriously.[123]

According to T.O. Mabbott, the tale is a "repulsive masterpiece."[124] Poe's central object is no doubt to create a sense sof horror, and in doing this he has carefuily established the circumstances and prepared our minds by means of several significant methods. The narrative is given a historical authenticity. The narrator tells us that he is giving the facts "as far as I comprehend them myself." In the opening paragraph he tells us that the extraordinary case of M. Valdemar has given rise to excited discussion and even grabled or exaggerated accounts. The case would have been taken for a miracle; but the narrator in effect gives a convincing account of it and makes an impossible thing seem entirely plausible under the circumstances of the case.[125] In short, Poe's sucess lies in adopting a procedure that is strictly accurate in detail and circumstances. He calls the tale a "hoax." In his letter of Jue 15, 1846, to Joseph M. Field, Poe quotes Elizabcth Barrett Barrett's words about the tale: "The *certain* thing in the tale in question is the *power* of the writer and the faculty he has of making horrible improbabilities seem near & familiar."[126] However, this tale is different from tales like "The Balloon Hoax" in that it contains the semblance of emotional excitement. There is an attempt at gradual intensification of horror through the indistinct replies of Valdemar and the desription of his changing aspect: "...so hideous beyond conception was the appearance of M. Valdemar at this moment, that there was a general shrinking from the bed" (II, 330), and "...there issued from the distended and motionless jaws a voice—such as it would be madness in me to attempt describing" (II, 331). Again, the incidents of the swooning of the medical student and the fleeing of the nurses quicken the pace of the story. The final "hideous voice" of Valdemar has a shocking effect on the narrator: "For God's sake!—quick!—quick!—put me to sleep—or, quick!—waken me!—quick!—*I say to you that I am dead!*" (II, 334). This outburst, at which the narrator is "thoroughly unnerved, and for an instant remained undecided as to what to do," propares the reader for the final experience.

The effect of this tale, however theatrical, is not a pleasant or a shocking surprise but a loathsome horror verging on the ludicrous. Neither incident nor character in this piece is though-provoking as in the serious tales like "The Fall of the House of Usher." In addition, the narrator of the case of M. Valdemar tries to produce an effect on the reader when he says, "I now feel that I have reached a point of this narrative at which every reader will be startled into positive disbelief It is my business, however, simply to proceed" (II, 330). Readers of Poe's day were enthralled and not disgusted by this graphic horror; the newspapers and novels of the day hardened them (as do our violent TV films today).[127]

II

In addition to the several tales of Poe that fall predominantly in one group or another, there are certain tales with unique features, defying a strict classification. Tales such as "The Assignation", "The Man of the Crowd", and "William Wilson" are cases in point. However, since these tales have some Gothic lineaments, they are analyzed in this section. They are too limited in number to be treated in a separate chapter.

"The Visionary, ("The Assignation"), first published in 1834, is essentially a romantic story. As Roy P. Basler says, the protagonist is modeled on Lord Byron.[128] The tale is in the first–person–periphral narrtion like "The Fall of the House of Usher". The narrator here is the author's deputy who imposes a point of view on the narrative: the incidents are presented through his consciousness. His stance is that of an interested, even engrossed, spectator who fully participates in the events and is profoundly affected by them. His keen participation in the incidents gives the narrative a depth of intimacy. Yet the first–person–peripheral narration is by its very nature a device for maintaining distance. The narrator is at the same time in and out of the events and his understanding of them is limited and incomplete. His understanding of the character too, is distant and he is thus fallible. But this distance in the present tale is perhaps required by the very nature of the material. Someone has to survive to report the deaths.

The background of the incidents and the behavior of the characters must be shrouded in a veil of mystery. The protagonist is reluctant to disclose his identity and background and tries to mystify the narrator in this regard. While the narrator in "The Fall of the House of Usher" is intimately associated with the central character and right from the beginning his role is clear and definite for us, the narrator in "The Assignation" comes into action only after the drowning scene, offering the services of his gondola to the hero who "spoke of our former slight acquaintance in terms of great apparent cordiality." Thus his distance from character and event increases and he is uneliable. The author's attempt to present the character's behavior in a state of ambiguity and the suggestive hints thrown by him in the course of the narration contribute to the mystery. The solution to the mysterious nature of the incidents sudenly comes to the narrator when at the end, "a consciousness of the entire and terrible truth flashed" (I, 273) on him.

The nature of the assignation has at once flashed upon the reader too. Both the lady and the lover appoint an assignation in death through an intuitive understanding of each other's meaning. In the light of the conclusion, the strange exultation of the lover is also clarified for the reader as well as for the narrator in retrospect. The lover has evidently been preparing for the assignation, "...for the wilder visions of that land of real dreams whither I am now rapidly departing" (I 272-273). The epigraph to the tale is also illumined:

> Stay for me there! I will not fail
> To meet thee in that hollow vale.

Thus the technique of the tale is one of suggestion and mystery which are best preserved by the peripheral role that the narrator assumes.

The opening incident of the baby drowning is at once a dramatic beginning to the tale and a necessary crisis which brings the lovers together at an intensely emotional moment, and thus prepares them for the assignation. The episode also provides the necessary background for the assignation, introducing the husband of the lady as a tyrant. This highlights the characters of the lady and the lover. In addition, the apostrophe at the opening of the tale itself introduces the mysterious and romantic character of the hero: "Ill-fated and mysterious man! bewildered in the brilliancy of thine own imagination, and fallen in the flames of thine own youth!" (I, 258). The trepidation with which the character speaks (to the narrator) is not Gothic in the sense that it is a permanent trait of the character but occasioned by the special circumstances o the situation. He is only exulting in his idea of an assignation with his beloved. The mystified narrator understands the implications of the character onlyat the end, as the reader does. And the introduction of the verse quotation, though not fully understood by the narrator, only serves to suggest the romantic nature of the character and of his background. The poetic lines here serve the same purpose as those in "The Fall of the House of Usher" do—where the poem "The Haunted Palace" sketches the character of Usher himself. Despite his dreamy nature, the character in "The Assignation" does not experience sublunary visions as the Gothic character of Usher does. He is somewhat akin to the Poe heroes in the major tales in that he possesses an absorbing and passionate love of art. The chamber in which the narrator finds himself along with the hero is richly decorated with paintings and magnificent settings. Even the external setting, with "the deep midnight, the Bridge of Sighs, the beauty of woman, and the Genius of Romance" (I, 259) remind us of Byron's Venice. This is not a Gothic tale but part of the Eastern Orientalism that Byron's *Childe Harold* and *Lara* and plays make so popular—along with Moore's *Epicurean* (an Eastern novel) which influenced Poe's poetry and tales.

While romantic isolation marks the condition of the chracter in "The Assignation", a terrible sense of loneliness in the midst of crowds, reminding the reader of the plight of modern man, characterizes the protagonist in "The Man of the Crowd" (1840). Like many of the Poe tales, "The Man of the Crowd" opens with an epigraph and a philosophical disquisition of an idea. The quotation from La Bruyere, "*Ce grand malheur, de ne pouvoir etre seul*" (That is the great misfortune—not to be able to be alone), contains the motto of the piece. The opening paragraph outlines the moral-psychological idea of which "The Man of the Crowd" is the illustration. The idea set forth here is the convulsion of a moral conscience under the pressure of an undivulged guilt. Arthur H. Quinn sums up the theme of the story thus: "...a powerful story of a human being, driven by the search for some lost companion, or by the memory of a crime, who walks through the crowded streets of London without cessation, dreading to be alone."[129] In the words of T.O. Mabbott,

> Here is a powerful treatment of the mystery hidden in every human soul, which no other soul ever knows completely. Some of what is hidden is evil, at least in tendency. It may be observed that the protagonist, who is never named, and is unknowable apart from the crowd, himself is neither rich nor poor; rather, he wears a costume suggesting both wealth and poverty. Is he Everyman?[130]

Although Poe has not rated this tale high, there is obviously some serious message in it.

Like the typical tales of Poe, "The Man of the Crowd" undertakes to follow out a central motif set forth at the opening. The conclusion of the story fully substantiates and completes the central idea set forth earlier. To that extent the tale is successful in what it undertakes to do. But the narrative hardly deserves to be called a tale. There is no logical structure with mutually dependent incidents and characters. It is rather a pen-picture or a psychological portrait rendered in a suggestive manner. The behavior and movements of the man cause as much curiosity in the reader as they do in the narrator. And throughout the story the author keeps us in breathless suspense and promisesto lead us to some crashing climax. However, this never happends: and the end comes about in a rather tame fashion. Even the psychological study of the character, Gothic in a sense, is rendered not in any effective dramatic terms—the author does not attempt to reveal the inner drame of the character—but as an outward observation of behavior. Poe's descriptive powers are well exemplified in the picture that he gives of the passing pageant of the crowd with a minute study of the individual movements of different types of persons, the Man of the Crowd having been in the foreground. The effect of the whole scene on the reader is indeed pictorial. The restless wandering of the man through the streets of London and the narrator's hot chase of him are fraught with suspense. Nevrtheless, this suspense should only have been meant as a preparation for a truly dramatic finale. There is, however, no such dramatic conclusion. The position of the narrator in this tale deserves special comment. He is different from the narrators in "The Assignation" and "The Fall of the House of Usher" who have an actual role to play in the course of the events. Here the narrator is more of a raconteur, being nearer to the author himself, as in "A Descent into the Maelstrom". He relays the effect of the story successfully.

Speaking of the depiction of "the power of a moral idea upon the human soul," Arthur H. Quinn says that "the incidents (in this tale) are contributory to that idea, and are not of importance in themselves."[131] Strictly speaking, there are, in this tale, no incidents of the kind one notices in the other tales of Poe. The entire story consists of a single events of the narrator's pursuit of The Man of the Crowd. It records no development and leads toward no climax. The tale is rather a sketch of a man in psychological isolation.

The first–person–narration of "William Wilson" (1840) commences with a sketch of the character and family backgrounds of the narrator. The image of him that is given to us is that of a remorse-stricken person reflecting upon his past life and present predicament. We are at once made aware of the workings of an acute moral sense in him. In this respect the character of William Wilson is perhaps slightly more complex than the Gothic characters who are more pathological than morally sentient. Wilson shares the Gothic imagination and sensibility that he has inherited through his family—a propensity to "sublunary visions and wild sensations." In the description of the setting of the tale also Poe employs the usual Gothic *decor*—the quaint old building with its "incomprehensible subdivisions," its "terror-inspirating aspect" and its "windings," borrowed from the elizabethan mansion accross from Dr. Bransby's school in Stoke Newington, which Poe attended.

It is against this background of character and setting that the other "William Wilson" is projected. However, this proection is not entirely in the private psychology of the narrator but is in terms of a character that has an objective existence and reality. Even though Poe builds up a close allegorical parallel in the character of the other Wilson—such that it might have been a subjective projection of the inner psychology of the narrator—the character is presented to us in completely realistic terms. The other WIlson bears a close resemblance to the narrator in many outward and inward traits, a resemblance that strikes the narrator with a mysterious significance to his own self—a resemblance that also attracts the notice of his schoolmates. Yet the other Wilson is set up as an antagonist or an anti-self that assumes an ironic posture toward him, perhaps something like the "real Me" of Whitman's poem that

> ...stands yet untouch'd, untold,
> altogether unreached,
> Withdrawn far; mocking Me with mock—
> Congratulatory signs and bows
> With peals of distant ironical laughter...[132]

The other Wilson's voice is significantly enough "a very low whisper," and "it grew with the very echo of my own." Poe mentions "Bi-part soul" in "Lionizing" and in "The Murders in" "The Rue Morgue" and makes use of the idea in "The Fall of the House of Usher". T.O. Mabbott sums up the idea of "William Wilson". "Each man has only half a complete soul, and the pair has but one conscience, which abides wholly in the half that belongs to the whisperer.[133] The continuing theme of the tale is of course the impingement of the anti-self and his intrusion upon the life and personality of the narrator. In the beginning the other Wilson is merely a disturbing and challenging presence to the narrator. The horrid experiences of the chamber at the Bransby school reveal to him the other Wilson in striking resemblance to himself, so that he flees from him (the other Wilson) as from an unknown terror. Wilson's subsequent movements are only attempts to avoid confrontation with his other self.

However, Wilson flees in vain from his harassment, while the terror of the alter ego persistently dogs his path. He flees from place to place, seeking refuge from his tormentor, "my arch enemy and evil genius"–through Vienna, Berlin, and Moscow. There are three major confrontations: the first at Eton, the second at Oxford and the third and the final at Rome. In all these confrontations, the visitation of the other self is for the purpose of chastising the narrator and exposing his fraud. As elsewhere, here too, Poe invests the details with considerable psychological significance. In the first instance, the visitor gesticulates to Wilson with an uplifted finger (of admonition). He speaks in his characteristic whisper. He is only half-revealed in dim light. And on the last occasion he wears a mask of black silk. All these various details give the image of the other Wilson the character of a subjective projection, investing it with the symbolism of a psychic experience. The last and the eventful scene of this psychic drama takes place when, in the Rome scene, the narrator finally comes to grips with his phantom and plunges his sword into his bosom. And he is brought to a shock of recognition that he and his double are after all the same.

Thus the incidents following the Bransby school scene portray the intense inner drama of Wilson's mind and his confrontation with his other self. Whereas the account in this part of the tale is rather in terms of an inner psychological drama, the characterization of the other Wilson in the earlier part is clearly in objective realistic terms. The other William Wilson in the earlier phase is an objective character, one of the schoolmates; but in the latter phase he is transformed into a phantom. It is of course to be admitted that even the earlier objective portrayal of his character is fraught with a definite psychological meaning for the narrator. The significance of the tale lies in the transformation of the actual and material into the fantastic and psychological—the abrupt shift from the physical to the psychological plane of reality. Unlike the other tales of psychological interest, in this tale Poe balances external realism and psychological realism, avoiding the extremes of morbidity.

In his review of Nathaniel Hawthorne's *Twice-told Tales*, Poe notices "a very flattering coincidence of thought" (VII, 36) between "William Wilson" and "Howe's Masquerade". In both the tales the protagonist is confronted by his double under similar circumstances. The *Doppelganger theme was* popular in the nineteenth-century literature. R.L. Stevenson's *Dr. Jekyll and Mr. Hyde* is a well-known example. The theme was better exploited subsequently by Henry James in *Jolly Comer* and Joseph Conrad in *The Secret Sharer*, bringing to it a greater psychological depth. In Conrad's *The Secret Sharer*, the captain sees in the fugitive officer the image of what he could have become. The method of psychological analysis, of preoccupation with the internal world of men and women, was the method Dostoyevsky also developed in his works. In the character of the hero in *Poor Folk* he projected the first of a long series of "Doubles" the split-personality types. Poe's William Wilson is a precursor to all these "Doubles" in literature.

The foregoing analyses of Poe's major and minor Gothic tales shed light on the different aspects of his narrative technique such as the telling methods, openings and endings, incident and tone, suspense and suggestion, symbolic and pictorial devices and the dramatic quality. Poe does not employ all these technical elements in any single tales, but uses them in varying combinations in different tales. He himself has outlined some of the possible ways in which elements like tone and incident may be manipulated singly or in combination. He differentiates between tales in which the effect is wrough through incident, and those in which it is wrought through tone, and yet others in which both incident and tone combine to produce the desired effect.

The telling methods in Poe's tales of the Gothic type are mainly of four categories. Most of these tales are narrated by the central character himself, who actually goes through the incidents of the story and relates them to the reader. It is clear that Poe deliberately chooses the protagonist as narrator to create the maximum intensity because the narrator himself is at the heart of the conflict, and he presents a point of view that is vital to the emotional content of the narrative. Poe's handling of the protagonist-narrator device in tales like "The Cask of Amontillado", "The Tell-Tale Heart", "Ligeia", and "The Black Cat" secures for the narrative a high degree of dramatic immediacy. The story is narrated with great emotional excitement and the reader's involvement in the course of the events is complete. Critics of the psychoanalytical school are fond of maintaining that Poe's protagonist-narrators are little more than maddened versions of Poe himself. James W. Gargano in his illuminating study refutes this charge and maintains that poe is a deliberate craftsman, "who employs the neuroses of his characters with probing intelligence. He permits his narrator to revel and flounder into torment but he sees beyond the torment to its causes."[134] In spite of the objective method of Poe's narration, his presence in the tales at times becomes rather palpable. For instance, the apostrophe to the Baron's mother in "Metzengerstein" is structurally unrelated to the main incident of the tale. The prolonged theorizing of "The Imp of the Perverse" destroys the balance between the narrative interest and the interest of the idea that the tale exemplifies. In his more successful tales like "Berenice" Poe of course manages to subordinate the theorizing to the main business of the tale and to make it contribute directly toward the central effect.

A second method that Poe employs in telling his story is to have the peripheral narrator speaking in the first person. In tales like "The Assignation" and "The Fall of the House of Usher" this keeps the narrator at a considerable distance from the inner torments of the central character, and contributes to the sense of mystery that is so vital a part of the effect of those tales. In "The Assignation" the narrator is an implicated but helpless interpreter, who attempts to clarify the story for the reader. In "The Fall of the House of Usher", however, he shows a greater degree of participation and is more deeply involved in the predicament of the central character, but since he is largely a confused spectator, his point of view is unreliable. Allen Tate says that the point of view in this tale is that of Usher himself in spite of the fact that the story has been narrated by a secondary character.[135] It is true that Usher looks at the events and the physical surroundings as indicative of an impending catastrophe for himself. His words to the narrator are significant: "'In this unnerved—in this pitiable—condition, I feel that the period will sooner or later arrive when I must abandon life and reason together, in some struggle with the grim phantom, FEAR'" (I, 138-39). Also his actions like the drawing of a picture with the background of a rectangular vault, his rhapsody on "The Haunted Palace", his delight in reading ancient books and finally his emotional outburst in the climactic part of the story, reveal a point of view that is definitely his own. Nevertheless we should notice the importance of the narrator's point of view which serves to heighten the effect of terror through suggestion and suspense. Till almost the middle of the story the point of view is essentially that of the narrator himself. Right from the opening paragraph, the manipulation of the reader's mood is achieved through the effect that the entire surroundings and characters produce upon the narrator's mind. Broadly speaking, we can say that the tale has two points of view—one is that of the narrator and the other, Usher's own. However, despite the presence of a dual point of view, the final effect of the story is unified and single.

"The Masque of the Red Death" is the only instance of the omniscient narrator among the Gothic tales. The choice of the omniscient author narration in this instance is fully warranted by the nature of the theme. The doom of Red Death overtakes all the characters of the story and there is no survivor at all to tell the story. Implied, of course, is the allegory of a universal doom for all of us.

A fourth position is that of the mere recorder—an unidentified individual whose presence is not felt by the reader. The narrator in "Hop-Frog" is strictly a reconteur and renders an eyewitness account of the incidents. He is neither the central character nor a dramatized secondary character as in "The Fall of the House of Usher". However, he seems to have been connected with the court. Even though in the earlier part of the tale his presence is felt more distinctly, the latter part does not reveal him much. It sounds like the voice of the omniscient author. The narrator knows things which only one standing near the king and his jester all the time would know, and yet, when the scene shifts to the masquerade room, he speaks of all the characters, king, jester, Trippetta, ministers, and masqueraders, in the third person. The transition is artfully handled, and the reader gains a panoramic view of the room.

Yet a more interesting narrative method, used in "A Descent into the Maelstrem," is the double-narrator: a raconteur and the central character narrator. The story in this tale moves in two concentric circles. The shocking experience related by the fisherman, the actual appearance of tho whirlpool and the surrounding seas in the story are conveyed to the reader through the reactions of the listener (the raconteur).

Poe's narrative methods do not exhibit the same complexity of interest as those of Henry James. As James' aim in his tales, as well as in his novels, is the unfoldment of the consciousness of his characters, he makes subtle shifts of point of view of sometimes provides a multiple centre of interest. But in Poe there is only a single point of view that produces a single and unified impression. Whatever narrative medium he employs, he does it with rare ingenuity. While maintaining that "in Poe's work narration is itself often problematic," John Michael says that "reflection and narrative form an ineluctably joined double movement, an 'enchanted circle' of reflection that carries narrator and reader together toward the limit of cognition. In their very narration, Poe's tales enact the search for the grounds of thinking and the self."[136] Jonathan Auerbach examines a similar problem in the relation of narrative to personal identity by analyzing the repeated instances in Poe of first person story tellers "whose precarious identities largely depend on the alienating act of inventing some coherent literary form to contain and explain themselves."[137]

In his Hawthorne review Poe says that the very initial sentence should indicate the effect intended to be produced. Thus a good short story should have a beginning that foreshadows the course of the later events. This is well exemplified in most of the major Gothic tales. Poe adopts various kinds of story-opening. They can be broadly classified into four categories: reflective, dramatic, atmospheric, and matter-of-fact. In all of these categories, the introductory paragraph gives as much information as is required, thus drawing the reader into the situation. In the first of these types, the tale opens with a philosophical reflection on some theory (like metempsychosis, misery, evil, etc.) which receives exemplification through the later events until finally the conclusion reinforces the idea. However, there are instances in which the openings are not fully justified and borne out by the later events of the tale. The theorizing part (obviously authorial) in "The Imp of the Perverse" and "The Premature Burial" becomes a little overdrawn and tedious unlike the brief opening paragraphs of the major Gothic tales. The conclusion of "The Sphinx" again does not carry out the expectation aroused by the opening. The tale has a Gothic opening but ends in a disappointing rationcination.

The second method of opening a tale is *in media res*. The story starts abruptly either with an apostrophe (as in "The Assignation" and "William Wilson") or with a character-sketch (as in "Morella" and "Ligeia"), or with an excited speech by the narrator which at once draws us into the midst of an action. "The Cask of Amontillado" and "The Tell-Tale Heart" are the best illustrations of the dramatic opening.

"The Fall of the House of Usher" and "The Masque of the Red Death" open with a description of the physical surroundings (of the setting) and of the narrator's reactions to them. Thus the author builds up the tone of the narrative. Wayne C. Booth calls the device the "mood-building" method:

> Every adjective and detail intended to set our mood is a part of the growing mood and experience of the central character; the rhetoric now seems functional, "intrinsic." It is no longer simply directed outward—as if it were a drug that could be injected into the spectator on his way into the theatre.[138]

In some of his openings, Poe skillfully plays upon the reader's nervous sensibility, inducing the desired mood by means of suggestive detail. The descriptions in the course of the narrative serve as interpretative accompaniment to achieve subtle intensification of the sensation. In "The Fall of the House of Usher" the peripheral narrator's reactions to the appearance of the mansion and its surroundings help build up the mood, but in in "The Masque of the Red Death" the omniscient author gives a vivid description of the physical horrors arising out of the pestilence.

Yet another method is the matter-of-fact opening with no dramatic abruptness or reflection or mood–building. "The Oblong Box" opens with an account of a voyage from Charleston to New York. In "Ms Found in a Bottle" the narrator gives the details of his birth and personal life. "The Black Cat," which turns out at the end to be a tale of horror, opens with a "homely" account of a succession of natural causes and effects. The tone of voice of the narrator is matter-of-fact and contrasts sharply with the excited openings of tales like "Berenice." "The Facts in the Case of M. Valdemar" too develops into a fully Gothic narrative, but it opens in a matter-of-fact way with the narrator trying to present before us the facts of the case with the ostensible detachment of a newspaper reporter. In both the cases the particular attitude of the narrator, the claim of homely origins in the case of "The Black Cat" and the claim of a veracious account of a case of measmerism in "The Facts in the Case of M. Valdemar," is evidently a strategy to secure the effect of a surprise ending. The openings of these tales are in sharp contrast to those of "The Fall of the House of Usher" and "The Masque of the Red Death" where even the initial sentence foreshadows the ending.

Poe says that the conclusion of a tale should fully bear out its beginning. In his own practice he achieves remarkable success with his story-endings. Such tales as "The Fall of the House of Usher", "Berenice", and "The Facts in the Case of M. Valdemar" have climaxes that are arresting in their effect. But the conclusion of "Morella," like that of "The Cask of Amontillado", is more gradual. The entire plot of "The Cask of Amontillado" is one prolonged climax, but even within its own movement the story records a peak point that is marked by the chaining of Fortunato and the ultimate horrifying act of his entombment. The conclusion of "The Black Cat" is clear in its effect, but that of "Ligeia," though fully justified in terms of the tale, produces a confused response on the part of the reader. "Hop-Frog" is marred by a defective conclusion that is not promised by the beginning. The conclusion of "The Man of the Crowd" is rather disappointing, for it does not fulfill the reader's expectations. The effect of "Shadow" is blurred at the end by a too obvious allegorizing. However, in spite of these occasional shortcomings, most of Poe's tales end well.

Poe insists on a strict causal relation of the incidents of the tale and follows out this principle in his major Gothic tales. In fact, his observance of it makes for great theatrical effect. The unity of plot in his tales arises out of (i) a strict causal relationship of incidents, and (ii) harmony of character and incident. "The Fall of the House of Usher" and "Ligeia" have mutually dependent incidents that make the story move with rapidity and intensity. "The Cask of Amontillado" is a little drama in itself; in fact, it has only one prolonged chain of episodes, Montresor leading his unsuspecting victim to his doom. The tale achieves dramatic effect through the harmonious relationship of character and incident, and the skillful management of dialogue. "Morella" is successful within its own limited form, the two main incidents of the heroine's death and the scene of the daughter's baptism emerging directly from the character. "The Tell-Tale Heart" achieves dramatic quality through the device of a prose monologue, although the device is not fully exploited. The climactic incidents show the author's masterly rendering of the incidents of the tale. "The Black Cat" is remarkable for the strickly causal ordering of its incidents.

Killis Campbell says that Poe "was never expert in the management of dialogue."[139] However, Poe does employ dialogue to great effect in "The Cask of Amontillado" Again, in certain scenes of "Morella" and "The Fall of the House of Usher" too the dialogue reveals character-motivation and furthers action. In subsequent chapters we shall observe the functional use of dialogue in tales like "The Gold-Bug" and "Bon-Bon". On the whole, it is difficult to conclude that Poe is inexpert in the management of dialogue, even though he does not make use of the device frequently.

In his more successful Gothic tales like "The Pit and the Pendulum", "The Masque of the Red Death", "The Fall of the House of Usher," and "Ligeia", Poe makes the setting contribute directly to the effect. But in "William Wilson", the setting of the Bransby School does not quite harmonize with character and incident. The external setting of wilson's school is not in harmony with his inner life. However, this dichotomy of the real and the fantastic establishes the peculiar nature of the tale. "Morella" depends mainly on character and incident and is successful even without any external Gothic decor. Through setting as much as through the peculiar mental state of his characters, Poe achieves atmospheric effects in his major Gothic tales.

Suggestion and suspense are devices employed by Poe to build up the rising emotion of his tales. By these means the reader is kept in a state of poised expectancy as to what is going to happen. The information deliberately withheld from the reader keeps him in a state of anticipation and uncertainty as to the outcome. This is a sure way of creating the maximum emotional tension in the tale. Poe uses the device of suspense in achieving this end in the Gothic tales as much as in the ratiocinative tales. He displays remarkable skill in keeping the reader in a state of high excitement in his major tales like "Ligeia" and "The Fall of the House of Usher." In "The Facts in the Case of M. Valdema" he gives us no inkling as to what will happen at the end and achieves unqualified success in keeping the reader in suspense. In his method Poe seems to have been influenced by Mrs. Radcliffe to whom he makes a direct reference in "The Oval Portrait."

Suggestion, like suspense, keeps the reader in a state of expectation. While dropping a few hints, the author leaves the rest of the details to the reader's imagination. In many of his tales Poe fully exploits the Gothic power of suggestion, casting a hypnotic spell over his reader; especially significant in this respect are tales like "The Masque of the Red Death," "Berenice," and "Ligeia". Even the earliest tale, "Metzengerstein," abounds in suggestive details (like the figure of the horse) that create a sense of horror in the tale.

In addition to suggestion, association plays a significant part in the creation of the mood and the ultimate effect. We find many eminent modern writers using this technique, perhaps derived from Poe's early model. For example, Elizabeth Bowen's "The Cat Jumps" describes a group of people staying in a house in which a gruesome murder was once committed. Just before the characters retire for the night, the author gives a description: "The house, fingered outwardly by the wind that dragged unceasingly past the walls, was, within, a solid silence: silence heavily as flesh." The words "fingered," "dragged," and "Flesh," by association remind us of the former context and create an impression of horror. Poe's tales like "The Black Cat," "The Tell-Tale Heart," and "Berenice" display such a technique.

Poe's use of symbolism in his tales adds to the significance of the associative images. However, symbolism, instead of making the tales vague, contributes to dramatic effect. Poe's tales abound in color symbolism producing both visual and emotional effects on the reader.[140] Out of all the colors, blackness finds a predominant place in Poe's tales as in those of the major American writers like Nathaniel Hawthorne and Herman Melville. harry Levin has discussed in considerable detail the significance of blackness in the works of these nineteenth-century writers.[141] In "The Fall of the House of Usher," the fissure in the mansion symbolizes the tottering condition of the hero's mind. And in "The Masque of the Red Death," the chiming clock symbolizes the time concept. The clock symbol is also used in "The Devil in the Belfry" for comic purposes. In addition to these, Poe uses the symbols of light and shade in "Ligeia" and "The Fall of the House of Usher" and different colors in "The Masque of the Red Death." The device of the light and shadow—chiaroscuro, the quality that Poe finds so attractive in *Peter Snook*—is commonly employed in the fiction of Hawthorne and Cooper.[142] As Hervey Allen says, poe always seems "to have visualized with a keen eye for shadow and color, and with sufficient vividness to make him desire to reproduce his impressions."[143] This is a result of Poe's interest in contemporary art. He considers the tale as a painting—an arrangement of details in space to convey an idea. In "Ligeia," the temporal movement in the story action is limited. While time passes, the writer summarizes events instead of presenting them in detail. Percy Lubbock calls it the "Pictorial method." In his words, it is a method "to view the past retrospectively and discourse upon it, to recall and meditate and summarize. That is picture-making in its natural form, using its own method."[144]

Sometimes Poe's presentation of character and situation is highly impressionistic. His description of the fast–moving crowds in "The Man of the Crowd" or the gigantic rotating black funnel in "A Descent into the Maelstrom" leaves an indelible impression on the reader's mind. In "William Wilson," the protagonist is pictured as moving from place to place with great momentum. The motion of the background, whether it is Bransby's, Eton, or Oxford, or the various other European cities, gives an impression similar to the rapid shifting of scenic views in motion pictures. While the reader keeps on looking at the picture of the character, the background changes swiftly. We know vaguely where the action is taking place, but we have no distinct idea of the specific locale.

When Fyodor Dostoyevsky finished his first story, *Poor Folk* in 1845, Vissarion Belinsky, the leading critic read the manuscript with great enthusiasm and praised Dostoyevsky's skill in portraying truth in art. Regarding this appreciation, Dostoyevsky wrote to his brother:

> They (Belinsky and others) find in me a new and original spirit in that I proceed by analysis and not by synthesis, i.e., I plunge into the depths, and while analyzing every atom, I search out the whole: Gogol takes a direct path and hence is not so profound as I.[145]

This "Plunging into the depths" of the human psyche, proceeding by analysis, is what Poe achieves in his Gothic tales. The ultimate effect of his tales of terror on the reader is similar to what Ernest J. Simmons calls, referring to *Crime and Punishment*, "the characteristic spiritual glow" illuminating "the darkest recesses of the minds of these tormented and suffering men and women."[146] We have D.H. Lawrence's testimony to the effect of the Gothic tales when he calls Poe "an adventurer into vaults and cellars and horrible underground passages of the human soul."[147] Poe's heroes like Roderick Usher and the narrator of "Ligeia" are "tormented and suffering" individuals. Reading about them is, indeed, an adventure into the "horrible underground passages of the human soul." These protagonists are artists or scholars, desperately struggling to find the meaning of life. Their beloved too are intellectual women, in a similar state of inexplicable suffering. An absence of psychological adjustment of these characters constitutes the essential drama of Poe's Gothic tales.

Characters in Poe's tales are often alienated personalities, their physical appearances symbolizing the states of their minds. Events tend to be unusual, being perverse, violent, or shocking. The characters' disposition is toward fear, terror, horror, insecurity, and the failure of love. Therefore, problems are seen within the individual's soul or unconscious rather than in external terms. In portraying complex or distroted emotion, the submerged psychic states, Poe has affinity with Hawthorne whom he calls "a man of rare genius."[148] Moreover, in thus revealing phases of buried thought or feeling, constance Rourke says, both are close to the "rude fantasy making of the pioneer."[149] Allen Tate is in agreement with Miss Rourke when he says, in a letter to Donald Davidson, "Poe's 'nervous man' is our ancestor, however, clumsily he creates him."[150] Harold Bloom is right in admiring "the psychological dynamics and mythic reverberation" of Poe's stories.[150A]

In his "Marginalia" (No. 150), Poe says that certain "fancies" exist "at those mere points of time where the confines of the waking world blend with those of the world of dreams" (VII, p 312). He is attracted to this "point of blending between wakefulness and sleep" (VII, 314). However, he adds that he would proceed to prevent "the lapse from this border-ground into the dominion of sleep." Thus, he can startle "from the point into wakefulness, *and thus, transfer the point itself into the realm of memory*–convey its impressions, or more properly their recollections, to a situation where (although still for a very brief period) I can survey them with the eye of analysis." This is crucial to an understanding of Poe's rationalistic conception of dream experiences rendered in tales like "The Pit and the Pendulum," "A Descent into the Maelstrom," and *Pym.* Poe's "point of blending between wakefulness and sleep" is similar to Hawthorne's conscious sleep of the haunted mind. Such an experience is rendered skillfully in tales like "Berenice" and "The Pit and the Pendulum." Sigmund Freud regards the dream as "a sort of substitute for the thought processes, full of meaning and emotion."[151] The dream, as being "full of meaning and emotion" is thus a device employed by Poe in his major Gothic tales to produce emotional effects. In these tales the protagonist undergoes great emotional stress and the author successfully dramatizes that emperience.

Poe's territory, a nightmare landscape, is unnamed and indistinct. It is rendered perceptible through symbols of intense and sometimes unidentifiable fear. Thus the symbolic mode in Poe serves to enhance the emotional tension of his tales. However, symbolism, instead of making these Gothic tales vague and indistinct, serves a dramatic purpose in producing a definite psychological effect on the reader. The physical and psychological experiences of Poe's characters—guilt, persecution mania, and claustrophobia—are universal dream experiences. In his attempts to depict these subterranean experiences, Poe exploits the Gothic mode.

Poe uses different devices like opening, conclusion, character, incident, suggestion, suspense, symbolism, allegory, and narrative points of view within the limits of the tale. These fictional devices are employed in different tales for different kinds of effect. In the major Gothic tales, the devices are managed exquisitely despite occasional faults. The minor tales and sketches are more happazard in composition and seem to be too brief and sketchy to merit serious attention. In the major tales, there is generally a proper integration of theme and technique. But in the minor tales and sketches, the author seems to be in great haste, without conscious effort to impress the reader.

NOTES

1. Arthur H. Quinn, *Edgar Allan Poe: A Critical Biography* (New York: Appleton–Century–Crofts, Inc., 1941) 289. According to Quinn, Sir Walter Scott's essay, "On the Supernatural in Fictitious Composition" is Poe's source for the terms "Arabesque" and "Grotesque". Scott says that the tales of E.T.W. Hoffman are grotesque, resembling the arabesque in painting, in which "strange and complicated monsters are introduced." See Sir Walter Scott, "On the Supernatural in Fictitious Composition," *Foreign Quarterly Review*, I, (1827): 81-82.
2. L. Moffitt Cecil, "Poe's 'Arabesque'," *Comparative Literature*, XVIII (1966): 55-70.
3. G. R. Thompson, *Poe's Fiction: Romantic Irony in the Gothic Tales* (Madison: The University of Wisconsin Press, 1973) 70.

4. Robert D. Jacobs, *Poe: Journalist & Critic* (Baton Rouge: Louisiana State University Press, 1969) 166n.
5. See John Ruskin, *The Complete Works of John Ruskin,* ed. E. T. Cooke and Alexander Wedderburn, Vol. II, *The Stones of Venice*, Ch. IV, "The Nature of Gothic." (London: G Allen, 1904).
6. See Wolfgang Kayser, *Grotesque in Art and Literature,* Trans., Ulrich Weistein (1963; rpt. New york: McGraw-Hill, 1966).
7. See Stuart Levine, *Edgar Poe: Seer and Craftsman* (Deland: Everett/Edwards, Inc., 1972).
8. See Joseph M. Garrison, "The Function of Terror in the Work of Edgar Allan Poe," *American Quarterly,* XVIII, No. 2 (Summer, 1966): 136-50.
9. Quoted in R.A. Foakes, ed. *Romantic Criticism, 1800-1850* (London: Edward Arnold Ltd., 1968) 176.
10. Poe's acquaintance with "Monk" Lewis is evident from his letter of June 26, 1849 to George W. Eveleth. See *Letters*, II: 449-50.
11. Lowry Nelson, "Night Thoughts on the Gothic Novel," *The Yale Review*, LII, No. 2 (Winter, 1963): 263.
12. See J.M.S. Tompkins, *The Popular Novel in England, 1770-1800* (1932; rpt. Lincoln: University of Nebraska Press, 1961); Montague Summers, *The Gothic Quest: A History of the Gothic Novel* (1938; rpt. New York: Russell and Russell, 1964); D.P. Verma, *The Gothic Flame* (London: Arthur Baker Ltd., 1957); Edith Birkhead, *The Tale of Terror: A Study of the Gothic Romance* (London: Constable and Co., 1921); Kenneth Clark, *The Gothic Revival: An Essay on the History of Taste* (1928; rpt. London: Constable, 1950); Arthur L. Cooke, "Some Side Lights on the Theory of the Gothic Romance," *Modern Language Quarterly*, XII (1951): 429-36; Paul Frankl, *The Gothic: Literary Sources and Interpretations Through Eight Centuries* (Princeton: Princeton University Press, 1960); Robert D.Hume, "Gothic versus Romantic: A Revaluation of the Gothic Novel," *PMLA*, 84 (1969): 282-90; Robert L. Platzner and Robert D.Hume, "Gothic versus Romantic': A Rejoinder," *PMLA*, 86 (1971), 266-74; Arthur O.Lovejoy, "The First Gothic Revival," in *Essays in the History of Ideas* (1948; rpt. New York: Putnam's, 1960); Clara F. McIntyre, "Were the 'Gothic Novels' Gothic?" *PMLA*, 35 (1921): 644-47; W.D. Robson-Scott, *The Literary Background of the Gothic Revival in Germany* (Oxford: Clarendon Press, 1965); Richard P. Benton, ed. "The Gothic Tradition in 19th-Century American Literature: A Symposium," *The Emerson Society Quarterly*, XVIII (1972): 5-123.
13. Oral Summer Coad, "The Gothic Element in American Literature

Before 1835," *The Journal of English and germanic Philology,* XXIV (1925): 72.

14. James K.Keech, "The Survival of the Gothic Romance," *Studies in the Novel,* VI, No. 2 (Summer, 1974): 134.
15. D.P. Varma, *The Gothic Flame*, 225.
16. *Ibid.*, 211.
17. "Foreward" to *The Gothic Flame*, viii. Craig Howes and Kent Ljungquist in their brilliant studies have shown Poe's familiarity with the Burkean sublime. See Craig Howes, "Burke, Poe, and 'Usher': The Sublime and Rising Woman," ESQ: *A Journal of the American Renaissance*, 31 (1985): 173-89 and Ch. I of Kent Ljungquinist, *The Grand and the Fair: Poe's Landscape Aesthetics and Pictorial Techniques* (Potomac, Md: Scripta Humanistica, 1984).
18. Quoted in George E. Woodberry, *The Life of Edgar Allan Poe,* I, 223.
19. *Letters*, I, 121.
20. Robert D. Jacobs, *Poe: Journalist & Critic,* 165n. In disclaiming Germanism, Poe evokes the Support of Washington Irving. As he says in his letter to Joseph Evans Snodgrass, "I am sure you will be pleased to hear that Washington Irving has addressed me 2 letters, abounding in high passages of compliment in regard to my Tales... Irving's name will afford me a complete triumph over those little critics who would endeavor to put me down by raising the hue and cry of *exaggeration* in style, of *Germanism* and such twaddle. You know Irving leads the school of the *quietists*." *Letters*, I, 121.
21. D.P. Varma, 130. Joseph M. Garrison uses the terms as distinct from each other, even though he does not elaborate. See Joseph M. Garrison.
22. G.R. Thompson, 69.
23. Irvin Malin, *New American Gothic* (Carbondale: Southern Illinois University Press, 1962) 79.
24. Thomas Hubert maintains that "certain so-called Southern qualities and attitudes may be found in writers like Melville and Hawthorne, the latter of whom, for instance, satirized with Poe the early nineteenth-century's infatuation with the machine." Thomas Hubert, "The Southern Element in Poe's Fiction," *The Georgia Review,* XXVIII, No. 2 (Summer, 1974): 201. In an interesting article, Edward Stone says that the Southern Gothic, which attained intensity in the writing of Poe, has flowered into greater diversity in the writings of the twentieth-century writers like George Washington

Cable and William Faulkner, all dealing with a basic "concept of the human personality." Edward Stone, "Usher, Poquelin, and Miss Emily: The Progress of Southern Gothic," *The Georgia Review* (Winter, 1960): 433-43.

25. Thomas O. Mabbott, "Introduction," *Collected Works of Edgar Allan Poe* (Cambridge, Mass: The Belknap Press of the Harvard University Press, 1978), II, 15. Hereafter referred to as *Collected Works.*
26. Edd Winfield Parks, *Edgar Allan Poe as Literary Critic* (Athens: University of Georgia Press, 1964) 24.
27. Arthur H Quinn, *Edgar Allan Poe* 192-93.
28. T.O. Mabbott, ed. *Collected Works of Edgar Allan Poe,* 15.
29. *Letters*, I: 77-78.
30. Joseph T. Shipley, ed. *Dictionary of World Literature* (New York: The Philosophical Library, 1943) 233.
31. Herbert Read, *English Prose Style* (Boston: Beacon Press, 1952) 125.
32. Charles Brockden Brown, *Wieland* (Garden City, N.Y.) Doubleday and Co., Inc., 1962) 12.
33. T.O. Mabbott, ed. *Collected Works,* II, 133.
34. George E. Woodberry, *Life,* I, 306.
35. T.O. Mabbott, ed. *Collected Works* II. 574.
36. *Ibid.*, 576.
37. Charles Brockden Brown, *Edgar Huntly* (New York: The Macmillan Company, 1928) 107.
38. *Letters*, I, 175.
39. *Ibid.*, 258.
40. Joseph P. Roppolo, "Meaning and 'The Masque of the Red Dealth," *Tulane Studies in English*, XVIII, 1963: 69.
41. T.O. Mabbott, ed. *Collected Works*, II, 667.
42. For a close study of the tale see Walter Blair, "Poe's Conception of the Incident and Tone in the Tale," *Modern Philology* (May, 1944): 228-40.
43. Joseph Patrick Roppolo.
44. Roppolo's description of Prospero as "a hero or demigod" of a myth is only reading more into the tale than is warranted. Prospero is, in fact, a victim to a horror experience along with the rest of the company. There is nothing particularly heroic about his action.
45. T.O. Mabbott, ed. *Collected Works,* II, 668.

46. Kermit Vanderbilt, "Art and Nature in 'The Masque of the Red Death'," *Nineteenth-Century Fiction*, Vol. 22, No. 4 (March, 1968): 379.
47. David Thorburn and Geoffrey Hartman, eds. *Romanticism: Vistas, Instances, Continuities* (Ithaca: Cornell University Press, 1973) 64.
48. T.O. Mabbott, ed. *Collected Works*, II, 679.
49. George E. Woodberry, *Poe* (1885), 120-121; *Life* (1909), I, 220-31.
50. T.O. Mabbott, ed. *Collected Works*, II, 392.
51. Caroline Gordon and Allen Tate, *The House of Fiction* (New York, 1950) 116.
52. Wayne C. Booth, *The Rhetoric of Fiction*, 203.
53. See Ian Walker, *Modern Language Review,* October 1966.
54. Richard Wilbur, "The House of Poe," *Anniversary Lectures*, Library of Congress (1959) 28. (reprinted in Eric W Carlson's *The Recognition of Poe*, 1966 255-77.
55. *Letters*, I, 161. according to J.W. Ostrom, Poe's charge of Plagiarism by Longfellow was unfounded. 161n.
56. See E. Arthur Robinson, "Order and Sentience in 'The Fall of the House of Usher," *PMLA,* Vol.76, No.1 (March 1961), 68-81. Robinson argues that Poe's use of expressions like "Order" and "Sentience" brings out the strange harmony between the decayed mansion and the gloomy atmosphere around it, that binds together even the fantastic elements of the plot.
57. Darrel Abel, "A Key to the House of Usher," *The University of Toronto Quarterly*, January 1949.
58. T.O. Mabbott, ed. *Collected Works,* II, 395.
59. J.O. Bailey, "What Happens in 'The Fall of the House of Usher?'," *American Literature*, January 1964.
60. D.H. Lawrence, *Studies in Classic American Literature* (1923); rpt. New York: The Viking Press, 1968 76.
61. Frederick Crews, *The Sins of the Fathers: Hawthorne's Psychological Themes* (New York: Oxford University Press, 1966) 271.
62. In his letter of September 21, 1839 to Philip P. Cooke, Poe says that Washington Irving "speaks with enthusiasm of a late tale of mine, 'The Fall of the House of Usher' " (*Letters*, I, 118). Poe had reviewed *Astoria* in *Southern Literary Messenger* of January 1837 and his admiration for Irving is evident from the fact that

he solicited an article from the "Pioneer" for his projected *Penn Magazine*. (See his letter of June 21, 1841 to Washington Irving in *Letters*, I, 161-63).

63. Joseph Warren beach, *The Twentieth–Century Novel: Studies in Technique* (New York: Appleton–Century Crofts, 1932) 343-44.
64. *Letters*, II, 329. See also Poe's letter of January 8, 1846 to Evert A. Duyckinck: "undoubtedly the best story I have written." (*Letters*, II, 309).
65. Arthur H. Quinn, *Edgar Allan Poe*, 269.
66. George E. Woodberry, *The Life of Edgar Allan Poe*, I, 227.
67. Poe subsequently published this as a poem entitled "The Conqueror Worm" in *Graham's Magazine* for January 1843.
68. See Donald R. Swanson, "Poe's 'Conqueror Worm'," *The Explicator*, XIX. No. 7, Item 52. Swanson analyzes the poem as a theatrical performance in four acts, beautifully integrated.
69. T.O. Mabbott, *Works*, Vol. 2, 331.
70. James Schroeter, "Poe's 'Ligeia'," *PMLA*, LXXVII, (December, 1962): 675.
71. Roy Basler, "Poe's 'Ligeia'," *PMLA*, LXXVII (Dec., 1962): 675.
72. T.O. Mabbott, ed. *Collected Works,* II, 307.
73. Vincent Buranelli, *Edgar Allan Poe* (New York: Twayne Publishers, 1961) 73.
74. T.O. Mabbott, ed. *Collected Works,* II, 334n and 308.
75. Charles Brockden Brown, *Edgar Huntly* (New York: The Macmillan Company, 1928) 90.
76. *Letters*, I, 118.
77. Quoted in T.O. Mabbott, ed. *Collected Works*, II, 307.
78. *Letters*, I, 118.
79. See Joseph Andriano, *Our Ladies of Darkness: Feminine Daemonology in Male Gothic Fiction.* University Park: The Pennsylvania State University Press, 1993.
80. T.O. Mabbott, ed. *Collected Works of Edgar Allan Poe,* II. 308.
81. D.H. Lawrence, *Studies in Classic American Literature*. 84.
82. *Letters*, I, 118.
83. *Letters*, I, 78.
84. See Roy P. Basler in *College English,* April, 1944. Again in *PMLA*, December 1962 he replies to James Schroeter's contention in *PMLA*, September 1961. Schroeter, defending the romantic view, refers to interpretations of the story as one of magic by Woodberry, Clayton Hamilton, and A.H. Quinn.

85. *Letters*, I, 78.
86. *Ibid.*, 118.
87. *Ibid.*, 77-78. In this connection Poe says: "Generally, people praise extravagantly those of which I am ashamed, and pass in silence what I fancy to be praiseworthy." It is evident from this that "Morella," published in 1835, is, in Poe's own opinion, superior to "Ms Found in a Bottle" (1833) in the quality of the Gothic effect.
88. T.O. Mabbott tells us that "Morella" "makes use of a widespread superstition that gods and men must answer when the right names are spoken. Poe also seems to know of a superstition that it is a most unusual, even supernatural, child who takes its first breath after its mother breathes her last". *Collected Works*, II, 221.
89. *Letters*, I, 118.
90. Henry James, "The Art of Fiction," *Henry James: Representative Selections*, ed. Lyon R. Richardson (New York: American Book Company, 1941) 86.
91. *Letters*, I, 58.
92. *Ibid.*, 57.
93. Constance Rourke, : *American Humor: A Study in National Character* (New York: Harcourt, Brace and Company, 1931) 184.
94. T.O. Mabbott, ed. *Collected Works,* II, 207.
95. *Letters*, I, 258.
96. T.O. Mabbott, ed. *Collected Works,* III, 847.
97. Jeffrey Meyers, *Edgar Allan Poe: His Life and Legacy* (New York: Charles Scribner's Sons, 1992) 137.
98. *Ibid*.
99. *Ibid*.
100. George E. Woodberry, *Life*, II, 231. Mary E Phillips says that the tale, dramatized as "Fortunato and I," was presented at *The Little Theater* in Philadelphia. See Mary E. Phillips, *Edgar Allan Poe the Man* (Chicago: John C. Winston Co., 1926), II, 1181.
101. Charles W. Steele, "The Cask of Amontillado," *The Explicator*, (April, 1960). Also see Dana D. Nelson, "The Haunting of White Manhood: Poe, Fraternal Ritual, and Polygenesis," *American Literature*, Vol. 69, No. 3 (September 1997): 517.
102. John Gardner and Lennis Dunlap, eds. *The Forms of Fiction* (New York: Random House, 1962), 23-24. See also Karl Beckson and Arthur Ganz, *A Reader's Guide to Literary Terms* (New York: The Noonday Press, 1960) 195.

103. George E. Woodberry, *Edgar Allan Poe* (1885), 82; *Life* (1909), I, 127.
104. T.O. Mabbott, ed. *Collected Works,* II, 187.
105. See Burton R. Pollin, *Studies in Short Fiction*, Vol. 12.
106. George E. Woodberry, *Edgar Allan Poe* (1885): 82; *Life* (1909), I, 127. It is difficult to agree with Arthur H. Quinn who says that the tale is a satire on democracy. Quinn seems to exaggerate the reference to democracy made by Poe, ignoring the dominant theme of the story. See Arthur H Quinn, *Edgar Allan Poe*, 499.
107. T.O. Mabbott, ed. *Collected Works*, III, 1245.
108. The first version was called "Life in Death." Mabbott calls the tale "one of the briefest and best known of the arabesques." (*Collected Works*, II, 639). Margaret Alterton points out a parallel between the opening of Poe's "Life in Death" and that of a story called "Buried Alive" in *Blackwood's* for October 1821. ("Origins of Poe's Critical Theory," 20).
109. Margaret Alterton and Hardin Craig Eds. *Edgar Allan Poe: Representative Selections*, 517. See also Sam S. Baskett, "A Damsel with a Dulcimer: An Interpretation of Poe's 'Eleonora'," *Modern Language Notes*, LXXIII (May, 1958): 332-38.
110. See Oswald Doughty, "Coleridge and 'The Gothic Novel' or 'Tales of Terror'," *English Miscellany,* 23, 1972: 125-48.
111. Burton R. Pollin, *Discoveries in Poe* (Notre Dame: University of Notre Dame Press, 1970) 38.
112. T.O. Mabbott, ed. *Collected Works*, II, 637.
113. See Poe's review of *The Gift for 1842* in *Graham's Magazine*, November 1841.
114. T.O. Mabbott, ed. *Collected Works*, II, 635.
115. George E. Woodberry, *Poe* (1885), 168.
116. T.O. Mabbott, ed. *Collected Works*, II, 636-37.
117. Burton R. Pollin says that in this tale, the theme of dance prominently appears and that it "borrows its basic plot and masquerade situation from an article about the death of a ballet dancer from fire, printed in the *Broadway Journal* of 1 February, 1845; this article included a ball or masquerade episode about the King of France and his friends taken from the *Chronicles* of Froissart. Poe calls Hop–Frog's inamorata 'Trippetta', a dancelike name, probably after Milton's line "Come and trip it as yet go' (L'Allegro). More significantly, it is at the height of the ball, just after midnight, that the king and his seven ministers enter in their constumes of flax and tar, to be burned to death by the vengeful court jester." Burton R. Pollin, "Poe and the Dance,"

Insight and Outlooks: Essays on Great Writers (New York: Gordian Press, 1986) 137.

118. T.O. Mabbott, III, 1343.
119. *Letters*, II, 425.
120. Quoted in Arthur H. Quinn, *Edgar Allan Poe,* 470.
121. *Letters*, II, 329. See also Poe's letter of June 15, 1846 to Joseph M. Field in which he refers to the "most admired disorder". (*Ibid.*, 320).
122. *Letters*, II, 433. See also Poe's letter of Evert A. Duyckinck wherein he refers to the excitement the tale caused in London press. (*Ibid.*, 336) In contrast to the verisimilitude in "Valdemar Case" Poe seems to admire Defoe's "Robinson Crusoe" whose "design was far more to please, or excite, than to decieve by verisimilitude."
123. Arthur H. Quinn, 470.
124. T.O. Mabbott, ed. *Collected Works,* III, 1228.
125. *Letters*, II, 320. In the "Fourth Supplement to *The Letters of Poe,"* John W. Ostrom quotes from Poe's letter of January 10, 1846—*ante* April 11, 1846 referring to "Mesmeric Revelation" and "Valdemar": "In the case of Valdemar, I was actuated by similar motives, but in this latter paper, I made a more pronounced effort at verisimilitude for the sake of effect. The only material difference between the two articles is that in one I believe actual truth to be involved; in the other I have aimed at merely suggestion and speculation. I find the Valdemar case universally copied and *received as truth*, even in spite of my disclaimer." John W. Ostrom, "Fourth Supplement to *The Letters of Poe,*" *American Literature*, Vol. 45, IV (January, 1974): 528-29.
126. See *Letters*, II, 337, 349.
127. Poe's statement in his letter of December 30, 1846 to Arch Ramsay of Scotland helps us in assessing the ultimate effect of the tale: "Hoax' *is* precisely the word suited to M. Valdemar's case..... The article was generally copied in England and is now circulating in France. Some few persons believe it — but/ do not — and don't you". (*Letters*, II, 337). However, Robert Collyer, the eminent Mesmerist, wrote to Poe from Boston on December 18, 1845: "Your account of M. Valdemar's case has been universally copied in this city, and has created a very great sensation." (Quoted in T.O. Mabbott, ed. *Collected Works,* III, 1230).
128. See Roy P. Basler in *American Literature,* May 1937, and Richard P. Benton in *Nineteenth-Century Fiction,* September, 1963.
129. Arthur H Quinn, Edgar *Allan Poe*, 310.

130. T.O. Mabbott, ed. *Collected Works,* II, 505.
131. Arthur H. Quinn, Edgar *Allan Poe*, 310.
132. "As I Ebb'd with the Ocean of Life." *Walt Whitman: Representative Selections,* ed. Floyd Stovall (New York: American Book Company, 1934) 183.
133. T.O. Mabbott, ed. *Collected Works,* II, 425.
134. James W. Gargano, "The Question of Poe's Narrators," *College English,* XXV, No. 3 (December, 1963): 181. See also Floyd stovall, "The conscious Art of Edgar Allan Poe," *College English*, XXIV, No. 6 (Marc, 1963): 417-21.
135. Allen Tate, *The Man of Letters in the Modern World: Selected Essays, 1928-1955* (1936; rpt. New York: Meridian Books, 1955) 140.
136. John Michael, "Narration and Reflection: The Search for Grounds in Poe's 'The Power of Words' and 'The Domain of Arnheim'," *Arizona Quarterly*, Vol. 45, No. 3 (Autumn 1989): 4.
137. Jonathan Auebach, *The Romance of Failure: First Person Fictions of Poe, Hawthorne, and James.* (New York: Oxford University Press, 1989) 26-27.
138. Wayne C. Booth, *The Rhetoric of Fiction,* 202.
139. Killis Campbell, *The Mind and Art of Edgar Allan Poe,* 68.
140. See Wilson O Clough, "The Use of Color Words by Edgar Allan Poe," *PMLA*, XV (March, 1930): 598-613.
141. See Harry Levin, *The Power of Blackness: Hawthorne, Poe & Melville* (London: Faber and Faber, 1958). For an interesting study of the suymbolism of whiteness in Poe see Edward Stone, *Voice of Despair: Four Motifs in American Literature* (Athens: Ohio University Press,. 1966) 92-93. Professor Stone says, "With poe whiteness conveys terror, whether aesthetically or metaphysically."
142. For a somewhat detailed study of the device in Copper's fiction see Donald A. Ringe, "Chiaroscuro as an Artistic Device in Cooper's Fiction", *PMLA*, LXXVIII, 1963: 349-57.
143. Hervey Allen, *ISRAFEL: The Life and times of Edgar Allan Poe* (New York: Holt, Rinehart and Winston, 1926) 81.
144. Percy Lubbock, *The Craft of Fiction* (1921; rpt. London: Jonathan Cape Ltd., 1932) 255.
145. Quoted in "Introduction," Ernest J. Simmons, ed. *The House of the Dead* by Fyodor Dostoyevsky (New York: Dell Publishing Co., Inc., 1959) 6.
146. *Ibid.*, 14.

147. D.H. Lawrence, Studies *in Classic American Literature*, 81.

148. Letter to James R. Lowell, *Letters*, I, 261. Poe's admiration for Hawthorne is also evident from the fact that he wanted to engage Hawthorne as a permanent contributor to his projected *Penn Magazine* (together with others like Cooper). See Poe's letter to James R. Lowell, *Letters,* I, 222.

149. Constrance Rourke, *American Humor: A Study of the National Character* (New York: Harcourt, Brace and Company, 1931) 191.

150. *The Literary Correspondence of Donald Davidson and Allen Tate*, ed. John Tyree Fain and Thomas Daniel Young (Athens: University of George Press, 1974) 350.

150A. Harold Bloom, ed. *The Tales of Poe* (New York: Chelsea House Publishers, 1987) 4.

151. Sigmund Freud, *On Dreams*, trans. James Strachey (New York: Norton, 1952) 11. Poe's description of the dream experience in "Marginalia" as the "point of blending between wakefulness and sleep" rendered "with the eye of analysis" reminds us of what Freud said later in his essay, "Creative Writers and Day-dreaming": "The writer softens the character of his egoistic daydreams by altering and disguising it, and he bribes us by the purely formal—that is, aesthetic—yield of pleasure which he offers us, in the presentation of his fantasies." (Sigmund Freud, Standard *Edition of the Complete Psychological Works*, London: The Hogarth Press, 1953, IX, 153.) Based on Freud, Norman Hollad shows how the unconscious can be transformed into intellectual meanings: "The story 'means' in that it transforms its unconscious fantasy into social, moral, intellectual, and even mythic terms." (Norman Holland, *The Dynamics of Literary Response*, New York: Oxford University Press, 1968, 27-28). The Oneiric elements that Patrick F. Quinn discusses at length, like these fantasies dealt with by Holland based on Freud, are rendered into objective phenomena rationally presented as dream symbols. Thus, instead of taking the reader into the private world of the author's subjectivity, these dreams constitute objective fictional aspects of an empirical structure of the tale.

4

COMIC SENSE

"...the ludicrous heightened into the grotesque; ...the witty exaggerated into the burlesque..."

Letter to Thomas W. White
August 30, 1835

Critics have differed widely concerning Poe's humor. Generally his laughter is dismissed as hysterical, his tales invoking not the comic muse but the macabre. Thus Arthur Ransome says that "his attempts to be funny are like hangman's jokes."[1] In the opinion of Constance Rourke, "His laughter was of a singular order: it was inhuman, and mixed with hysteria."[2] Rourke relates Poe to the more callous aspects of the South-western comic mode. Brom Weber, however, thinks that Poe is "one of our major humorists."[3]

In the comic tales Poe deals with matters of current interest like exploration, mesmerism, and balloons to capture what George E. Woodberry calls the "contemporaneous mind." At his foster-father's house, at the University of Virginia, and later at Baltimore and Philadelphia, Poe is said to have come across the popular modes of comic story-telling. Constance Rourke, however, maintains that "The gamut of his moods might have been drawn from the West, plumbing horror, yet turning also to a wild contrived comedy."[4] But, Edwin Fussell who deals with the influence of the West on Poe in some detail, says that only a few comic tales contain marginal Western humor—"The Man that was Used Up" (Indian fighting), "Von Kempelen and His Discovery" (California Gold Rush), and "The Thousand-

and-Second Tale of Scheherazade" (natural wonders in the West).[5] Benjamin Franklin Fisher IV says: "Poe's merging of the realistic with the weird is well known, and a like blending often increases artistic dimension in Southwestern devil stories."[6] Poe's early tales deal wittily and ironically with aspects of American life and character. The later work fuses the humorous with the Gothic, producing what Poe himself calls the "grotesque" effects. It is in this type of writing that Poe's humor is somewhat disturbing. Brom Weber recognizes this element:

> ...the critically humorous spirit of Poe is disconcerting because it harks back to a darkness associated with Puritan orthodoxy, displays itself in fantastic grotesqueries abjured by a realistic temper, delights in blending humor with such abhorred topics as death, and insanity in violation of a humanitarian spirit,...[7]

Thus scholars have been mainly concerned with the "critically humorous spirit of Poe" that verges on the grotesque. But Poe's humor has several facets like the burlesque, parody, and social comedy in addition to the grotesque. The essential comic sense of Poe emerges only on an objective study of these aspects of his humorous writing.

Referring to Poe's letter to Thomas W. White,[8] Stephen Le Roy Mooney divides the tales into four categories: 1) the horror tale: the fearful colored into the horrible; 2) the grotesque tale, a heightening of the ludicrous; 3) the burlesque tale, an exaggeration of the witty; and 4) the mystical tale, a working out of the strange and the singular.[9] Thus Mooney treats the "grotesque" and the "burlesque" as two categories. In fact, together with the social comedies, they fall under the larger category of the "Comic Sense" of Poe. Mooney is not convincing when he maintains that "Some degree of comedy is intended in all four categories." Such an interpretation misses the real significance of the major Gothic tales wherein Poe vigorously strives for a concentrated effect.

Dewayne August Peterson questions Arthur H. Quinn's classification of Poe's tales on the ground that "Four Beasts in One" is called an "Arabesque" in Poe's letter of May 4, 1833 to Joseph T. & Edwin Buckingham.[10] While his study deals with the grotesque tales (meaning the comic), Peterson groups these with the serious tales like "Ligeia," "The Fall of the House of Usher," and "William Wilson," saying that the latter tales prove that Poe is "a master of the contemporary school of grotesque fiction which dominated the literary magazines."[11] In saying so, Peterson fails to distinguish the more serious nature of the major Gothic tales like "Ligeia" and "The Fall of the House of Usher" from the lighter fiction. In the serious tales referred to by Peterson, Poe is not so much satirizing the contemporary magazine fiction as he is adopting its style to his own serious writing. In the lighter tales like "A Predicament," however, he parodies the magazine style and subject matter. More recently, in his anthology entitled *The Naiad Voice: Essays on Poe's Satiric Hoaxing,* Dennis W. Eddings maintains: "Rather than looking for elements that separate the comic and the serious in Poe, we need to seek that which unifiesthem."[12] Such a view, similar to Clark Griffith's suggestion[13] that "Ligeia" is a carefully concealed satire that pokes fun at the very thing it purports to be, misses the very focus of the comic in Poe.

Referring to the humor of his early tales in his letters, Poe uses terms like "bizarreries," "grotesque," "serio-tragicomic," "banter," "extravagances," "joke," and "quiz" in a rather general way. From this it is evident that not all of his comic writing should be taken as "grotesque." Poe obviously intends some gradation in his humorous writing when, ion his letter to Thomas W. White, he refers to "the ludicrous heightened into the grotesque" and "the witty exaggerated into the burlesque."[14] However, it will be more appropriate to classify the comic tales under the sub-divisions "Grotesque," "Burlesque and Parody," "Hoax," and "Social Comedy."

Even though Poe has no systematic theory of the comic, he does make a few occasional statements on it. For instance, commenting on fancy and imagination, he says:

> When...Fantasy seeks...incongruous or antagonistical elements...we laugh outright in recognizing Humor... but when either Fancy or Humor is expressed to gain an end.. it becomes, also, pure Wit or Sarcasm, just as the purpose is well-intended or malevolent.[15]

Thus Poe is not unaware of the finer aspects of the comic sense. In his review of August us Lonystreet's *Georgia Scenes* (1835) he confesses that even though he "laughed immoderately" over the book, he is not "used to the perusal of similar things," and that personally he is not "of the merry mood." Nevertheless, in spite of his apparent taste for the sharp and the pungent in humor, Poe prefers to temper it with wit. Hence he greatly admires the "hidden humor" of Charles Lamb and of Washington Irving. He finds in *Bubbles from the Brunnens of Nassau* (1836) "the same covert conceit, the same hidden humor" as Lambn and Irving,

> the same piquant allusion, which, while you read, place the author bodily before you, a quiet old gentleman fond of his ease, but founder of his jokes—not a broad, forced, loud, vacant-minded joke, but a quiet, pungent, sly, laughter-moving conceit, which, at first stirrings the finest membrances of your pericardium, at length sets you out into a broad roar of laughter.

Reviewing *Henry Cockton's* Harry Lorrequer (1836) Poe says that a book, even a humorous one, needs action, "to the extent of its thought, independent of its deed." Thus true to the "Common-Sense" spirit of his writing, Poe insists upon "thought" even in humorous writing.

A close study of the significant comic tales under the headings of "Grotesque," "Burlesque and Parody," "Hoax," and "Social Comedy" brings out the variety of Poe's technique in this type of his compositions. It is noteworthy that a sizeable part of his fiction consists of the comic tales; there are as many as twenty such pieces as against twenty four or so Gothic and five or six mystery and ratiocinative tales.

Grotesque: A Twilight Region

The term "grotesque", derived from the Italian, has been intractable and the attempts of philosophers, scholars, and critics to define it have not been really successful. *La grottesca* and *grottesco* refer to *grotta* (cave) and designale a certain ornamental style which came to light in the fifteenth century during the excavations in Rome and in other parts of Italy. This style constituted an unknown ancient form of ornamental painting.

John Ruskin, in The Stones of Venice (1851-1853), says that the true grotesque plays with the fearful and the awesome, that it recognizes the moral nature of the universe. Grotesque to Coleridge, however, is different. As he says, "When words or images are placed in unusual juxtaposition rather than inconnectiou, and are so placedomerely because the justaposition is unusual—we have the odd or the grotosque."[16] To Coleridge the grotesque is concerned with the chimerical and spectacular characters and events employed simply to produce sensational effects or to "excite bodily disgust, but not moral fear."[17] Philip Thomson defines the term as "the unresolved clash of incompatibles in work and response."[18] Thomson maintains that "there is almost always a comic element in the grotesque" and that "'grotesque' in everyday speech refers to something which the speaker fins simultaneously funny and repulsive."[19]

The "grotesque" of the kind present in Poe's "King Pest" and "The System of Dr. Tarr and Prof. Fether" can be traced into the works of modern writers like Brecht, Genet, Ionesco, and other members of the "Theater of the Absurd."[20] Karl S. Guthke describes this as the theater of the "grotesque-absurd." As he says, "the grotesque is by and large, the outward appearance of the absurd, that is to say, the disorienting perception of the absurdity of the world expresses itself in the modern 'theater of the absurd' by means of distortion of reality which is grotesque." Thus in the new drama, horror and ludicrousness are mingled and it envisions "an absurdity, usually of comic dimension..."[21] Ultimately, the world of the grotesque-absurd is weird and distorted.

Poe's grotesque does not reach the "sublime incongruity" that G. Wilson Knight refers to in his essays, "*King Lear* and the Comedy of the Grotesque" and "The Lear Universe" in *The Wheel of Fire*. According to Wilson Knight, in Lear's grotesque, "the comic and the tragic rest both on the idea of incompatibilities, and are also, themselves, mutually exclusive: therefore to mingle them is to add to the meaning of each; the result is but a new sublime incongruity."[22] William Van O'Connor's description of the term is interesting:

> The grotesque, as a genre or form of modern literature, simultaneously confronts the antipoetic and the ugly and presents them, when viewed out of the side of the eye, as the closest we can come to the sublime. The grotesque affronts our sense of established order and satisfies, or partly satisfies, our need for at least a tentative, a more flexible ordering.[23]

This "Affronting" or "our sense of established order" is felt when one goes through tales like "Dr. Tarr and Prof. Fether" and "King Pest" even thought in these tales one does not come across the experience of the sublime.

Wolfgang Kayser maintains that the grotesque is an artistic expression of the sense of alienation that grips man when faith in a natural order is destroyed. And he identifies the term with the Gothic.[24] according to him, Poe uses the word "grotesque" in the sense used by Sir Walter Scott (in his essay on E.T.A. Hoffman) and in "The Masque of the Red Death," Poe gives an authoritative definition of the term entirely through examples:

> Be sure they were grotesque. There were much glare and glitter and piquancy and phantasm—much of what has been since seen in "Hernani". There were arabesque figures with unsuited limbs and appointments. There were delirious fancies such as the madman fashions. There were much of the beautiful, much of the wanton, much of the *bizarre*, something of the terrible, and not a little of that which

> might have excited disgust. To and fro in the seven chambers were stalked, in fact, a multitude of dreams. And these—the dreams—writhed in and about, taking hue from the rooms, and causing the wild music of the orchestra to seem as the echo of their steps (I, 312).

If this is "grotesque" it is because Poe is here commenting on the absurd situation of Prince Prosper and his companions trying to avoid death but getting trapped in the very chambers of death The situation brings together the actual and the imagined states of the characters. While we have to give due allowance to ironic comments like this on the part of the author, even in an otherwise serious tale, the serious and the grotesque cannot totally be identified, as Kayser does. The Gothic tale as a whole cannot be treated as an ironic presentation. G. R. Thompson too goes contrary to Poe's own opinion (regarding" a vast variety of modes") in saying that the *grotesque* and *arabesque* "refer to a single psychological effect or response"[25] and that Poe is essentially a satiric ironist in his Gothic tales.

Donald H. Ross has suggested that the "grotesque"--a juxtaposition of inharmonious parts, some real, some imaginary—need not be concerned with the accepted dualisms. The grotesque may be explored with the hope of discovering it as a unique and unalloyed *mode* of human expression. As Ross says, "a major function of the grotesque, even in its superficial aspects, is to mock dualistic concerns, to disparage all polarities by encompassing them in a larger framework."[26] It is true that the grotesque, like the Gothic, is very much a part of the human experience. And Poe's concern as a writer is to present these facets of man's life in this world.

Poe's own statements about "grotesque" are scattered. In his review of "Zinzendorff and other Poems," he says: "The conclusion of this is bathetic to a degree bordering upon the grotesque" (VI, 97). Thus the grotesque implies The bathetic, containing things downright earthy and producing a humorous reaction on the reader's part. This element of "bathetic" in the grotesque is further explained in the review of Drake and Halleck (1836): "In the second stanza, 'the thunder-drum of Heaven' is bathetic and grotesque in the highest degree—a commingling of the most sublime music of Heaven with the most utterly contemptible and commonplace of Earth" (VI, 104). In talking of "the ludicrous heightened into the grotesque" or "the witty exaggerated into the burlesque," Poe obviously means something different from "the fearful colored into the horrible."[27] Thus the grotesque is closer to the comic than to the horrible. This is further evident from Poe's statement in his letter to Beverley Tucker: "Moreover—are you *sure* Jeffrey was never jocular or frivolous in his critical opinions? I think I can call to mind some of the purest *grotesque* in his Reviews—downright horse laughter."[28] The essence of the grotesque lies in a combination of " the most sublime" and "the most utterly contemptible and commonplace of Earth." This is almost Poe's conception of the grotesque, with its basic dualistic concerns—a combination of the high and the low. The quality of such a dualism has been evident in the passage from Poe's "The Masque of the Red Death" referred to above.

While conceding that Poe's statement on the comic is not entirely helpful in arriving at a satisfactory conclusion of his humor, Burton R. Pollin says that "to Poe the *grotesque* was humorous. This may also imply that there may have been a trace of cruelty or malice in Poe's wit, at times."[29] Constance Rourke, however, concludes that Poe belongs to the tradition of the West and the frontier, because of his tall tales and his hoax tendencies. While Miss Rourke is not entirely unconvincing when she says that Poe's grotesquerie "lies midway between the comic and the terrible,"[30] it is difficult to agree with her when she asserts that "with Poe the horrible was always with in view." A close analysis of the representative comic tales of Poe makes it evident that his comic sense has several facets including the grotesque. A tale like "The Man that was Used Up" brings Poe's humor close to the Bergsonian conception in that the human is presented in mechanistic terms, the discrepancy producing laughter that is different form the merely repulsive. Walter F. Taylor has said that Poe not only mocks the fiction of his day but even some of his own sentimental writings. Taylor's argument is based on Poe's letter of 1835 to Thomas W. White, indicating the concealed satire of his stories.[31] Satire is certainly a significant aspect of Poe's humor. He says that the satirist should avoid rage in his sarcasm: "Coarse and malignant" satire demonstrates "less of the power than the *will* for causticity." Thus it is, as in the late "abortive satires of Byron (especially "English Bards and Scotch Reviewers") and Pope's "The Dunciad"—"frequently most feeble when it attempts to be most severe." The satirist, Poe adds, should not give way to "gross obscenity and filth," which, like invective, is only "the awkward left arm of the Muse."

Both in its character-portrayal and in its incident, "King Pest" (1835) develops genuine narrative interest. Through its entire development the tale shows a strong comic objective. Ruth Leigh Hudson says that in this tale Poe burlesques Disraeli's *Vivian Gray*.[32] However, the tale acquires an independent interest in its description, character, and incident wherein Poe establishes a clear tone of the "grotesque." Human traits are distorted to the extent that Legs and Hugh Tarpaulin and the six courtiers of King Pest are presented in grotesque expaggeration. The incidents of the tale, despite the description of the pestilence, are burlesque. But their burlesque nature is overwhelmingly subordinated to the power of description of the pestilence which forebodes terror. While dismissing "King Pest" as being "certainly one of the least valuable of Poe's stories," T. O. Mabbott reports that it horrified Robert Louis Stevenson.[33] Elsewhere Mabbott calls the tale "a wild parody on the British magazinists."[34] According to Constance Rourke, the tale "is one of the most brilliant pure burlesques in the language, transmuting terror into gross comedy, as it had often been transmuted in the Western tall tales."[35] Despite the author's attempt at such a "transmutation," the terrible is always visible behind the comic and this is what makes the effect of the tale ultimately grotesque.

The circumstances connected with the escape of the characters from the ale-house and their running into the plague district and the strange experiences that follow are all given the distinct aspect of a Laurel and Hardy comic fantasia. However, Poe's humor here has about it a strong touch of barbarity. Such are the descriptions of the plague district and of the ghostly characters of the court of King Pest. The grotesquerie is nowhere so clearly brought out as in the comic dialogue that ensues between Legs and Tarpaulin and King Pest, and above all in the fantastic finale itself.

The development of the tale as well as the details of description and characterization have a strong allegorical suggestion. In the subtitle Poe himself calls "King Pest" "A Tale Containing an Allegory." But it is somewhat difficult to place any clear interpretation on its allegorical meaning. Probably it is Poe's satire on the subtitles of British magazine tales of those times. We know for certain that in creating monstrosities like Legs, Tarpaulin, King Pest and the others, Poe must have been satirizing something. But what is it that he is satirizing? The epigraph to the tale, "The gods do bear and will allow in kings,/ The things which they abhor in rascal routes" might be the key to the allegory. Poe might have been thinking mainly of rulers in general in presenting the grotesque distortions of the characters of King pest and his court. But even then no precise equation between character and its allegorical significance would seem to fit the details.[36] And, again, where do the characters, of Legs and Tarpaulin fit in and what is their exact significance? Thus no precise interpretation of the allegory in the tale seems possible. Whatever Poe's intention might have been in "King Pest," it would seem more likely that in it he was writing something that is grotesque just for the sake of being grotesque.

Arthur H. Quinn thinks that "The System of Dr. Tarr and Prof. Fether" (1845) is clever but "not improtant."[37] George E.

Woodberry calls it an "absurd madhouse grotesque.[38] According to Wagenknecht, Poe's "comic use of lunacy... comes pretty close to eighteenth-century brutality."[39] But T. O. Mabbott calls it "one of Poe's best humorous pieces."[40]

In this tale Poe might have intended a satire of the mad houses of his time or he might have meant to suggest that even those people who look upon themselves as being exclusively rational are after all crazy. William Whipple argues that in this tale, Poe's satire is at two levels: 1) on the management of mental hospitals; 2) on the narrator himself. Whipple's study is concerned with the views of Poe's friend, Dr. Pliny Earle, a resident physician at the Frankford Asylum who later moved to New York as superintendent of the asylum at Bloomingdale.[41] While the element of satire is present in the tale, what makes it interesting is the grotesquerie of character and incident. Brom Weber is correct when he says that the tale illustrates "how persistently and even sensibly Poe insisted upon the necessity for laughter even in chambers of horror."[42]

The circumstances of the tale center around a ludicrous situation: that of the inmates of a lunatic asylum capturing power and setting up a government of the mad. In developing this situation, Poe follows his own principle of heightening the ludicrous into the grotesque. The ludicrousness of the situation is caused by the astounding incongruity in the behavior of the character of the madhouse. The behavior of Monsieur Maillard himself is a supreme example of this incongruity. Here is a man who, having gone completely crazy himself, assumes the perfect appearance of a rational individual and plays that role with the absolute method and consistency of a rational individual and plays that role with the absolute method and consistency of a rational human being. Not only does he conduct himself before his guest with perfect balance and decorum, but he lays claim to certain original ideas in regard to the treatment of lunatics. It is only at the end when the truth of the matter is revealed to us that the almost unbelievable grotesquerie of this character comes to light. In the behavior of the other inmates of the madhouse, too, there is a strong element of the grotesque. These people enact the most incredible drama of madness in the confirmed belief of their own absolute sanity. The revelation of the true state of affairs is a perfect *coup de theater* and comes on us with a suddenness that we are not prepared for. The great success of the narrative is owed to the manner in which the author has preserved the mystery till the very last moment. This sense of mystery and the final explanation produces laughter ultimately directed toward the narrator himself.

The part played by the narrator contributes greatly to the preservation of this mystery. The whole story turns on the ingnorance of the travelling companion of all that happened to Maillard, the superintendent. Neither the narrator nor the reader suspects the superintendent to be insane. Right from the time of his entry into the asylum, the narrator of course meets with incidents that arouse his suspicion—like the strange behavior of the people at the dinner. But his suspicions are at every step effectively cancelled by the perfectly rational manner and self-assurance of his host. This makes the narrator unsuspecting right up to the end when there arises a great confusion with the rushing in of "a perfect army of what I took to be Chimpanzees, Ourang Outangs, or big black baboons of the Cape of Good Hope"—the sane keepers of the asylum decorated in those shapes and thrust into the cells. This completes the grotesquerie of the tale. The secret of the whole grotesque business is well kept right up to the end, when the reader is given an account of the narrator regarding the true state of affairs.

Poe called "The Angel of the Odd" (1844) "an extravaganza." According to Gerald E. Gerber, the tale "provides additional evidence of Poe's well-known dislike for the spirit of social reform," burlesquing "both the ideal of perfectibility and those reformers whose schemes were calculated to improve mankind."[43] T. O. Mabbott calls the tale "a bit of good-natured buffoonery, probably the most pleasantly absurd story Poe ever wrote."[44] In "Lionizing," Poe makes fun of "a human-perfectibility man." In "Fifty Suggestions" he tells us about reformers:

> The world is infested, just now, by a new sect of

> philosophers, who have not yet suspected themselves of forming a sect, and who, consequently, have adopted no name. They are the *Believers in everything Odd*. Their High Priest, in the East, is Charles Fourier—in the West, Horace Greeley...The only common bond among the sect, is Credulity:-let us call is Insanity at once, and be done with it.[45]

The opening paragraphs of the tale are in a lighthearted tone, revealing the narrator in his dining room in a chilly November afternoon and commenting upon certain fantastic newspaper accounts concerning some "odd accidents." This setting gives the proper occasion for the introduction of the Angel of the odd into the scene. The sudden retort, "Mein Gott, den, vat a vool you bees for dat!" takes the narrator by surprise and leads to a dramatic entry of the Angel on the scene. Further, the almost unintelligible language that the Angel speaks contributes to the comic effect as in the Germanic dialect of "Devil in the Belfry." The very appearance of the Angel is grotesque and brings to mind a delirious vision. By the time the Angel enters, the narrator is surrounded in his dining room by "miscellaneous bottles of wine, spirit, and *liqueur*," and this fantastic shape may have been a delirious distortion of these things. The incidents of the tale are incredible. The Angel of the odd, like the characters of the court of King Pest, is a grotesque conception: in its appearance it seems to be a dream-distortion or a delirious vision. The language that the Angel speaks resembles some highly distored dream talk "Angel" establishes the mock-serious tone. In short, the entire series of incidents in the tale would be possible only as dream distortions.[46] However, the narrator is not going through a dream; and though his first encounter with the Angle happens in a state of reverie induced by the intoxication of liquor, he goes through the other experiences as if they had really happened to him.

The extraordinary series of comic incidents that ensue are an outcome of the heated exchange that the narrator has with the devilish "Angel." The narrator cannot help the feeling that "...I gleaned from what he said that he was the genius who presided over the *contretemps* of mankind, and whose business it was to bring about the *odd accidents* which are continually astonishing the sceptic" (IV,150). The subsequent events—the "*odd accidents*"—fully substantiate this feeling on his part. By an "odd accident" the clock stops while he is engaged in his dialogue with the Angel, and this results in his missing his appointment with the insurance company. The account of the house catching fire and the narrator coming down from the window by a ladder is mock-serious in the extreme. The Angel confronts him again in the form of a huge hog, wallowing in mud, that uses the ladder the ladder for scratching his left shoulder. This results in the narrator's headlong fall. His subsequent remarks reveal an attitude of humorous detachment: "this accident, with the loss of my insurance, and with the more serious loss of my hair, the whole of which had been singed off by the fire, predisposed me to serious impressions, so that, finally, I made up my mind to take a wife" (IV, 153). Here comedy arises from the way serious matters are treated in a lighter vein. Purely comic in nature are the incidents of the narrator's wooing a rich widow as her eighth husband and his wig falling off by accident, thus resulting in an unfortunate termination of the affair, and that of "a small particle of some foreign matter lodging in the corner of my eye," resulting in missing her in an avenue thronged with the *elite* of *the* city.

"A Predicament" (1838), purposely written by Poe as an illustration of the type of sensational tale described in "The Psyche Zenobia" ("How to Write a Blackwood Article"), is a parody of the Gothic horror tale. In his review of Hawthorne's *Twice-Told Tales* published in Graham's in May 1842, Poe said that a skillful writer would fit his materials into a preconceived design to evoke a specific mood or tone. The method of tale-writing that Poe enunciated on the basis of his reading of *The Blackwood's Magazine* was parodied earlier in "The Psyche Zenobia" ("How to Write a Blackwood Article") published in *American Museum* of Baltimore for November 1838. In "The Psyche Zenobia," Mr. Blackwood offers good instruction to Psyche Zenobia, but since the latter is fool, her story is ridiculous, in spite of the repulsive elements typical of the British magazinists. "A Predicament" is an illustration of the method learnt by Psyche Zenobia from Mr. Blackwood. The tale is in a highly exaggerated style, describing the incredible and absurd experiences of the character.

The opening itself establishes the humorous tone of narration:

> It was a quiet and still afternoon when I strolled forth in the goodly city of Edina. The confusion and bustle in the streets were terrible. Men were talking. Women were screaming. Children were choking. Pigs were whistling. Carts they rattled. Bulls they bellowed. Cows they lowed. Horses they neighed. Cats they caterwauled. Dogs they danced. *Danced*! Could it then be possible? *Danced*! Alas, thought I, *my* dancing days are over! Thus it is ever (IV, 212).

Having set the tone of narration, the author skillfully describes incident and character. The portraits of Diana, the lapdog, and Pompey are obviously comic caricatures. Diana is five inches in height with her head somewhat bigger than her body and her tail being closely cut off. The Negro servant is three feet in height and about eighty years of age. This is a purportedly comic portrait of a fitting companion for Psyche Zenobia in her incredible misadventures. Psyche Zenobia's assumption of an abrupt tone of seriousness in the middle of a lighthearted talk intensifies the comic effect of the narrative.

Another device used in the tale for comic effect is the method of contrast, juxtaposing things lofty and ludicrous. Psyche Zenobia passing beneath the portal of the cathedral and emerging within the vestibule is compared to the immense river, Alfred, passing "unscathed, and unwetted, beneath the sea." While Psyche Zenobia is gazing at the spiral staircase that appears to have had no end, "an accident occurred of too momentous a nature in a moral, and also in a metaphysical point of view, to be passed over without notice." It is Diana smelling a rat while Psyche Zenobia herself could not do so. We are told that this is like the fact that some persons can smell the sweet and very powerful perfume of the Prussian Isis while others fail to do so. Following the accidental head-on collision of Pompey with Psyche Zenobia on the floor of the belfry, the latter "tore out a vast quantity of black, and crisp, and curling material," and tossed it with disdain. The material got stuck up among the cordage of the bell and started dangling. The reactions of Psyche Zenobia are significant:

> I fancied it still alive. I fancied that it stood on and with indignation. Thus the *happydandy Flos Aeris* of Java bears, it is said, a beautiful flower, which will live when pulled up by the roots. The natives suspend it by a cord from the ceiling and enjoy its fragrance for years (IV, 217).

The humor here arises out of the juxtaposition of the high and the low. Further, Psyche Zenobia contemplates the great figures upon the dial-plate saying, "how intelligent, how intellectual, they looked! And presently they took to dancing the Mazurka, and I think it was the figure V who performed the most to my satisfaction." Lighthearted and witty remarks like these contrast sharply with the perilous situation in which the character finds herself, and the result is humor.

The satire in this tale is many-pronged. Poe is considerably inventive in transforming several "piquant" examples of Blackwood. The Muses Melete, Mneme, and Aoede have been changed into the Furies Melty, Nimmy, and Hetty. The Persian iris becomes the "Prussian Isis." Mr. Blackwood, referring to Voltaire's tragedy, quotes "*Aussi tendre que Zaire*" because foreign tongues make the articles more glittering. This phrase is applied to a chicken humorously. Psyche applies the phrase to Pompey in a mangled form: "*Ossi tender que beefsteak.*" Poe himself noted in "Marginalia" that "misapplication of quotations is clever, and has a capital effect when well done."[47] Poe also uses many figures of speech like bathos, Pompey "shut his two eyes as if he were endeavoring to crack nuts between the lids." Rhetorical devices like repetition contribute to the humor of the tale: "Thus it is said," "I entered the ominous archway! I entered," "The ticking...amused me. *Amused* me, I say..." "my lamentable situation. Lamentable indeed!" etc.

The last part of the tale takes a grotesque tun Due to the pressure of the machine on Psyche Zenobia's neck one of the eyes rolls down from the socket into the gutter, running along the eaves of the main building. In addition to this, the eye from the gutter winks and blinks at the character. And finally the very head of Psyche Zenobia is separated from the body and rolls down into the street. These unbelievable incidents give a more serious turn to the story. The dialogue between the headless character and her head is the culmination of this fantastic series of events. Thus the tale ends as the highly incredible grotesquerie of the type seen in "King Pest."

Walter F. Taylor says that Poe, being no popular humorist like Irving, occasionally wears the jester's motley. Referring to "A Predicament," he says that the tale is "not humorous, but callously grotesque."[48] However, the grotesquerie that the tale develops toward the end is well balanced by the several humorous situations in the course of the tale. Thus Burton R. Pollin is more convincing when he asserts that the tale is "a well-executed, deftly constructed, highly unified short story, whose quality is sensationalism 'a la Blackwood's,' is only one phase of its varied humor and its stylistic ingenuity."[49]

"Bon-Bon" (1835) is a satirical sketch rather than a narrative, but it is considerably entertaining. Vincent Buranelli calls it a farce and says, "Whether Poe was really capable of writing farces for the stage is debatable. He certainly was capable... of writing farces for the magazines."[50] T.O. Mabbott, calling the tale "one of Poe's best comic stories," says that it has been played on the stage in New York, with dialogue "word for word" from Poe.[51] The situation of the hero's encounter with the devil is rendered in purely objective terms as a dialogue.

Dialogues like the following are entertaining:

"The—hiccup!—soul," replied the metaphysician, referring to his MS, "is undoubtedly—"

"No, sir!"

"Indubitably—"

"No, sir!"

"Indisputably—"

"No, sir!"

"Evidently—"

"No, sir!"

"Incontrovertibly—"

"No, sir!"

"Hiccup!—"

"No, sir!"

"And beyond all question, a—"

"No, sir, the soul is no such thing!" (IV, 38).

However, the dramatic situation serves as a pretext for a series of satirical comments on the pretensions of scholars and philosophers The piece presents a weird fantasy that achieves effect through exaggeration.

The tone of exaggeration and absurdity in the tale is reflected in the portrait of the character as well as in the general style of the narrative. Poe here uses nearly all the patent devices of the comic art: high-sounding or queer names, stilted, pretentious language with its ponderous periods, its use of parallel, rhythmic structures, and its choice of impressive learned words and phrases.

The initial circumstance itself, of Pierre Bon-Bon the *restaurateur* being also a philosopher of great pretensions, has a touch of the grotesque. Bon-Bon, we are told, is an expert not only in the making of omelettes but in discoursing upon philosophy, Nature, and Soul. It is suggested that Kant himself is indebted to him for his metaphysics. Equally famous with his omelettes are the ideas of Bon-Bon:

> Bon-Bon was Ionic—Bon-Bon was equally italic. He reasoned *a priori*—he reasoned also *a posteriori*. His ideas were innate—or otherwise. He believed in George of Trebizond—he believed in Bossarion. Bon-Bon was emphatically a—Bon-Bonist (IV, 23).

The same satirical vein is evident in the delineation of Bon-Bon's appearance.

> Bon-Bon was barely three feet in height, and if his head was diminutively small, still it was impossible to behold the rotundity of his stomach without a sense of magnificence nearly bordering upon the sublime. In its size both dogs and men must have seen a type of his acquirements; in its immensity a fitting habitation for his immortal soul (IV, 26).

The grotesque nature of the character is thus evident here in the juxtaposition of the sublime and the ridiculous. Bon-Bon's cafe itself is a curious melange of kitchen properties, dishes, and *the bibliotheque* of the *QEuvres de Bon-Bon*. The mid-night encounter with the devil presents a very lively comic dialogue on various philosophical matters. The general tone is that of grotesque humor, even of savage uproarious laughter. Poe's talent for comic dialogue is nowhere better demonstrated than in the dialogues between Bon-Bon and the Devil.

Burlesque and Parody

According to Joseph T. Shipley, the term "burlesque" originally denoted "a robust spirit of humor rather than a literary method. Synonymous with 'droll,' it implied the strongly ludicrous... Burlesque is now used for poetry, fiction, and drama in which customs, institutions, persons, or literary works—individually or types—are made to appear ridiculous by incongruous imitation."[52] The comic effect is produced by a deliberate disproportion between the style and the sentiments, presenting the trivial with ironic seriousness or the serious with grotesque levity. Frequently its purpose is critical or satirical, but it may aim to amuse by extravagant incongruity. Such a purely fantastic piece is called an extravaganza.

Richmond p. Bond says: "Burlesque consists in the use or imitation of serious matter or manner, made amusing by the creation of an incongruity between style and subject."[53] This incongruous use or imitation can be seen in Butler's *Hudibras* or Pope's In *The Rape of the Lock*. While in some burlesques a relatively trifling subject is ludicrously elevated by the style of presentation, in some a relatively important subject of cutting of a lock of hair is elevated by the epic style of presentation, but in Hudibras the lofty pretensions of Puritanism are degraded. In the words of John D. Jump, the former is "high burlesque" and the latter "low burlesque."[54]

Associated with the burlesque as a form of literary satire is parody. Gilbert Highet in *The Anatomy of Satire* draws a distinction between the "burlesque" and what he calls the "mock-heroic parody." According to him, "A mock-heroic parody takes a theme which is usually trivial or repellent and treats it with elaboration, grandeur, and feigned solemnity. A burlesque treats its subject with ridicule, vulgarity, distortion, and contempt."[55] More specifically, Highet calls "parody" "one of the chief shapes which satire assumes," and defines the term as "imitation which, through distortion and exaggeration, evokes amusement, derision and sometimes scorn."[56] John D. Jump defines parody as the "high burlesque of a particular work (or author) achieved by applying the style of that work (or author) to a less worthy subject: e.g., Fielding's *Shamela*."[57] Thus parody is an aspect of the burlesque and is more specific than burlesque.

In his letter of February 11, 1836 to John P. Kennedy Poe says:

> You are nearly, but not altogether right in relation to the satire of some of my Tales. Most of them were *intended* for half banter, half satire—although I might not have fully acknowledged this to be their aim even to myself. "Lionizing" and "Loss of Breath" were satires properly speaking—at least so meant—the one of the rage for Lions and the facility of becoming one—the other of the extravagances of Blackwood.[58]

It is well known that *Blackwood's Magazine* was a source of Poe's serious as well as comic writing. Tales like "Bon-Bon," "Lionizing," "Loss of Breath," and "King Pest" constitute the bulk of Poe's "Tales of the Folio club." These seventeen tales, as Poe says in his letter of September 2, 1836 to Harrison Hall, "are of a bizarre and generally whimsical character."[59]

"Lose of Breath" (1832) is sub-titled "A Tale Neither in nor out of 'Blackwood'." George E. Woodberry sees in the tale "a parody on the inane jargon (as it was then thought) of German metaphysics."[60] There is exaggeration in the rendition of both incident and tone. The circumstance of Mr. Lackobreath's loss of breath and its accidental appropriation by Windenough, and the final transaction of its delivery back to its owner by Windenough and the series of adventures that Lackobreath goes through including his mutilation and hanging—are all manifestly absurd happenings that contribute to the humor of the tale.

Michael J.S. Williams says, "in 'the Man that was Used Up' and "A Predicament," language is presented as prior to, indeed as determining, events in the world."[61] The tone of narration is absurd. Though the narrator is telling us of a most notorious misfortune, the tone is mock–serious. In the midst of the most excruciating circumstances, the narrator finds the presence of mind to make light-hearted comments, to indulge in metaphysical reflection, and in quips and turns of expression. When he gets kicked out of the cab breaking both of his arms and the largest of his trunks falls on his head, he remarks that he "fractured (his) skull in manner at once interesting and extraordinary." As the two greedy cats fight for a bite of his nose he remarks that they "betook themselves of the indecorous contention for the paltry consideration of my nose." The knot of the halter as he is hanging causes him "very little inconvenience" as he has no breath to be suspended. As he is hanging,

> The populace *encored.* Several gentlemen swooned; and a multitude of ladies were carried home in hysterics. Pinxit availed himself of the opportunity to retouch,

> from a sketch taken upon the spot, his admirable painting of the "Marsyas Flayed Alive" (IV, 85).

When he finally arranges the transaction with Windenough for the return of his breath, he says: "Preliminaries being at length arranged, my acquaintance delivered me the respiration; for which (having carefully examined it) I gave him afterward a receipt" (IV, 90). Thus Poe has himself written an absurd composition with the intention of parodying the absurd stuff of *Blackwood's Magazine*.[62] The narrative belongs to a familiar species of literary parody, but as narrative too is possesses a certain charm and liveliness of manner.

Poe called "The Devil in the Belfry" (1839) an "extravaganza." George E. Woodberry calls it a "grotesque sketch."[63] According to N. Bryllion Fagin, the story is "one of Poe's lighter performances, and any effect he intended to create is hardly impressive."[64] However, T. O. Mabbott calls it one of the better grotesques, "a bit of harmless buffoonery, unmarred by repulsive elements."[65]

The author claims historical authenticity about the inhabitants of a certain small town who have for generations existed in a state of isolation from the outside world. The tale is told from an omniscient point of view. The inhabitants of the small town are a people whose lives are dominated by the twin images of the time-piece and the cabbage. The image of the time-piece suggests the kind of mechanical, repetitive, time-ridden world in which these people live. Cabbage (symbol of German diet) suggests the paradoxical nature of a life that vegetates, a world that never changes but grows without producing events. The devil who enters the Belfry and upsets the rhythm of their life might symbolize the impingement of the external world and the destruction of their time-concept. In brief, the tale may be taken as a satire on the time-consciousness of the American bourgeoisie. T.O. Mabbott reports that Professor Carl Schreiber told him he thought the story satirized an excessive emphasis laid on puntuality in Philadelphia.[66]

Poe's treatment of the tale throughtout is in a vein of burlesque. The incidents are incredible and exaggerated. The people's obsession with time is such that they have in their houses and environs recurring images of time. Every house has a clock on it and every man carries a watch in his pocket and even their pigs have watches (and cabbages) tied to their tails. The people of Vondervotteimittiss (Wonder What time it is) are so self-satisfied with their own little world that they pass resolutions in their town council "That it is wrong to alter the good old course of things;" "That there is nothing tolerable out of Vondervotteimittieess;" and "That we will stick by our clocks and cabbages" (IV, 108). The satirical purpose of the tale becomes quite manifest here, and the entire happening connected with the devil in the belfry is given a comic-allegorical significance. In short, Poe succeeds in creating a brilliant caricature of the people and life of the small town. And the last scene of the story in which the clock strikes thirteen is highly comic. T. O. Mabbott says that clocks do strike thirteen on rare occasions, and the phenomenon is interpreted as a sign of death or very bad luck. Mabbott adds: "Poe's dull worthies observe only that the thirteenth hour must mean it is one in the afternoon."[67] Archer Taylor tells us that "When the clock strikes thirteen" is a location for never.[68]

"Never Bet the Devil Your Head" (1841) is a literary satire which purports to ridicule things in general like the New England Transcendentalists, the German idealists, and Carlyle. But in particular, it is a satire on the demand of the critics that every fiction should have a moral. In the sub-title Poe calls the piece "A Tale with a Moral." Obviously, he is here ridiculing the absurd habit of reading a moral Into every tale:

> These fellows ("modern Scholiasts") demonstrate a hidden meaning in "The Antideleevians," a parable in "Powhatan," new views in "Cock Robin," and transcendentalism in "Hop O' My Thumb." In short, it has been shown that no man can sit down to write without a very profound design. (IV, 124-25).

Poe intends the tale as a direct reply to his critics who

complained that he had never written a tale with a moral. He seems to tell them that if one were to write a fully moral tale it might only be such an absurd thing as the story of Toby Dammit. The story of Toby Dammit offered by Poe might thus be a parody of a tale with a moral. But while this is the main focus of the satire, Poe also uses the opportunity to mack the persons, systems, and institutions that he disliked. He insert wry comments on Coleridge, Kant, Carlyle, Emerson, the Transcendentalists, at the homeopathists, and the contemporary journals like "The Dial" and "The North American Quarterly." Referring to "Never Bet the Devil Your Head," Poe says in his letter of September 19,1841 to Dr. Joseph Evans Snodrass:

> You are mistaken about "The Dial." I have no quarrel in the world with that illustrious journal, nor it with me. I am not aware that it ever mentioned me by name, or alluded to me either directly or indirectly. My slaps at it were only in "a general way." The tale in question is a mere Extravaganza levelled at no one in particular, but hitting right and left at things in general.[69]

Obviously, Poe is hitting at those commentators who give a profound meaning to mere extravagances of imagination.[70]

In the portrayal of Toby Dammit Poe uses the familiar burlesque paraphernalia, the essence of which is an unbelievable distortion of character-traits and incidents and the highly exaggerated tone of language—all of which are calculated to produce humorous effects. Burlesque wit is evident when the narrator says:

> I remonstrated—but to no purpose. I demonstrated—in vain I entreated—he smiled. I implored—he laughed. I preached—he sneered. I threatened—he swore. I kicked him—he called for the police. I pulled his nose--he blew it... (IV, 127).

But the narrative also develops a ludicrous situation in the encounter of Toby Dammit with the old gentleman the Devil, and in his absurd bet about leaping across the turnstile and the consequences that follow. The Devil's repetition of "*ahem*" as some kind of refrain makes the tone of narration mock-serious. It is like the "Nevermore" used in "The Raven" for an altogether serious purpose of heightening the emotional tension in the protagonist as well as in the reader. Here the word is repeated. In the tale there is a touch of the allegorical bout the encounter. The gentleman in black suit who incites Toby Dammit into his reckless adventure and finally walks with his head away is obviously the Devil himself.

The tale ends on a preposterous not. Poe makes consummate use understatement in describing the circumstances of Toby Dammit's self-destruction and the incidents tat follow. After the jump over the stile Toby Dammit comes down heavily on the ground and lies still, and concludes that his feelings had been hurt. But the truth is that the poor fellow had been deprived of his head, which could not be found anywhere around, and "He did not surnine long his terrible loss." In his letter of April 30, 1835, to Thomas W. White, Poe speaks of the "witty exaggerated into the burlesque" as a way to attain clebrity in the Magazines. In "Never Bet the Devil Your Head" he does succeed in achieving the burlesque wit. T. O. Mabbott concedes that this tale "conforms very well to the author's peculiar ideas of what constituted humor. Relatively few readers share his belief that *any* impossible combination of events is laughable.[71] nevertheless, Poe creates humor in his comic in his comic tales by means of incongruities.

Social Comedy

While in the tales of the Grotesque like "King Pest" and "The System of Dr. Tarr and Prof. Fether" Poe takes the reader to the verge of the terrible, in tales like "The Spectacles," "Three Sundays in a Week," and "The Man that was Used Up," treating his subject in a lighter vein, he creates the world of social comedy. These lighter tales should convince us that Poe's comic sense has several interesting strands and that he is really capable of depicting fun for the sake of fun.

Both "The Spectacles" (1844) and "Three Sundays in a Week" (1841) are tales in a light-hearted vein. In his letter of

March 30, 1844 to James R. Lowell, Poe calls "The Spectacles" "a somewhat extravagant tale."[72] George E. Woodberry describes it as "an extremely weak piece of humor."[73] T.O. Mabbott dismisses it as "one of the least meritorious."[74] However, Burton R. Pollin feels that even this minor tale is significant.[75] The tale is probably a satire on romantic love at first-sight presented through the character of the young man who, in the blindness of his passion, falls in love with an eighty-year old hag who finally turns out to be his own great-grandmother. The central idea of the tale is that of mistaken identity. The situation turns upon a rather preposterous comic conspirsy to feed his passion with the intention of fooling him.

The success of the story lies in tricking the reader too, along with the character. In fact, the truth of the story is known from the beginning only to the lady herself and to the narrator's friend. Throughout the course of events the reader feels that he is reading a romantic story of love-at-first-sight. The author cleverly manages the events of the tale, like the happenings in the opera house, the correspondence of the youth with the lady, and the final experience of the character. The young man is unsuspecting even when the lady speaks of "age." He is under the impression that she is only a few years older than himself. Even the miniature that the lady presents to him fails to make his realize the truth. The reason for all these happenings is the defective vision of the young man; and when on wearing the spectacles he realizes that he has after all been flirting with an old lady, it is a shocking experience for him. At this point the whole plot of the great–grandmother and the narrator's friend is explained.

According to T. O. Mabbott, "Three Sundays in a Week" is Poe's "only tale that can possibly be read as a simple happy love story. Probably because of its superficial comedy—reminiscent of 'Lionizing'—it has been more popular with ordinary readers than with professed critics."[76] The story turns upon a clever trick played by a young grandnephew in collusion with a young lady and his naval friends to win his grandducle's consent for his marriage. But tne tale is a rather thin affair, and though it provides an interesting comic portrait of the granduncle the other characters are not drawn vividly. Nevertheless, the action is rather amusing. It led Jules Verne to create his Around the world In 80 Days, because of the usc of time around the globe in travelling.

In both "The Spectacles" and "Three Sundays in a Week" there is a highly exaggerated humor turning on fantastic names and phrases. The narrator in "The Spectacles" traces his descent to the "Moissart, Voissart, Croissart, Froissart" line, and the granduncle Rumgudgeon[77] in "Three Sundays in a Week" is a "hard-hearted, dunderheaded, obstinate, rusty, crusty, musty, fusty, old savage." The humor arises here from the author's play on words. The narrator calls his granduncle Rumgudgeon "a little, pursy, pompous, passionate, semicircular somebody, with a red nose, a thick skull, along purse, and a strong sense of his own consequencc." The humor of the tale results from the narrator's attempts to get the consent of Rumgudgeon to marry Kate.[78]

Poe thought of "The Man that was Used Up" (1639) so highly that he gave it a place of honor second to "the Murders in the Rue Morgue" in both *Phantasy-Pieces* and *Prose Romances.* (1843) However, the tale has baffled critics. Arthur H. Quinn says, "There may be some profound meaning in this satire upon a general who is made up of cork legs, false teeth, and other artificial limbs, but it escapes the present writer."[79] Walter F. Taylor, while admitting that Poe, apart from any satirical purpose, "could construct situations that are themselves intrinsically humorous," dismisses "The Man that was Used Up" as "merely a dressing-up of the old joke about the person with the false teeth, the cork leg, and the glass eye."[80] Thus in Taylor's view this tale, instead of being "intrinsically humorous," exemplifies "the cheapest methods of the vaudeville gag and slapstick." But a close reading of the tale convinces us of the "intrinsic humor" of the character and situation. According to Henri Bergson, "The attitudes, gestures, and movements of the human body are laughable in exact proportion as that body reminds us of a mere machine."[81] In this Bergsonian sense, the dressed-up man in Poe's tale does produce laughter although is has escaped the attention of critics like A. H. Quinn and Walter F. Taylor. T. O. Mabbott, however, sees an important thoughtful element in the tale. As he puts It, "The author asks the ancient question, 'What is Man?' —and considers the problem of identity. The body may be diminished, the spirit is still whole."[82] However, it is interesting to sea the relevance of the "artificial" man who is now seen as prosthetically possible. It is a satire on "progress."

The conception of "the man that was used up" is comic in its unbelievable distortion; and the tone of the narrative is one of exaggeration. This not of exaggeration is evident in the names that the author has chosen for his characters and incidents. The hero is Brevet Brigadier General John A. B. C. Smith; the narrator's sculptor-friend is called Chiponchipino. The other names that occur are Dr. Drummummup, Miranda Cogenscenti, Miss Thabita Tea, Mr. Tattle, Mrs. O'Trump, Mrs. Piroutte, Miss Bass Blue, etc. The mechanical repetition of this dreadful business of the Bugaboo and Kickapoo by the various characters that the narrator encounters, itself produces patently ludicrous effect.[83] The several personages in the tale are in fact so mechanical both in their behavior and utterance that they give the impression of comic automata. There is also a touch of the comic in the ironic contrast between the narrator's passionate curiosity to unravel the mystery about the General and the almost consistent manner in which his curiosity is thwarted by the persons who might have told him more about the General, but who keep repeating parrot-like the same eulogistic exclamations. The fulfillment of the narrator's curiosity comes as an anti-climax to the persistently built up impression of the General as a great hero. The comic effect of the tale is one that is wrought largely through the tone of exaggeration that the author assumes throughout the story.

The tale also has a clearly satirical motive. It purports to expose the utter hollowness and falsity of a man who puts on an *air distingue* and passes for a person of great distinction and heroism, though in actuality he is a pathetic figure assembled out of artificial limbs. Poe might have intended this comic portrait as a satire on the "wonderfully inventive age" of "Parachutes and rail roads--man-traps and spring-guns," and today on prosthetics. This might be inferred from many incidental references in the dialogues to this subject of modern inventions. But the focus of interest is not on inventions but on the pathetic incongruity between appearance and reality in the character of the General, between what he is taken to be and what he actually is. Whatever the theme of the satire. Poe's intention is clearly to expose sham and this object he achieves with considerable success.

Hoax

In addition to the grotesques, burlesques, parodies, and social comedies, Poe has also written a few scientific hoaxes that greatly influenced writers like Jules Verne. In these hoaxes, combining realism and fantasy, he creates a fascinating world of make-believe. The effect wrought by these tales on the reader is ultimately one of wonder at Poe's skill at verisimilitude and his sense of humor. Hoax, one can say, is a part of Poe's larger concern with playing upon the mind of the reader, more specifically his credulity.

Referring to Poe's involvement with matters of contemporary interest like exploration, treasure-hunting, and balloons. Constance Rourke says, "He turned to comedy; as by instinct he turned to the hoax."[84] Hervey Allen refers to Poe's "childish and almost unbalanced delight in a hoax of any kind."[85] However, there is something more than the "childish" and the "unbalanced" in Poe's hoax. It is a conscious attempt on his part skillfully and intentionally to hoodwink his readers. It is a part of the very dramatic nature of his presentation. Daniel Hoffman, referring to works like "Hans Pfaall," calls the author "Hoaxiepoe" and concludes that in "Hans Pfaall", "the sensibilities of Hoaxiepoe vibrate to the same terrors as do the tales of Horror-haunted Edgar."[86] Hoffman's whimsical description of Poe does not, however, convince us. Poe's hoax has a unique place in his comic imagination

G.R. Thompson views the hoax in the light of romantic irony, as "a kind of supreme irony in which the writer mocks perceptive 'eirons' like himself, and even, therefore, himself."[87] Poe, of course, quite enjoys writing hoaxes, but he has not obviously thought of the "supreme irony" hidden in these writings. His purpose in writing these hoaxes is primarly to laugh with the reader as well as at him.

The method of verisimilitude employed in Poe's tales is an aspect of his scheme of comic fiction. This is evident from his reference to "the idea of imparting very close verisimilitude to what I should write—that is to say, so close as really to deceive." (VIII, 138). Poe's hoaxes are intended to "deceive" the reader by means of verisimilitude.

Poe writes in his letter to the *Columbia Spy* concerning the reception of "The Balloon Hoax" (1844):

> The "Balloon Hoax" made a far more intense sensation than anything of that character since the "Moon-Story" of Locke. On the morning (Saturday) of its announcement, the whole square surrounding the "Sun" building was literally besieged, blocked up—ingress and egress being alike impossible, from a period soon after sunrise until about two O'clock P.M. In Saturday's regular issue, it was stated that the news had been just received, and that an "Extra" was then in preparation, which would be ready at ten. It was not delivered, however, until nearly noon. In the meantime I never witnessed more intense excitement to get possession of a newspaper.[88]

"The Balloon Hoax" is certainly one of the most entertaining adventure stories written by Poe. His introductory note describes the theme of the piece which is in the form of a journal account of a voyage of Mr. Monck Mason and friends across the Atlantic in three days: "Astounding News by Express, *via* Norfolk!—The Atlantic Crossed in Three Days! Signal Triumph of Mr. Monck Mason's Flying Machine!." The "Balloon Hoax" was only called thus years later (after Poe's death) being presented originally as a newspaper scoop.

The story consists of two parts, the first giving a sketch of the balloon with scientific detail and the second giving an account, in journal method, of the actual voyage across the Atlantic. All this is Poe's method of verisimilitude to make the incidents at once striking. The description of the actual crossing of the ocean is thrilling in its detail. The tale is a hoax in that the author describes the crossing of the Atlantic by a fictional aeronaut as though he is reporting an actual happening. In addition to the details regarding the balloon and the modes of ascent and descent with an apparent scientific accuracy, Poe also gives details of the voyage in a journal method giving the whole narrative the semblance of truth. The prophetic tone of narration is clear when he concludes: "This is unquestionably the most stupendous, the most interesting, and the most important undertaking ever accomplished or even attempted by man."

Another tale which greatly excited the contemporary reading public is "The Unparalleled Adventure of One Hans Pfaall" (1835).[89] Constance Rourke says that the tale bears "a close resemblance to the more elaborate and finished tall tales of the West."[90] The highly fanciful nature of the tale is indicated in the epigraph:

> With a heart of furious fancies,
>
> Whereof I am commander,
>
> With a burning spear *and a horse of air,*
>
> To the Wilderness I wander

"The Balloon Hoax" was only called thus years later (after Poe's death) being presented originally as a newspaper scoop. Hans Pfaall, the narrator, says that this wandering to the "wilderness" from Rotterdam by a balloon finds all Europe "in an uproar, all physics in a ferment, all reason and astronomy together by the ears." The tale consists of an account of how the adventurous Hans Pfaall surprises his friends and neighbors by taking off by a balloon. A major part of the story is supposedly a letter written by Hans Pfaall to Van

Underduck and Rubadub, President and Vice–President of the States' College of Astronomers in the city of Rotterdam regarding his voyage to the "wilderness" of the sky by the balloon. The narrator's dream relates to a trip across the ocean to London where the Lord Mayor and other dignitaries greet him, but he proceeds to Paris where the balloon changes to a long horn, the small end toward the earth, and he drops out of his dream.

The voyage, described in greater detail than in "The Balloon Hoax," has humor of a high order. Replete with extensive terminology of aerial navigation, the tale produces an effect of verisimilitude. In the words of Hervey Allen, "The clever, and 'imaginative realism' of Poe's style was successful in temporarily cozening the multitude who read, gaped and believed."[91]

Burton R. Pollin includes "Hans Pfaall" in the *Collected Writings* under "The Imaginary Voyages" along with *Pym* and "Julius Rodman." He maintains that it is not a "hoax" and that Poe was not writing a "parody of the romantic moon voyage," as Bailey, A. H. Quinn, and Marjorie H. Nicholson thought.[92] On the other hand, "What makes this unusual and strangely like Poe's account is the fictional tone and the many touches of graphic description of natural phenomena, such as the varying clouds and ocean and the attempts to show the development of an obsession with flight in an apt layman. It is surely one of the stimuli for Poe's exploiting a growing popular interest and also a source for some of his specific details."[93]

In 1861, Fyodor Dostoyevsky, praising "The Balloon Hoax" for its realistic "fantasticalness," said that the tale was "so realistic and truthful that at least for a couple of hours everybody was convinced of the reported fact and only later investigation proved it to be entirely invented."[94] Humor in Poe's hoaxes arises from the reader's ultimate realization that he is after all fooled by the author. Scientific hoaxes like "The Balloon Hoax" and "Hans Pfaall" are interesting not only as comic writings but as forerunners of the science-fiction fantasies so popular today. Poe's originality in writing this type of fiction is evident from his letter of September 11, 1835 to John P. Kennedy:

> Have you seen the "Discoveries in the Moon"? Do you not think it altogether suggested by *Hans Pfaall*? It is very singular—but when I first purposed writing a Tale concerning the Moon, the idea of *Telescopic* discoveries suggested itself to me—but I afterwards abandoned it. I had however spoken of it freely, & from many little incidents & apparently trivial remarks in those *Discoveries* I am convinced that the idea was stolen from myself.[95]

Poe is here accusing Richard A. Locke, the author of *Discoveries*, of plagiarism. Whether it was a case of plagiarism or not, subsequent writings in similar vein by various authors in the world have proved that Poe was a trend–setter.

The foregoing analyses of Poe's comic tales bring to light several interesting devices used by the author to produce humorous effects. In all these tales there is a firm narrative structure—though in some it is more conspicuous than in others—and there is incident and character, worked out in some detail. One aspect of Poe's comic art in his grotesque tales is his employment of "improbability" as a recurring device (e.g., "Loss of Breath" and "The Angel of the Odd"). "Loss of Breath" depicts the improbable and often ludicrous adventures of Mr. Lacko' breath from the time he loses breath while haranguing his bride until Mr. Windenough restores it. In "The Angel of the Odd" the Angel is an incredible figure composed of various containers of alcohol. The story relates the oddest and the most improbable series of incidents. However, these two tales burlesque the fantastic plots of the popular grotesque fiction of Poe's time. "A Predicament," in which Psyche Zenobia attempts to produce the type of fiction taught by Mr. Blackwood, is a tale not of terror but of a series of grotesque situations and improbabilities. Incidents like Psyche Zenobia's eyes and head rolling down the clock-tower into the gutter and the character holding dialogue with her head are unbelievable in the extreme and only create grotesque effects.

In addition to the improbability of action, Poe makes use of unbelievable physical distortions of the characters for producing grotesque effects. Certain parts of the human body are presented in abnormal dimensions, thus giving a queer look to the character. For instance, the courtiers of King Pest have their bodies unusually distended and the effect they produce is something less than terror and more than comedy. A number of badly formed human figures are presented in these tales. The major representatives are Hugh Tarpaulin, Bon-Bon, the inhabitants of Vondervotteimittis and M. Valdemar, a living corpse. The reader cannot ignore the repulsive aspect of these characters. But this emphasis on a particular distortion only produces humor. Ultimately the violence and suffering presented in these tales produce amusement because they are patently absurd and unnatural. At the same time details from the world of actuality remind the reader of a stark reality which is not fully concealed by the absurdity. In addition to violence and suffering, death also is an aspect of Poe's grotesque humor. The devil stands for a link between humor and death in some tales like "Bon-Bon" and "Duc del'Omelette." Thus death in the grotesque tales is a source of laughter. Duc del'Omelette's daring comic escapades are presented against a background of the hell-torments of lost souls. "Bon-Bon" depicts a fine admixture of philosophy and devilry. The climax of the ridiculous in the story is reached when the devil classifies Greek and Latin philosophers according to the delectability of their souls. In both tales the grotesque humor mainly arises out of the dialogue between the human character and the devil which sounds like a parody of the dialogue between Dr. Faustus and Mephistopheles even though Poe never alludes to Goethe's *Faust*.

"The Spectacles" and "Three Sundays in a Week" achieve their effects through light–hearted incidents and dialogues between the characters. Despite the fact that they lack the power of expression and spirited quality of Poe's other comic tales like "Bon-Bon" and "The Man that was Used Up," they do have considerable interest for the reader. This kind of joke at the reader's expense is attempted in "The System of Dr. Tarr and Prof. Fether" too, where the mystery Is aimed as much at the reader as at the narrator. In the Gothic and the Ratiocinative tales the mystery intensifies the effect of terror, but in the comic tales the device is employed mainly for ludicrous effects.

Both incident and tone in Poe's comic tales are exaggerated to the point of absurdity. For instance, in "The Angel of the Odd" and "A Predicament" the character adopts a mock-serious attitude toward distressing experiences such as a serious injury or mutilation of the body. In "The Angel of the Odd" the humor also arises out of the odd accidents that the narrator undergoes. The tone of "The Man that was Used Up" is established by the exaggerated and mechanical repetition of the mention about the "Bugaboo and Kickapoo Campaign" by persons who are themselves mechanical. This produces a comic effect in the Bergsonian sense of the human resembling the mechanical. The incidents in tales such as "Loss of Breath", "King Pest", "The Angel of the Odd," and "A Predicament" are highly incredible and grotesque in the extreme. In "A Predicament" the humor also arises out of a juxtaposition of things lofty and ludicrous. Again in some tales the characters are made to speak in a language that they are least acquainted with and about things which are not expected to be known to them. "Bon-Bon" is an instance of this type. The comic devices used in the tales are puns, misquotations, and queer names of the characters. For instance, the repetition of "Moissart, Voissart, Croissart, Froissart, etc." in "The Spectacles" produces laughter. In "The Man that was Used Up," Brigadier General John A.B.C. Smith and Dr. Drummummup are typical. Legs, Tarpaulin, King Pest, and Queen Pest in "King pest" and Lacko'breath and Windenough in "Loss of Breath" are some more of the comic characters in the tales.[96] In addition to these names, certain serio-comic verbal exchanges such as those between the devil and the philosopher Bon-Bon produce laughter.

Walter Blair says that the framework narrative is typical of the American humorous writing and discusses the use of the technique in the works of writers like T. B. Thorpe.[97] Poe's "Hans Pfaall" too adopts the same techniques for humorous effect even though Thorpe was mainly after Poe. The tale deals with subjects like gravitation, astronomy, the topography of the moon, the construction of ballons, and the effects of atmospheric pressure. This show of learning is superbly fitted into the framework of a letter describing Hans Pfaall's adventures. The parallelism is interesting.

Just as in the Gothic tales the settings contribute to the effect of terror so also in the humorous tales the descriptions of the physical settings produce grotesque humor. "King Pest" and "The Duc del'Omelette" have settings that emphasize death. But the incidents are so absurd and improbable that the effect is humorous. In "Bon-Bon" the incongruity of the Physical setting corresponds to the incongruity of Bon-Bon's philosophical-gastronomical proficiency. Tales such as "The Spectacles" and "Three Sundays in a Week" are entirely in a light-hearted tone and their settings are matter-of-fact. The tone and setting of "Four Beasts in One" and "The Devil in the Belfry"—two of the political satires—are as absurd as the character and action. All of the houses of Vondervotteimittis are precisely uniform inside and outside, with grotesque decorations of clocks and cabbages. These settings, like those previously mentioned, produce humorous effects. In fact, the settings of most of Poe's comic tales are far removed from the realities of conventional life. However, in a large number of the tales the setting serves as the background for the freakish and humorous actions of the characters.

Common to all the types of humorous tales in Poe's writing is satire. The author satirizes the institutions, customs, manners, habits, characters, and convictions of the Americans of his time. Northrop Frye calls the satire that deals with mental attitudes the "Menippean Satire" and says that in such a satire, "Pedants, bigots, cranks, parvenus, virtuosi, enthusiasts, rapacious and incompetent professional men of all kinds, are handled in terms of their occupational approach to life as distinct from their social behavior."[98] In this sense Poe's satire in several of his humorous tales is "Menippean Satire." Thus in tales such as "A Predicament," "The System of Dr. Tarr and Prof. Fether," "Loss of Breath," and "Never Bet the Devil Your Head" Poe is satirizing the mental attitudes of profestionals.

According to Walter Blair, the humor of exaggeration is typically American. Poe's tales abound in the use of this device. Mark Twain was to use the device effectively in *A Tramp Abroad* (Ch. XVII): "His breath bred pestilence and conflagration, and his appetite bred famine." In "Mellonta Tauta" Poe views nineteenth-century America as a part of ancient history. The story is set in 2843 A.D. With a perspective similar to the "lunatics" fancied by Washington Irving's Knickerbocker, Poe presents the citizens of America as savages and their democratic institutions as disruptive mob rule.

NOTES

1. Arthur Ransome, *A History of Story-telling* (London, 1909) 251.
2. Constance Rourke, *American Humor: A Study of the National Character,* 148.
3. Brom Weber, ed. *An Anthology of American Humor* (New York: Thomas Y. Crowell Company, 1962) 226.
4. Constance Rourke, 147.
5. Edwin Fussell, *Frontier: American Literature and the American West* (Princeton: Princeton University Press, 1965) 148n.
6. Banjamin Franklin Fisher IV, "Devils and Devilishness in Comic Yarns of the Old Southwest," *ESQ*, Vol. 36, i (I Quarter 1990), 41.
7. Brom Weber, 226.
8. *Letters*, I, 57-58.
9. Stephen LeRoy Mooney, "Poe's Grand Design: A Study of Theme and Unity in the Tales," Diss. University of Tennessee, 1960. 45.
10. Dewayne August Peterson, "Poe's Grotesque Humor: A Study of the Grotesque Effects in His Humorous Tales", Diss. Duke University 1962. 12.
11. *Ibid.*, 18.
12. Dennis W. Eddings, ed. *The Naiad Voice: Essays on Poe's*

Satiric Hoaxing. (Port Washington, N.Y.: Associated Faculty Press, 1983) 156.

13. See Clark Griffith, "Poe's 'Ligeia' and the English Romantics," *University of Toronto Quartely,* 24 (October 1954): 8-25.
14. *Letters*, I, 57-58.
15. Stedman and Woodberry, *The Works of Poe,* VIII, 15.
16. *Lectures on Shakespeare* (London, 1951), 260.
17. *Ibid.*, 280.
18. Philip Thomson, *The Grotesque* (London: Methuen and Co., Ltd., 1972), 27.
19. *Ibid.*, 50.
20. See Martin Esslin, *Theatre of the Absurd* (London, 1962).
21. Karls S. Guthke, *Modern Tragicomedy* (New York, 1966), 73-74.
22. G. Wilson Knight, *The Wheel of Fire* (rev. ed.; London, 1949) 32-38.
23. William Van O'Connor, *The Grotesque, An American Genre* (Carbondale: Southern Illinois University Press, 1962), 19.
24. Wolfgang Kayser, *The Grotesque in Art and Literature,* trans. Ulrich Werssitein (Bloomington: Indiana University Press, 1963) 78.
25. G.R. Thompson, 116.
26. Donald H. Ross, "The Grotesque: A Speculation," *Poe Studies,* IV, No. 1 (June, 1971): 11.
27. *Letters,* I, 57-58.
28. *Ibid.,* 77.
29. Burton R. Pollin, "Names Used for Humor in Poe's Fiction," *Proceedings of Names Institute* at East Texas State University, (Fall, 1972): 52.
30. Constance Rourke, 148.
31. Walter F. Taylor, "Israfel in Motley," *The Sewanee Review,* XLII (July-September, 1934): 330-40.
32. See Ruth Leigh Hudson, "Poe and Disraeli," *American Literature,* VIII (January, 1937): 402-16.
33. T.O. Mabbott, ed. *Collected Works*, II, 238.
34. *Ibid.,* 679.
35. Constance Rourke, 147.
36. See T.O. Mobbott, ed. *Collected Works,* II, n16, 255. Mabbott says that the six Pests are type of people who are pests in the figurative sense of the word. All "dead" since they types of deadly futility.

37. A.H. Quinn, *Edgar Allan Poe,* 470.
38. George E. Woodberry, *Life,* II, 162.
39. Edward Wagenknecht, *Edger Allan Poe: The Man Behind the Logond* (New York: Oxford University Press, 1963) 57.
40. T.O. Mabbott, ed. *Collected Works,* III, 997.
41. William Whipple, "Poe's Two-edged Stiric Tale," *Nineteenth-Century Fiction,* IX (September, 1954): 121-33.
42. Brom Weber, 226.
43. Gerald E. Gerber, "Poe's Odd Angel," *Nineteenth-Century Fiction,* June 1968: 88-93.
44. T.O. Mabboth, ed. *Collected Works,* III, 1098.
45. "Fifty Suggestions," No. 28, *Graham's Magazine,* June 1849, 363.
46. T.O. Mabbott, ed. *Collected Works,* III, 1098.
47. Burton Rs. Pollin, "Poe's Tale of Psyche Zenobia: A Reading for Humor and Ingenious Construction," Papers on Poe, Essays in Honor of John Ward Ostrom (1972): 92-103.
48. Walter F. Taylor, 338.
49. Burton R. Pollin, "Poe's Tale of Psyche Zenobia: A Reading for Humor and Ingenious Construction": 92-93.
50. Vincent Buranelli, *Edgar Allan Poe,* 42. Buranelli quotes John P. Kennedy's advice to Poe in a letter of September 19, 1835 that Poe try to write "fraces after the manner of the French Vaudevilles." The playlet, by William Barstow, was given a special benefit performance at the Little Theatre, Sunday evening, February 29, 1920. Mr. F.C. McCarthy had the title role, the playwright the part of the devil. See also Mary E. Phillips, *Edgar Allan Poe the Man* (Chicago: The John C. Winston Co., 1926), I, 427. Mary E. Phillips says: "The *New York Tribune,* November 23, 1919, notes of 'Bon-Bon' and other tales, as a 'story by Poe done word for word into a Play.' ...In 'Bon-Bon' the spoken lines of conversation are as *written by Poe.* Description of characters and setting are as he pictured them."
51. T.O. Mabboot, ed. *Collected Tales,* II, 119-20.
52. Joseph T. Shipley, ed. *Dictionary of World Literature* (New Jersey: Littlefield, Adams and Co., 1960) 79.
53. Richmond P. Bond, *English Burlesque Poetry* (Cambridge, Mass, 1932) 3.
54. John D. Jump, *Burlesque* (London: Methuen & Co., Ltd., 1972) 2.

55. Gilbert Highet, *The Anatomy of Satire* (Princeton: Princeton University Press, 1962) 105.
56. *Ibid.*, 69.
57. John D. Jump, *Burlesque,* 2.
58. *Letters*, I, 84.
59. *Letters*, I, 103.
60. George E. Woodberry, *Life,* I, 130.
61. Michael J.S. Williams. *A World of Words: Language and Displacement in the Fiction of Edgar Allan Poe.* (Durham: Duke University Press, 1988) 51.
62. Walter F. Taylor says that in this tale Poe was satirizing his own preoccupation with premature burial. See Walter F. Taylor, "Israfel in Motely," *The Sewanee Review XLII* (July-September, 1934): 330-40.
63. George E. Woodberry, I, 199.
64. N. Bryllion Fagin, 204.
65. T.O. Mabbott, ed. *Collected Works,* II, 362.
66. *Ibid.,* 364.
67. T.O. Mabott, ed. *Collected Works,* 375, n7.
68. Archer Taylor. *American Notes and Queries,* January 1944.
69. T.O. Mabbott, ed. *Collected Works,* II, 620.
70. *Ibid.*, 619.
71. *Ibid.*
72. *Letters,* I, 247.
73. George E. Woodberry, *Poe* (1885), 246.
74. T.O. Mabbott, ed. *Collected Works,* III, 883.
75. Burton R. Pollin, "The Spectacles' of Poe-Sources and Significance," *American Literature* 38 (May 1965): 185-90.
76. T.O. Mabbott, II, 648.
77. See Burton R. Pollin, "Names used for Humor in Poe's Tales," *Proceedings of Names Institute* at East Texas State University, (Fall 1972): 51-57.
78. T.O. Mabbott, II, 648. Mabbott says: "The natural phenomenon on which the plot is based ossomething noticed when Spanish and Portuguese Navigators reached China by different routes." William T. Bandy tells us that Jules Verne's *Around the World in Eighty Days* was inspired by Poe's "Three Sundays in Week." William T. Bandy, "The Influence and Reputation of Edgar Allan Poe in Europe" (Lecture at the 37th Annual Commemorative

Program of the Edgar Allan Poe Society in October, 1959), Baltimore, 1962, 11.

79. Arthur H. Quinn, *Edgar Allan Poe,* 283.

80. Walter F. Taylor, 333.

81. Henri Bergson, "Laughtel," in *Comedy,* ed. Wylie Sypher (Garden City, N.Y.: Doubleday and Company, Inc., 1956) 79.

82. T.O. Mabbott, ed. *Collected Works,* II, 376.

83. T.O. Mabbott says: "The story was timely, for the newspapers were full of references to the troubles with Indians in Florida in 1839, in which the Kickapoo tribe was involved. Readers of historical sources will recall that prisoners were often mutilated by their captors, and some even survived scalping. There are also many allusions to the contemporary scene. The legal troubles of Captain Mann interested journalists in the City of Broterly Love. So many of the artisans mentioned can now be identified that it seems probable that all were real people although not all were Philadelphians." (*Collected Works,* II, 377).

84. Constance Rourke, 146.

85. Hervey Allen, *Israfel: The Life and Times of Edgar Allan Poe,* 463.

86. Daniel Haffman, *Poe Poe Poe Poe Poe Poe Poe* (Garden City, N.Y.: Doubleday and Comany, Inc., 1972) 158.

87. G.R. Thompson, *Poe's Fiction: Romantic Irony in the Gothic Tales* (Madison: The University of Wisconisn Press, 1973) 10.

88. Quoted in Arthur Quinn, 410. In fact, "The Balloon Hoax" was not entirely a flight of Poe's imagination. During those days there were serious plans both in America and in England, by respectable flyers, to cross the ocean by air. See T.O. Mabbott, ed. *Collected Works,* III, 1063.

89. Poe's meticulousness in the writing of even a piece in the lighter vein is evident from his letter of July 20, 1835 to Thomas W. White: "What Mr. Pleasants says in relation to the commencement of Hans Pfaall is judicisous. That part of the Tale is faulty indeed—so much so that I had often thought of remodelling it entirely. I will take care & have the Letter inserted in all the Baltimore papers." (*Letters*, I, 65).

90. Constance Rourke tells us that the tale bears "a close resemblance to the more elaborate and finished tall tales of the West." Constance Route, 146.

91. Hervey Allen, 470.

92. Burton R. Pollin, ed. *Collected Writings of Edgar Allan Poe,* I, 368.

93. *Ibid.,* 371

94. Quoted in Vladimir Astrov, "Dostoyevsky on Edgar Allan Poe," *American Literature,* XIV (March, 1942): 74.

95. *Letters,* I, 74. See also Poe's "Literati" article on Richard Adams Locke.

96. Burton R. Pollin, *Dictonary of Names and Titles in Poe's Collected Works* (New York: Da Cape Press, 1968). Later in an interesting article Pollin considers how the several names are "playfully and satirically inserted into his tales and criticism from 1832 to 1849." See "Names Used for Humor in Poe's Fiction," *Proceedings of Names Institute at* East Taxes State University, (Fall, 1972): 51-57.

97. See Walter Blair, *Native American Humor* (San Francisco: Chandler Publiching Company, Inc., 1960) 91-95.

98. Northrop Frye, *Anatomy of Criticism* (1957; rpt. New York: Athaneum, 1965) 309.

5

RATIONAL STANCE

> "These tales of ratiocination owe most of their popularity to something in a new key. I do not mean to say that they are not ingenious—but people think them more ingenious than they are—on account of their method or air of method."
>
> *Letter to P.P. Cooke*
> *August 9, 1846*

> "My main object, however, as you will readily understand, is the analysis of the *principles of investigation...*"
>
> *Letter to Joseph Evans Snodgrass*
> *June 4, 1842*

Poe calls the "analytic stories" published from 1841 through 1845 and included in Evert Duyckinck's collection to *Tales* (1845), "tales of ratiocination."[1] He employs the term "ratiocination" to describe his tales of the order of "The Purloined Letter", "The Murders in the Rue Morgue," and "The Gold Bug." The description at once brings out the distinction of this class of tales from the tales or terror. The tale of ratiocination appeals to the reader's intellectual curiosity, but the tale of terror appeals to his fear of the unknown, his dread of the supernatural. The tale of terror employs atmospheric suggestion and presentiment; the opening itself vaguely foreshadows the closing. The ratiocinaive tale, on the other hand, builds up an intellectual curiosity which is finally reward by a rational explanation and solution of the mystery.

In the ratiocinative tále, the complicated and ingenious mechanism of the plot is primary in importance; incident, character, and action are subordiante to it. In the tale of terror, character, situation, and atmosphere often predominate over all other aspects. Despite certain common elements like the rising emotion, the two types are opposed to each other. Another distinction is Dorothy L. Sayers': "The detective story seeks to leave nothing unexplained; the story of horror must always leave us guessing."[2] However, whatever the effect of the conclusion on the reader, both the ratiocinative tale and the tale of terror keep the reader engaged by means of mystery. Mystery in the tale of ratiocination and puzzle-solving is based on intellectual curiosity, but in the tale of terror it is one resulting from emotional involvement leading to fear. In the tale of terror, mystery raises more questions than answer, whereas in the tale of ratiocination, a rational explanation is offered toward the conclusion.

In his letter of August 9, 1846 to P.P. Cooke, Poe says:

> You are right about the hair-splitting of my French friend: - that is all done for effect. These tales of ratiocination owe most of their popularity to being something in a new key I do not mean to say that they are not ingenious—but people think them more ingenious than they are—on account of their method or *air* of method. In the "Murders in the Rue Morgue" for instance, where is the ingenuity of unravelling a web which you yourself (the author) have woven for the express purpose of unravelling? The reader is made to confound the ingenuity of the suppositious Dupin with that of the writer of the story.[3]

Thus in Poe's view the "ingenuity" of the tales of ratiocination depends largely on "their method or air of method." Poe implies here that he takes these tales as constituting but a phase of his mind. Hence his objection Duyckinck's collection: "He has what he thinks a taste for ratiocination, and has accordingly made up the book mostly of analytic stories. But this is not *representing* my mind in its various phase—it is not giving me fair play."[4] Poe has repeatedly stressed the "vast variety of modes" of his fiction that he referred to in his review of Hawthorne's *Twice-Told Talcs*.

While the major tales of ratiocination of the order of "The Purloined Letter" and "The Murders in the Rue Morgue" are interesting for the process of reasoning, the minor tales of the type are significant for the way mystery is sustained. In his review of Charles Dickens' *Barnaby Rudge*, Poe says:

> Every point is so arranged as to perplex the reader, and what his desir for elucidation:... The impression here skillfully conveyed is, that the ghost seen is that of Reuben Heradale; and the mind of the not-too-acute reader is at once averted from the ture state of the case—Now there can be no question that, by such means as these, many points which...would have been comparatively insipid if given in full detail in a natural sequence, are endued with the interest of mystery... The design of the mystery, however, being once determined upon by an author, it becomes imperative, first, that no undue or inartistical means be employed to conceal the secret of the plot; and, secondly, that the secret be well kept... A failure to preserve it until the proper moment of *denouement* throws all into confusion so far as regards the effect intended. If the mysterty leak out, against the author's will, his purpose are immediately at odds and ends; for he proceeds upon the supposition that certain impressions *do* exit, which do *not exist*, in the mind of his reder (VII, 49-52).

Poe thinks that Dickens' novel does not quite succeed in having a definite end in view. He doubts whether Dickens has sufficiently determined upon any particular plot while commencing the story. Also he maintains that Dickens has employed inartistic means in the concealment of the secret—means that do not finally lead to the conclusion. Dickens has, for instance, introduced extraneous material, historical details, such as the Gordon riots, into a story concerned with mystery. He fails to develop certain "dark hints," which a liberal hand, he has scattered throughout his story for misleading the reader. Poe concludes that *Barnady Rudge* is not a successful mystery novel.

The process of unravelling the mystery is detection. Poe employs the term "ratiocination" to describe this process because of his overriding concern with reasoning.[5] The term "detection," as used by the modern detective-fiction writers, involves not only the investigator's deductive reasoning based on the data available, but as predominantly, the dramatic hunt for the criminal.

The success of the ratiocinative tale lies in the precision and correctness of its logical deductions. The solution to the mystery comes through an exact reconstruction of the other man's mental processes. The writer of the ratiocinative tale presents us with the problem or an enigma and through a process of close deduction chalks ot the exact course of happening of the incident. His success lies in effectively concealing the secret of the plot till the proper moment at which the mystery is unravelled and all the facts of the case fall into place, illumining in a flash the significance of all the events retrospectively.

The ratiocinative tale differs from the Arabesque kind of its effect and in its mode of operation; but it resembles thae Arabesque in its relentless pursiut of a pre-established design. According to Poe, every fictional plot must be elaborated to its denouemnt with an "indispendable air of consequence, or causation by making the incidents, and especially the tone at all points, ten to the development of the intention" (VI 31). The logical process of the composition of "The Raver" described in "The Philosophy of Composition" is similar to the compositional method of a tale of the Arabesque or of Ratiocination: the work proceeds step by step to its completion with the precision and rigid consequence of a mathematical problem. Logical progression toward the plotted end is thus the underlying philosophy of poe's composition of the tale, as it is of the poem. But the difference is in the pattern of imagery and the sybolic use of language which predominate in the construction of the poem. Due to the very nature of its structure, the tale affords an opportunity for a variety of incident and character. Each one of Poe's tales is a strategy for securing a specific reader-response. In the Gothic tales the cumulative effect results in an intense stirring of the reader's emotions; the reatiocinative tales stimulate his intellect by means of a careful manipulation of suspense. According to Martin Price,

> It is our task to play against the author, remaining vigilant where he most wishes to lull our suspicions, refusing what strikes us as false leads, inventing surmises that go beyond his preferred evidence. Some detective stories persent a series of solution, each new one overturning and correcting the last, until that takes into account every prossibilty that has been raised.[6]

Such an interaction between the reader and the author is ever present in Poe's ratiocinative tales. By deliberately withholding certain important facts from the reader and throwing certain hints, the author "whats his desire for elucidation". This resutls is suspense for the reader and his attention is reveted to the course of the incidents. All tis is at the back of Poe's concern with producing an "effectt" on the readr. An exceptional analytical power enables him to achieve his literary objectives. As W.K. Wimsatt sayes, the ratiocinative tales demostrate this exceptional power of anlysis as opposed to the merely creative talent.[7]

The ratiocinative process is described in "The Murders in the Rue Morgue," "The Mystery of Marie Roget," and "The Purloined Letter". In these tales we are concerned not with how the mystery is "well kept" but with the imaginative processes of the reasoner, leading to *a posteriori* reconstruction of the events of the case. The opening paragraphs of the first of Poe's ratiocinative tales, "The Murders in the Rue Morgue" (1841), lay down the main principles of the ratiocinative method and advance the propositions in the light of which the business of detection is to be conducted. Poe tell us about the ratiocinative power of the human mind—the activity of the intellect which disentangles—the power in which the analyst glories. The epigraph from Sir Thomas Browne reinforces the idea that no human action, however remote, is beyond conjecture. The analyst is able, by a supreme exertion of his intellect, to arrive at conclusions which to the ordinary appehension may appear preternatural. But, as the author explians, "His results, brought about by the very soul and essence of metthod, have in truth, the whole air of intuition" (III 53). Thus, staring as an intellectual exercise, the ratiocinative method enters the realm of intuition. The results of the analyst are arrived at through a minute process of analysis, like the whist player who by his careful attention and inference, puts himself in full possession of the contents of the hands of the other party. The analytic power, the author explains, is not a simple ingenuity but a faculty that comes only to the truly imaginative. As Poe further expounds it in "The Purloined Letter," it consists in the rational reconstruction of the mental processes through which the other man, the opponent, arrived at a certain construction. This is made possible by "an identification of the reasoner's intellect with that of his opponent." And this calls for a profound imagination or a poetic-intuitive faculty that enables the reasoner to enter into the other man's mind and to re-enact the intricate movements of it. If this process is called "poetic," it is because the reasoner is able to see the connections between the apparently disparate objects of his investigation by means of a unifying vision that places him above the average men. However, the steps through which the conclusion is arrived at are mathematical in progression—the progression of a deductive reasoning. The primary condition in this process is imaginative (poetic) identification. Hence Poe calls for a union of these two faculties for any successful ratiocination.

Poe's ratiocinative faculty is at its best in the three major tales, "The Murders in the Rue Morgue," "The Mystery of Marie Roget," and "The Purloined Letter." As a tale of mystery and puzzle-solving, "The Gold Bug" is one of his most famous tales. Another tale wherein the element of mystery is of predominant interest is "Thou Art the Man," one of the neglected tales. Normally, critics take "The Oblong Box" as a minor Gothic piece. But the Gothic element in the tale is meager indeed. The centre of interest in the tale lies in how the mystery is "well kept" (from the narrator as well as from the reader). Hence the tale is considered at the end of the chapter asa tale of mystery. In the course of analysis of these tales, Poe's principle of mystery and ratiocination has been kept in mind.

In his letter of July 2, 1844 to James R. Lowell, Poe calls "The Murders in the Rue Morgue" (1841) one of his "best tales."[8] The tale employs all the detective-story devices like the detective's assistant who is impressed, bewildered, and finally enlightened by his friend, an often erring and overconfident police official, a wrong person arrested, the detective himself with his queer personal habits verging on eccentricity and the separate stories around the detective that lend an aura of mystery to the man. In this tale we have an introductory account of Dupin, the prototype of Conan Doyle's Sherlock Holmes. Dupin figures in all the three major tales with his energetic and imposing personality; he acquires a universal stature in the field of detective fiction at large. It was Poe who gave the detective a distinctive personality. T.O. Mabbott says that Poe derived his conceptionn of the detective from Voltaire's Zadig and the Princes of Serendip.[9] Scholars maintain that Poe was inspired by the Scripture and the Classics, Voltaire's *Zadig* (1748). Godwin's *Caleb Williams* (1794) and the sensational *Memoirs* (1828) of the French detective, Francois-Eugene Vidocg, and that Poe gave the detective tale an original and definitive form. According to Jacques Barzun, all that was subsequently done by other writers was only elaboration and complication.[10]

Poe's ratiocinative tales embody Dupin's masterful armchair detection, a logical deduction without much of a hectic outdoor hunting by the detective for clues. Of course,

"The Purloined Letter" has a little of such outdoor activity—Dupin visits the Minister's apartment for clues--but that too is accounted for by the detective himself in retrospect, while explaining the process of his deduction. Even in "The Murders in the Rue Morgue" this element is present—advertisement for the owner of the Ourang-Outang and the visit of Dupin and his companion to the scene of the tragedy. But it is reduced to a bare minimum. As Poe says in his letter of June 4, 1842 to George Roberts referring to "The Murders in the Rue Morgue," "Its theme was the exercise of ingenuity in the detection of a murder."[11] Whatever the "ingenuity" of the reasoner in this tale, Poe obviously rates it as inferior to "The Gold Bug."[12]

The pot of "The Murders in the Rue Morgue" unfolds with an itneresting episode in the course of Dupin's walk with his friend. In this episode, Dupin is able to enter the narrator's mind and "chime in" with his meditations by a remark about the little fellow Chantilly. This has all the appearance of a telepathic communion, but in actuality Dupin's thought-reading feat may betraced back link by link alonga long chain of reasoning based upon a closely attentive following-out of the movements of the other man's mind as well as his outward behavior. Dupin does, in explaining this to his friend, retrace the entire course of his meditations. Thus the episodic opening of the tale is intended to reveal the mental powers of the detective, preparing the reader to receive the more extraordinary things to follow. In the introductory paragraphs to "The Murders in the Rue Morgue," Poe maintains that "The analytical power should not be confounded with simple ingenuity."

Dupin's investigation of the mystery of the murders in the Rue Morgue exhibits the operations of the analytical mind. The reasoner follows a "retrograde" process of reconstructing the events a *posteriori* and mentally places himself in the exact circumstances in which the murders must have been committed and carefully observes every minute detail. Through a series of legitimate deductions he is able to fit the links together and arrive at a concusion as to the mode of the murder and the nature of the murderer. Certain inferences like the gruff voice heard by the neighbors and interpreted in different ways, the peculiar nature of the marks on the neck of (the dead body of) the daughter, the fact that her corpse has been thrust into the chimney with superhuman strengh, and the peculiar kind of hair found in the clutches of the corpse of the mother, lead him to the conclusion that the murderer is not human. The "grulft and shrill" voice is heard by the various people in the neighborhood. But each person thinks that it is in a language other than his own because he does not actually know the language in which the voice is heard. From this Dupin concludes that the voice is in no human language. All this ties in with the advertised fact that an Ourang-Outang has broken loose from the house of his sailor-master. Before this Dupin had already read some accounts of the monstrous Ourang-Outang of the East Indian islands, and he is able to understand the full horrors of the murder at once. He displays great acumen in his investigation regarding the mode of "ingress" and "egress" of the supposed murderer into the room, finally comming to the conclusion that only a creature with superhuman strengh could do that mighty feat. Another fact that confirms his belief that the murderer is not any human being is the lack of motive for anybody to commit such atrocities against the innocent women, and the fact that no costly article or money has been stolen from the apartment. The greasy ribbon with a sailor's knot proves that the owner of the animal is a sailor. All these suspicions lead to Dupin's advertisement for the owner. The astounding nature of this whole activity is that Dupin is not only able to work out all the steps of the case with the minutest precision, but he is also able to anticipate with a sureness of intuition the movements of the sailor. And the sailor does come in as anticipated by Dupin and at the very moment he is expected. This is the faculty that Poe "The Purloined Letter" calls "an identification of the reasoner's intellect with that of his opponent". John T. Irwin makes brilliant connection between Poe's "exposure" of Maezel's automaton chess player and the detective tales. According to him, both th chess player and Dupin are figurations of self-division and the mind/body proble: "The narrator's description of Dupin altered physical appearance as he exercise his analytic skill makes Dupin himself sound like an automaton... It is as if Dupin's body had suddenly become a physical medium for an alien spirit."[13]

Dorothy Sayers says that of the Dupin stories she finds "The Mystery of Marie Roget" (1842-43) "the most interesting of all to the connoisseur."[14] Richard P. Benton agrees with Sayers and maintains that the tale is "caviar for the gourment."[15] According to T O Mabbott, "This is a famous tale of historical importance, since it is the first detective story in which an attempt was made to solve a real crime. It has, I feel enjoyed a higher reputation among general readers than it deserves."[16] Richard Fusco tells us that between the original text fo the tale in *Snowden's Lady's Companion* of 1842-43 and the reappearance in the *Tales* of 1845, Poe's admiration for the rationcination theme altered, and "Marie Roget" reflected this change. Referring to Poe's letter of August 9, 1846 to P.P. Cooke wherein he refers to the public being carried away by "the method or *air* of method," Fusco says that Poe grew disenchanted with writing the tales of ratiocination."[17] It is more appropriate to say that Poe's "Marie Roget" is part of his attempts as a literary journalist to stimulate his reader's interest and demonstrate his own skills is solving an actual murder mystery, whatever his success in the process. Instead of taking it as Poe's "disenchantment," as Fusco suggests it is more appropriate to say that he deliberately plays the "detective" just as he plays the role of a solver of cryptograms elsewhere. In the process of writing such a detective tale, the kind of "several voices in the text" that a recent critic, Martin Roth refers to are inevitable.[18]

Poe says in his letter of June 4, 1842 to Georage Roberts that in "The Mystery of Marie Roget—A Sequel to the Murders in the Rue Morgue" he has "indicated the assassin in a manner which will give to the investigation of the actual murder of Mary Cecilia Rogers of New York a renewed impetus by domostrating "the fallacy of the general idea—that the girl was the victim of a gang of ruffians."[19] For this purpose he constructs an "ideal series of events which run parallel to the real ones,"[20] a fictitious tale whose exact parellel witht the real case of the murder of Many Rogers would be immediately recognized by Poe's readers. In a footnote to the tale Poe informs us that the subsequent developments in the case of Mary Rogers fully confirmed "not only the general conclusion but absolutely *all* the chief hypothetical details by which that conclusion was attained" (III, 100n). The series of hypotheses constitutes the theme of the tale. The main object of the tale, as Poe explains, "is an analysis of the true principles which should direct inquiry in similar cases."[21] In other words, it is to lay down the principles of correct analysis. One such principle that must guide analysis is what Poe calls in the initial paragraph of "The Mystery of Marie Roger" the "Calculus of Probabilities"—a term from the mathematical science which is applied in the gaugin of the most intangible elements of motivation and behavior. The essence of this method of calculation would lie in reasoning from known premises testable conclusion by a careful weighing of probabilities.

The analytical exercise of Dupin in the tales fully bear out this doctrine of Calculus of Probabilities. Dupin is confronted not only with the facts of the case of Marie Roget but with the several affidavits relating to the case and a host of often-misleading constructions placed by some newspapers upon the facts of the murder. He is faced with the enormous problem, not only of sifting the evidence but also of feeling his way unerringly through a bewildering variety of interpretations. In handling the case, he is guided by his power of calculating the probabilities combined with a sure insight into human motivation. With the supreme self-confidence and mastery that always characterize him, he rejects the improbable and chalks out the true line of probabilities. Dupin is able to achieve this great feat not only by his sound common sense and acute perception but also by his imaginative power of identifying himself with the minds of the other character and reconsturcting the exact course of their reasoing. Thus by an act of imaginative identification he is able to determine the behavior of both Marie Roget and the naval officer who killed her, in their own peculiar circumstances.

The difference between the present tale and "The Murders in the Rue Morgue" is given in Dupin's words:

> "I need scarcely tell you," said Dupin, as he finished the perusal of my notes, "that this is a far more intricate case than that of the Rue Morgue; from which it differs in one important respect. This is an *ordinary*, although an atrocious instance of crime. There is nothing peculiarly *outre* about it. You will observe that, for this reason, the mystery has been considered easy, when for this reason, it should have been considered difficult of solution." (III, 117).

The mystery regarding Marie Roget appearing to be "ordinary" eludes the Parisians; and the newspapers given various fantastic accounts regarding the second and final disappearance of the perfumery girl. Dupin's success lies in cancelling the various interpretations put forth by the journalist belonging to *L' Etoile, Le Commerciel,* etc. His ratiocination begins with countering *L' Etoile's* argument giving the impression that Marie is alive and that the dead body found in the river is that of somebody else. And he concludes that the murder might have taken place on the river's bank, or on the river itself, and that the body might have been thrown into the water. *Le Moniteur's* argument is cancelled by Dupin's detailed accounts regarding floating bodies. There cannot be any certainty when a corpse wil rise to the surface of the water since decomposition varies from body to body. In addition, only decomposition enables the corpse to have more specific gravity than the water displaced and thus to rise up and float. Dupin dismisses the insinuations levelled against Beauvais, who is after all a busy-body. He is able to reason against the opinion of *Le Commercial* that Marie "was seized by some gang of low ruffians not far from her mother's door" and that the knot tied around the body's waist with a piece of cloth torn from Marie's petticoat is done by "fellows who had no pocket handkerchiefs." It is well known, according to Dupin, that the ruffians are always sure to have at least handkerchief, if not anything else.

Dupin's suspicions are fixed upon the sailor of black complexion with whom Marie was seen at Madame Deluc's inn and which fact was later corroborated by the coach-driver. The sailor's knot that is found on the cloth wound round the waist of the corpse leads to this suspicion on his part. The fact that "the time elapsing between the first ascertained and second supposed elopement is a few months more than the general period of the cruises of our men-of-war," leads to the further certainty that the naval officer with whom Marie had a love affair is involved in the crime. Finally Dupin skillfully proves that the boat used for throwing the dead body into the river is a naval barge.

Thus by sifting the evidence from the various newspaper acconts with his skill at the "Calculus of Probabilities" Dupin arrives at a satisfactory solution to the mystery of Marie Roget.[22] An interesting feature of the tale is that it is wholly ratiocinative; there is no account of the reasoner going out of doors for inquiries or for an on-the-spot study of the case. However, critics generally find fault with the tale for its length. Thus, for instance, Arthur H. Quinn says: "It is too long and too much time is spent on upsetting false theories."[23] The very complexity of the evidence brings out the enormousness of the task that Dupin achieves in feeling his way through a bewildering mass of material. Besides, the tale can be defended on grounds of realism. Any murder mystery is bound to be just as complicated as that of Marie Roget. And what Dupin is faced with is what any investigator in his position would be faced with. The effect of the tale on the naval officer in the actual case of Mary Cecilia Rogers is stated in Poe's letter of January 4, 1848 to George W. Eveleth: "The 'naval officer' who committed the murder (or rather the accidental death arising from an attempt at abortion) *confessed* it; and the whole matter is now well understood—but, for the sake of relatives, his a topic on which I must not speak further."[24]

In spite of such assertain by Poe, T.O. Mabbott concldes on a close study of the case that Poe "did not solve the mystery."[25]

The great merit of "The Purloined Letter" (1845), according to T.O. Mabbott, "lies in the fascination of the purely intellectual plot, and in the absence of the sensational."[26] Poe himself calls the tale "the best of my tales of raiocination."[27] Like most detective tales, it adopts a two-fold stucture: the mystery and the ratiociantion that follows it. In "Thou Art the Man" the incidents receive a fuller development, contributing to the mystery, and the ratiociantion, though vital to the tale, is less elaborate. However, in "The Purloined Letter" the ratiociantive part becomes the centre of interest. There is, of course, a certain amount of drama in respect of "The Purloined Letter"—the vain attempts of the Prefect to recover it and the successful recovery of it by Dupin. But the ingenious reasoning of Dupin constitutes the major interest of the tale. Dupin's character is a masterly creation an with him we feel we are in the presence of a master brain. Our respect and admiration for his character will be inspired partly through the agony of the narrator himself whose function is to point up and highlight the utter intellectual superiority of the detective. One way in which his intellectual superiority is made to be felt is to contrast it with the prosaic, unimaginative, and rigidly mathematical brain of the Prefect. It is because of a combination of the poetic faculty of intution with the mathematical faculty that succeeds. And it is with these combined faculties that he achieves "an identification of the reasoner's intellect with that of his opponent."

In this tale, unlike in the other tales of ratiociantion, the culprrit is known. But the problem before Dupin is to secure the purlined letter from the possession of the Minister D—. The possession of the letter gives that man a certain power over the owner of the letter, a lady of the royal family; and he has been using the letter as a potent instrument of political blackmail. Before the fascinating process of detection by Dupin starts, we are given an account of the painstaking but futile methods used by the Perfect in ransaking the premises of the Minister. This is a familiar method employed in detective fiction to elevate the genius of the detective by exposing the comparative ineptitude of the police officals. The futile endeavours of the Prefect and Dupin's knowledge that the Minister is both a mathematician and a poet serve as starting points for the detective's reasoning. Dupin concludes that only a combination of the mathematical process of reasoning with the intuitive faculty will be helpful to him in his attempts to unearth the letter. It is by an intuitive perception that he is able to "admeasure" the man's movements and is able to interpret his frequent absence at midnight as deliberate ruses. It is again by such an insight that he is able to see the elusiveness of the obvious—that the opponent will, as a matter of course, be driven to "simplicity" as a device—that will escape the attention of the detective precisely because it is so simple and so very self-evident. Hence he concludes that the letter will be definitely in the Minister's hotel room at a place so conspicuous that it escape the notice of the Prefect. Subsequently Dupin pays a visit to the Minister's apartment with green glasses and notice a letter, solied and half-torn, at a conspicuous position in a rack. In all the ingenious reasoning of Dupin that leads him to this detection there is the remarkable yet basic understanding of human psychology and motivation. By means of this he is able to arrive at a conclusion that his opponent would behave like this in these given circumstances. Once these premises are established, the actual detection and exposure is an accomplished act. With his uncanny perception Dupin combines boldness and tact in handling the case. This is revealed in the dramatic circumstances of his recovery of the letter—he leaves a facsimile by creating a disturbance in the street only to distract the attention of the Minister, and makes away with the original (purloined) letter. These actions of Dupin are not presented in the story as separate events but are recounted by him in retrospection while he is explaining to his friend the process of his detection. Thus the tale exemplifies the technique of armchair detection perfected by Poe for the benefit of generations of detective-fiction writer.[28]

The twentieth-century theoretical breakthroughs have resulted in the Frechman Dupin being subjected to "hair-splitting" by the French Deconstructions and their American followers. There are three major cumulative series of interpretations, each successive reading commenting both on the story and on the previous readings in the series: Jacques Lacan's "Seminar on "The Purloined Letter" (1957), Jacques Derrida's "The Purveyor of Truth" (1975), Barbara Johnson's "The Frame of Reference: Poe, Lacan, Derrida" (1978), Johan T. Irwin's "Mysteries we Reread, Mysteries of Rereading: Poe, Borgers and the Analytic Detective Story" (1986), and *The Purloined Poe: Lacan, Derrida,* and *Psycoanalytic Reading Reading* (1988) edited by Johan P. Muller and William J. Richardson.[29] These studies present a lenghtly and complex argument in which "The Purloined Letter" is treated as a pretext, being read as a parable of the act of analysis. According to Lacon, the story consists of "two scenes, the first of which we shall straightaway designate the primal scene and by no means inadvertently, since the second may be considered its repetition."[30] Derrida in "The Purveyor of Truth" cites Lacon's multiple "acts of aggression" against him since the publication of *De la Grammatologies in Critique* in 1965. Thus Derrida takes the case of "The Purloined Letter" for one of the same reasons that Dupin did—the Minister once did Dupin "an evil turn" at Vienna, and Dupin sees the affair of the letter as an opportunity to settle scores with him. Whatever the parallel encounters of characters and critics involved, what is important is Lacan's idea of the triangular structure of each of the two scenes in the tale. The two scenes pointed out by Derrida are different from those dealt with by Lacan. According to Derrida, the scene in the royal boudoir and the subsequent scene at the Minister's residence are two narrated scenes within the framing artifice of the story. However, he maintains that the story itself consists of two scenes of narration—the first scene being the Prefect's initial visit to Dupin during which the Prefect recounts the events in the royal boudoir, and the second scene being the Prefect's subsequent visit during which Dupin recounts the events at the Minister's residence. As John T. Irwin ways, "Doubling tends, of course, to be a standard element of the analytic detective story, in that the usual method of apprehending the criminal involves the detective's doubling the criminal's thought processes so as to anticipate his next move and end up one jump ahead of him."[31] Some critics are still further than "one jump ahead" in describing Dupin himself as a criminal! What most of these ingenious studies of "The Purloined Letter" seem to miss is the focus of the tale—the analyst's process of reasoning to expose the criminal.

In the three major tales considered above ratiocination is of predominant interest, but in "The Gold Bug" and "Thou Art the Man" the preservation of mystery engages the reader's attention. In these latter tales the ratiocinative explanation of the mystery is but an appendage to the main interest of the mystery. While "The Gold Bug" is widely acclaimed as a tale of mystery and ratiocination, "Thou Art the Man" has not received much critical attention. "The Oblong Box" is normally dismissed as an insignificant piece. While the Gothic element in the tale is certainly meager, the actual center of interest lies in how the mystery is "well kept" (from the narrator as much as from the reader). Hence the tale is considered under tales of mystery at the end of this chapter.

"The Gold Bug" (1843), a prize-winning tale that brought considerable recognition to Poe, is one of the most popular stories in the world. In this tale the successful preservation of mystery and the following ratiocination are equally significant. What makes the tale so interesting is that in addition to mystery and ratiocination, there is fine drama involving incident, character, and dialogue. In this tale too, as in the Gothic tales and the tales of ratiocination, there is active reader-participation. And this is achieved by the way the element of mystery is skillfully handled by the author. This is, however, the kind of mystery that E.L. Mascall defines as being a puzzle.[32] Barton Levi St. Armand argues that Poe, in "The Gold Bug," achieves "mystification" by his use of alchemy.[33] However, it is not just "mystification" that Poe aims at in this tale. A close analysis of character and incident brings out the element of mystery and ratiocination based on Poe's interest in cryptography.[34]

In the first part of the tale, leading to the discovery of the hidden treasure, mystery is developed around the character of Legrand. The mystery operates at two levels: (i) the character of Legrand and his behavior, confusing the narrator and at times the reader; (ii) the mystery faced by the character himself in his search for the buried treasure. Legrand's character is presented from the points of view of the narrator and the Negro Jupiter. In the initial paragraphs the reader might develop the impression that Legrand is somewhat abnormal in mind. He is said to have belonged to "an ancient Huguenot family." The narrator, having got acquainted with him "by mere accient," finds that there is much in the recluse "to excite interest and esteem." He is "well educated, with unusual powers of mind, but infected with misanthropy, and subject to perverse moods of alternate enthusiasm and melancholy." These initial details might give the impression to the reader that the central character is crazy like Roderick Usher who is also well educated and belongs to an ancient family. Further, the epigraph to the tale clinches the impression: "What ho! What ho! this fellow is dancing mad!/He hath been bitten by the Tarantula." But the author's intention is to create a sense of mystery, and the strategy that he adopts for achieving this objective, to apply his words in the review of Dickens's *Barnaby Rudge*, is to have us believe that "certain impressions *do* exist, which do *not* exist, in the mind of his readers" (VII, 52). In spite of his apparent melancholy, Legrand, unlike Usher, is an extrovert, having been interested in gunning and fishing and in collecting shells or entomological specimens. In mystery and detective fiction, the detective is normally presented as being somewhat abnormal, his queer habits and behavior causing confusion to his down-to-earth companion and to the reader as well. This moodiness and apparent oddity of behavior are but preparations on the part of the detective for a profound intellectual activity. Combined with moodiness and irregular habits, there will be in the detective an unusual physical dexterity and love of adventure. These traits are very much present in Legrand, but the narrator misses the essential Legrand and misleads himself into taking his friend for mand.

Jupiter the faithful servant of "Massa Will" is deeply concerned about his master's well-being. He is much confused about Legrand's behavior and attributes it to the bite of the bug: "I'm berry sartain dat Massa Will bin bit somewhere 'bout de head by dat goole-bug." As Legrand explains in his letter to the narrator, his "ill looks" alone have saved him from being flogged by Jupiter for his erratic outdoor movements. In spite of anything, the simplistic Jupiter comes close to a clue to the mystery engaging the mind of Legrand while the narrator moves away from it on account of his assumed intellectual superiority. The word "gold" unwittingly used by Jupiter sets a chain of thought in Legrand's mind, leading to the great discovery. As for the "weight" of the insect, the narrator "could not, for the life of me, tell" why Legrand should agree with Jupiter in the matter. Legrand is concerned with the weight of the insect only to be shot through the left eye of the death's-head to locate the spot of the treasure. He could as well have used any heavy substance like a bullet, but heuses the bug only to make the narrator's (and reader's) confusion worse confounded.

Perhaps there is some justification for the narrator's misunderstanding of Legrand as being out of his wits: Legrand often slides into reveries in the course of his investigations. But Legrand himself explains the cause for his apparent insensibility: "The mind struggles to establish a connection—a sequence of cause and effect—and, being unable to do so, suffers a species of temporary paralysis."

The second part of the tale deals with the other level of the mystery: the mystery that Legrand himself is faced with and that he successfully solves. This mystery originates with the accidental discovery by Legrand that he is in possession of a pirate's parchment, which probably contains directions to a buried treasure. In fact, it is not the entomological specimen of the *scarabaeus* (the "goole-bug" as Jupiter calls it) that is really important for Legrand, but the piece of dirty paper (the parchment) picked up by him for holding the bug. When the confused Jupiter describes the insect as "goole-bug," the word starts in Legrand's mind a chain of association ultimately connected with the hidden treasure. After a discussion with Poe, Thomas Dunn English wrote in the *Aristidean* for October 1845:

> The bug, which gives title to the story, is used only in the way of mystification, having throughout a seeming and no real connection with the subject. Its purpose is to seduce the reader into the idea of supernatural machinery and keeping him so mystified until the last moment.[35]

Legrand is aware thatthe parchment (found on the coast near a boat) is normally used for a record of something to be "long remembered and carefully preserved". When it accidentally gets heated, the figure of the death's-head becomes visible. The death's-head is the emblem of the pirate; in all engagements of the pirate the flag with that emblem is hoisted. Having thus connected the bar and the death's-head. Legrand concludes that it must have belongedto a pirate. On the heated parchment he discovers the figure of a kid at thecorner of this slip, diagonally opposite to the spot where the death's-head is depicted. Thus the figure of the kid sounds to Legrand as a hieroglyphical signature, and he connects it with the pirate Captain Kidd whose name is commonly known.[36] The many stories current then about the treasure buried somewhere on the Atlantic coast by Kidd and his associates confirm Legrand's belief that the parchment containing the mysterious figure is a cryptogram relating to that treasure.

Legrand proceeds to solve the cryptogram assuming that it must be a simple one since, obviously, Kidd, with the crude intellect of a sailor, could not have constructed the more abstruse cryptograms. As for the language of the cipher, the principles of solution as regards the simple ciphers depend upon the "genius of the particular idiom." Legrand's decipherment of the cryptogram is superb. Having once done it, he does not take much time to understand the term, "good glass," "Bishop's Hotel," and "devil's-seat." The whole business of the cryptogram having been associated with a sailor, "good glass" is obviously a telescope. With some inquiry Legrand is able to make out that "Bishop's Hotel" means the high rock, *Bessop's Castle*. The "devil's seat" is but a niche in the cliff from where he looks at the thick forest with the telescope to locate the "death's-head" on the tree from where he should shoot a somewhat heavy substance with the help of a cord.

Hardin Craig calls "The Gold Bug" "possibly the most perfect of all the ratiocinative stories, always with the exception of "The Murders in the Rue Morgue"[37] In fact, this tale is of a different order from detective tales like "The Murders in the Rue Morgue" and "The Purloined Letter." Strictly speaking, it is a case of crytography preceded by a careful manipulation of mystery rather than of ratiocination as understood in the context of the detective tales. Ratiocination, as applied to crime detection, and as Poe has defined it at length in "The Purloined Letter" and "The Murders in the Rue Morgue" involves on the part of the reasoner a certain poetic/intuitive power of entering into the intricacies of other's minds, a deep insight into human motivation together with a careful calculation of probabilities in dealing with the available data. The unridding of a cryptogram proceeds in a more prosaic way employing statistical analysis. Starting with a tentative assumption, the process verifies the facts by a method of trial and error. By collating and analyzing the signs, it gives tentative values to them—values that can be verified later. In assigning these values to the "unknown quantities," it has of course to choose readings possible within the limits of its language and most self-evident. The reader of a cryptogram has to weigh probabilities in choosing his readings and must possess an insight into the rationale of the language of ciphers. He does not have to indulge in any flights of imagination or intutive flashes. Thus cryptography would be nearer to the mathematical faculty than to the poetic. The ratiocination in "The Gold Bug" is of this order. Dupin is both a poet and a mathematician, but Legrand, no doubt superbly ingenious in deciphering the riddle, does not possess the unifying vision of a poet. However, in "the exercise of ingenuity" Poe seems to have preferred "The Gold Bug" to "The Murders in the Rue Morgue" as he tells George Roberts in his letter of June 4, 1842.[38]

In the act of achieving his central effect in "The Gold Bug" Poe is able to invest his character with an amount of independent interest. All the three characters—Legrand, the narrator, and the Negro Jupiter—are individualized. Of particular significance is the life-like portrait of Jupiter who is a source of delightful comedy. The realism of the Negro's character is enhanced by the peculiar dialect he speaks. In addition to character, dialogue is managed skillfully. Consequently, action is presented in vivid terms. All in all, the tale is a remarkable combination of adventure, mystery, and ratiocination. In addition, it has considerable dramatic significance on account of dialogue and character. Small wonder that it was rendered as a stage-presentation by Silas S.Steele, a prominent playwright of Phiadelphia (and played at the Walnut Street Theater.[39] Poe was obviously happy when he called it "my most successful tale".[40]

Critics over the years have not paid proper attention to Poe's minor tale in the detective genre entitled "Thou Art the Man" (1844). George E. Woodberry calls it an "inferior grotesque."[41] William Bittner describe it as "almost a parody of the analytical detective story Poe had invented."[42] Arthur H. Quinn, while maintaining that in this story "the great master of ratiocinative stories burlesqued that branch of fiction," feels that Poe's use of the moral contrast is more important than the element of detection.[43] According to Stuart Levine, the tale is a "minor horror story," a satire on the tale of ratiocination itself.[44] A more recent critic, Richard Fusco says that "Thou Art the Man" indicates "Poe's contempt for detective stories."[45] A.E. Murch, however, seems reasonable in thinking that the tale is "a simple, straightforward detective story, and contains several features that were new in Poe's work."[46]

Even thogh "Thou Art the Man" does not contain the intellectual gymnastics of a Dupin, it neverthless has several technical features of the detective story as known to us today—a wealthy man is murdered while the criminal hoodwinks the public, posing as a respectable gentlemen, a wrong person is condemned to death, and a self-styled detective, an enthusiastic neighbor, shadows the criminal and eventually exposes him.[47] A close reading of the tale convinces us that in addition to containing these technical features, the tale conforms to Poe's own theory of mystery.

Poe explains the working of "mystery" in his review of Dickens's *Barnby Rudge;*[48] but he does not use the word as synonymous with "ratiocination." Ratiocination is the predominant factor in his major analytical tales, although he calls the story of Marie Roget "The Mystery of Marie Roget." In the minor tales like "Thou Art the Man" the successful preservation of mystery constitutes the major interest. Thus while generally the two terms, "mystery" and "ratiocination" might not be mutually exclusive, in Poe's tales of this order the one or the other element predominates. Mystery involves a clever manipulation, by the writer, of the events that appear to the reader as simply inexplicable. Ratiocination is the logical process whereby this mystery is unravelled by means of a methodical explanation of the logic of events in the story. In the typical mystery tale, every point contributes to the perplexity of the reader's mind, gradually intensifying his curiosity. The events of the story are so skillfully manipulated as to "avert" the reader's mind "from the true state of the case." And the secret of the plot must be "well kept" till the "proper moment of the *denouement*" without distracting the reader's mind with "undue or inartistical means."[49]

In the major ratiocinative tales of Poe the dramatic action is subordinated to the reasoner's logical deduction, a kind of practical mathematics. In "Thou Art the Man," however, the predominating interest is the dramatic action involving the hunt for the criminal and the manner of preserving the mystery. The ratiocinative process is subordinate to these other aspects.

In this tale, if we do not encounter the great Reasoner Dupin and his armchair detection, we have nevertheless another type of detective, an *amateur sans peur et sans reproche,* obviously an enthusiastic neighbor of the murdered man. The tale opens in a somewhat theatrical manner, but the narrator apologizes for discussing the event of Shuttleworthy's murder "in a tone of unsuitable levity." This is obviously an attempt on the author's part to tell us that there is something really serious behind the apparent levity. The "unsuitable levity" arises from the fact that the investigation is conducted by a self-styled detective, an enthusiastic neighbor of Shuttleworthy's and it might be possible that the narrator-investigator thus misleads the reader as to the tone of narration Being a close overseer of men and events, the narrator presents them in considerable detail and with authority, although he is neither a police official nor a professional detective.

The mystery of Shuttleworthy's murder is succesfully presented until the proper moment of *denouement.* The author works up our curiosity and excitement to a high pitch till the very conclusion of the tale when the incident of the *Chateau Margaux* box leading to the confession of the horror-stricken criminal comes on the reader with dramatic suddenness. In so leading us up to that point Poe successfully averts our attention from the real culprit and misleads us as to Pennifeather's behavior.

The picture of Goodfellow's character presented by the author is so exalted that it might not be possible to associate so noble a person with such a hienous crime. Goodfellow always acts with the kindest of intentions on earth. Referring to his name, the narrator wonders "whether it is a marvelous coincidence, or whether it is that the name itself has an iperceptible effect upon the character, I have never yet been able to ascertain" (III, 192). Coming from the mouth of the narrator-detective, thses words are meant to avert the reader's mind from the true state of the case. Though we are likely to suspect that the author overdoes his job, we are convinced of his skill giving us a "dark hint" as to the reality of the crimianl's character. If this eludes the reader as he goes through the story, at least toward the conclusion he does feel its effect. It is interesting to note that Goodfellow is held is high esteem by the public in spite of the fact that he has been in Rattleborogh "not longer than six months or thereabouts, and although nobody knew anything anout him before he came to settle in the neighborhood" (III, 192). This popularity is apparently a compliment to the man's good nature and his ability to win friends and admirers quickely. But the tone of narration suggests that Goodfellow might be an imposter cultivating Shuttworthy's friendship with an eye on his property.

By means of his assumed anxiety to remove public suspicion from Pennifeather, Goodfellow succeeds in appearing as not having had any ill-will against the young man. In the eyes of the public, he is always the honest old gentleman, "old Charely," who is the very emobodiment of moderation and Christian chanity. Again, when the citizens of Rattleborough demand an immediate investigation into the murder, it is "old Charley" who leads the hunt for the criminal. This is indeed a master stroke, for when the criminal himself joins the search party, he has done all that he can to avert everybody's attention from himself.

There are, however, two circumstances which might direct suspicion toword Goodfellow. The first is the little incident of Pennifeather knocking down old Charley and the latter swearing "summary vengeance" on the wicked young man, though at the moment he has "behaved with exemplary moderation and Christian charity." We might suspect that this incident would prompt Goodfellow to wreak vengeance upon Pennifeather. But the author is careful enough to explain it away as no more than "a natural and very justifiable ebullition of anger, which meant nothing, however, and, beyond doubt was no sooner given vent to than forgotten" (III, 196). The "summary vengeance" finally proves to be a fact in that Goodfellow transfers his crime his to Pennifeather in an absolutely calculated manner. The second circumstancce is Goodfellow's picking up the incriminating knife and his deliberate attempt at concealing it. This behavior on his part is taken by the public as a result of the benevolent old man's anxiety to save Pennifether.

Having successfully averted the reader's attention from the real culprit, the author directs his suspicion toward the wrong man. From the begining, he gives us the impression that Pennifeather is a violent, cantankerous young fellow, dissipated and not on good terms with his uncle. These facts might confirm our suspicions about him as the possible criminal. On hearing of the disappearance of his uncle, Pennifeather insists upon "making immediate search for the corpse of the murdered man." Considerable stress is laid on the "suspicious" manner of Pennifeather's insistence and our attention to its suspicious nature is pointedly drwan by Goodfellow's remark that it is "*a singular* expression, to say no more." Thus Goodfellow not only diverts our attention from himself but also points it toward Pennifeather. In fact, the people themselves wonder how Pennifeather is so much convinced as to think that his uncle is a "murdered man."

Once character and incident are established, the author prepares us for an effective *denouement*. As often happens in a crime story, the criminal, having taken the utmost care to divert attention from himself and having got the wrong man condemned, rejoices excessively and overreaches himself in a victory celebration. The incident of the Chateau Margaux box is the most dramatic in the story, leading to the sudden exposure of the criminal and his confession. Goodfellow, who often employs irony as a subtle means for incriminating Pennifeather is himself ultimately struck by irony when he calls upon the company to keep order "during the ceremony of disinterring the treasure." His own overconfidence and excessive enthusiasm finally expose him. Thus Poe handles all the details of the case with the utmost care and purposely misdirects the reader's attention so that when the final solution of the mystery is offered, it comes as a surprise mingled with horror. Even though the author nowhere explicity states it, this is also obviously the reaction of the guests at the party hosted by Goodfellow.

What remains for the author to do now is to explain character and incident in the light of the final solution of the mystery. At this point the ratiocinative process comes into play. In the brief final paragraphs the narrator-detective connets the various threads of the case and presents a thorough rational explanation of all the events that have taken place. The narrator's suspicions are aroused by Goodfellow's excesive frankness and the fiendish expression on his face when he threatens vengeance to Pennifeather.

A radical departure of the tale is that the narrator-detective arrives at certain conclusions an demonstrates them by means of dramatic incidents. As a result, the process of explanation at the end of the tale is minimized. Thus if we do not find in this tale the deductive reasoing of a Dupin, it is so because the tale constitutes a distinct type of detective fiction wherein the detective is an amateur. As for the rather comic tone of the story, the narrator, in apologizing for the "unsuitable levity," tells us that it is deliberate. The lighter treatment of the materials does not mar the effect of the mystery; on the contrary, it contributes to the theatrical effect of the story. N. Bryllion Fagin reports that in France Andre Antoine adapted the tale in 1889 for a dramatic performance. Fagin also refers to the "sensational effect" of the tale, comparing it with Amelia Reynold Long's *Death Looks Down* (1944).[50] The sudden sitting up of the corpse when the Chateau Margaux box is opened may be mere grotesquerie to all appearances. But its effect on the criminal's conscience[51] is one of intense horror, leading to his confession an death. Whatever the reaction of the sophisticated reader to the tone of Poe's narration in this tale, viewed from the point of view of the criminal and of the assembled guests, the effect is one of shock. Even if the reader is misled by the apparently comic tone of narration into dismissing the tale as a burlesque, the conclusion intensifies the effect of horror on account of the sheer contrast with the apparent levity of the earlier parts. Thus we can see reason in the narrator's initial apology for the "unsuitable levity" of his tone. If the reading of "ThouArt the Man" leaves us disappointed in comparison with the rich intellectual experience of the major ratiocinative tales like "The Purloined Letter," this slender piece nevertheless impresses us as a distinct type of detective story with a distinct kind of detective.

George E. Woodberry calls "The Oblong Box" (1844) an "inferior grotesque."[52] According to Arthur H. Quinn, it is "singularly uninteresting," and "suited quite well to *Godey's*."[53] While describing the tale as "one of Poe's less successful tales of horror," T.O. Mabbott admits, "It had some timeliness, for it must have recalled to its first readers a recent sensational murder case. The popular superstition involved was more prevalent in Poe's day than in ours, and thus better known."[54]

In fact, "The Oblong Box" is designed as a mystery tale and fully exploits the patent devices of the type: a sustained curiosity and a progressive heightening of tension leading to the resolution of the central mystery. Through the intelligence and curiosity of the peripheral narrator the deepening mystery finally finds its solution. He describes himself as a person "abnormally inquisitive about trifles; and I confess, with shame, that I busied myself in a variety of ill-bred and preposterous conjectures"(III, 234).

The initial presence of a mystery is created by the supernumerary stateroom which comes to the narrator as an intellectual challenge—an enigma to be solved: "It was no business of mine, to be sure; but with none the less pertinacity did I occupy myself in attempts to solve the enigma" (III, 234). The narrator tries many plausible solutions in a spirit of ratiocination; but one after another the solutions eliminate them and result in a heightened curiosity on his part. The curious circumstances of the extra stateroom, the suspiciousness aroused by the woman who is presented as Mrs. Wyatt, and the fact of the oblong box itself,—all these are arranged in a mounting scale of tension. The narrator is now determined to unravel the mystery: "I resolved to quiz him *well*, now and hereafter" (III, 237). But his attempts to penetrate Mr. Wyatt's secrets only result in a further mystification of his character; and the narrator is momentarily driven to the conclusion that Mr. Wyatt is mad. This does not, however, put an end to the narrator's pursuit of the mystery. Fresh circumstances involving the oblong box and Mr. Wyatt's nightly operations intensify the narrator's curiosity and heighten his sense of mystery. The movements of Mrs. Wyatt also arouse his strongest suspicions. At this point he attempts an explanation for the circumstance of Wyatt's opening of the box by telling himself that he was probably according to custom "merely giving the rein to one of his hobbies—indulging in one of his fits of artistic enthusiasm. He had opened his oblong box, in order to feast his eyes on the pictorial treasure within" (III, 242-43). But then there was nothing in this to make him sob. However, the narrator tries to explain it away as simply a trick of his own fancy. Though thus the curiosity on his part is momentarily suspended, he has not arrived at a completely satisfactory solution of the mystery. The concluding circumstance of the shipwreck and Mr. Wyatt's almost insane behavior in his frantic attempts to secure the oblong box and his death only tend to intensify the narrator's curiosity without offering him a solution. The mystery remains as baffling as it was in the beginning.

The solution to the mystery comes from the captain of the ship and leaves the reader disappointed. By the way the author handles the character of Mr. Wyatt and the mystery of the oblong box he has created a sense of the unfolding of some deep significance, of some complex psychology. But the actual solution that is offered frustrates much of that impression and gives a rather matter-of-fact ending to the tale. In his anxiety to render the explanation completely rational, Poe robs his tale of the promised depth. Mr. Wyatt, we are told, has acted with a perfectly practical motive in carrying the oblong box as he does. It is not only from an attachment to his dead wife but from an obligation to carry the corpse to her mother that Mr. Wyatt acts as he does. And there is after all no mystery about the oblong box as the captain has known all about it and Mr. Wyatt has arranged everything with him. However, the mystery is directed at the reader and our concern in analyzing the tale has been the manner in which it is sustained.

In spite of the fact that the narrator tells us at the end that he is still haunted by the nightmare of Mr. Wyatt's countenance and his hysterical laugh even days after the incident, he does not retrieve our lost impression, for the incident has lost its mystery through a too easy and plausible explanation. Curiously enough, the narrator himself seems to tell us that it has all been an excitement over nothing. If he got over-excited by a sense of mystery, it had been by his own wrong reasoning and his over-inquisitiveness: "My own mistakes arose, naturally enough, through too careless, too inquisitive, and too impulsive a temperament" (III, 248). In effect, it amounts to the author telling us that all that sense of suspense has been a mistake. The tale is the kind of mystery that tells us that after all there was no mystery. The author consistently builds up the mystery to a certain point; but this mystery is destroyed by the infringement of a matter-of-fact ending. All in all, "The Oblong Box" parodies the mystery tale, and the reader is beguiled as much as the narrator.

It may be worthwhile to consider the overall reader-response evoked by the tales of mystery and ratiocination. In the Gothic tale the mystery leading to the denouement leaves the reader thinking as to the ultimate significance of character and incident, but in the detective story, once the mystery is solved and the reader's rational faculty is given the fullest play, the "effect" disappears. In the words of David Daiches, "the mood of suspense can never be recaptured and the main interest of the story has disappeared."[55] Thus although Poe insists upon the "intensity of effect," it varies from one type of tale to another and from one tale to another within the same category. The Gothic tale too employs mystery to create the effect which remains long after the perusal. This kind of response is not evoked by the comic tale. In this type of tale, while we laugh with the characters, we laugh at them, from a distance as it were: there is not the kind of emotional involvement here as in the perusal of the Gothic tale. The detective tale, while arousing the reader's curiosity and involvement in a certain degree of mystery, leaves him completely satisfied without any further thinking on the solution of the story. If the ultimate "effect" of the detective story on the reader is not as thoughtful and sustained as that of the tale of terror, it is because of the "intensification of low mimetic," as Northrop Frye observes.[56] The detective is always an ironist to the extent that his words and actions till the final solution will have shades of meaning always confounding the other characters in the story as much as they confound the reader. Even the tone of narration has more than one level of meaning. T.S. Eliot notices some affinity between Sherlock Holmes and Roderick Usher: "There is a close similarity between the musical exercises of Holmes and those of Roderick Usher: those wild and irregular improvisations which, although on one occasion they sent Watson off to sleep, must have been excruciating to any ear trained to music."[57] Some critics have seen a similar affinity between Dupin and Usher. Of course, in both the Gothic character and the Reasoner there are certain superficial resemblances like the love of wild music and moodiness. However, they differ in their attitudes to things. The Gothic character is engrossed with the emotional, but the detective takes us into the realm of the intellect. While musicality or moodiness lulls the one into inaction, for the other it is but a preparation for the flights of the intellect.

NOTES

1. See Poe's letter of August 9, 1846 to P P Cooke, *Letters,* II, 328.
2. Dorothy L. Sayers, "Introduction" to the Third Series of *Great Short Stories of Detection, Mystery and Horror* (London: Gollancz, 1934).
3. *Letters*, II, 328.
4. Ibid.
5. P.P. Cooke, in his letter of August 4, 1846 to Poe, employed the term "detection" to describe Poe's "tales of ratiocination." See George E. Woodberry, II, 205.
6. Martin Price, "The Fictional Contract," in *Literary Theory and Structure*, ed. Frank Brady, *et al* (New Haven: Yale University Press, 1973) 153-54.

7. See W.K. Wimsatt, "Poe and the Mystery of Mary Rogers," *PMLA*, LVI, 1941, 230.
8. Letter, I, 258. In his letter to Joseph Evans Snodgrass, Poe refers to the contemporary popularity of the tale. (See *Letter*, I, 175).
9. "Introduction" to *Poe the Detective*: *The Curious Circumstances behind "The Mystery of the Marie Roget"* by John Walsh (New Brunswick; Rutgers University Press, 1968) 1.
10. Jacquies Barzun, *The Delights of Detection* (New York, 1961) 12. The critics who ackonwledge Poe as inventor of the detective story are Arthur Conan Doyle, *Though the Magic Door* (London, 1907) 114; Dorothy L.Sayers, *The Omnibus of Crime* (New York, 1929) 9-10; Ellery Queen, *101 Years' Entertainment: The Great Detective Stories, 1841-1941* (Boston, 1941) vi; Howard Haycroft, *Murder for Pleasure: The Life and Times of the Detective Story* (New York, 1941) 12; A.E. Murch, *The Development of the Detective Novel* (1958; rpt.: New York, 1968) 83; Julian Symons, *Mortal Consequences: A History–From the Detective Story to the Crime Novel* (New York, 1972) 29. However, there is a challenger to Poe's position: R.F. Stewart, '....*And Always a Detective': Chapters on the History of Detective Fiction* (North Pomfret, VT, 1980), Ch. 2.
11. *Letters,* I, 199.
12. *Letters,* I, 280.
13. John T. Irwin, *The Mystery to a Solution: Poe, Borges, and the Analytic Detective Story* (Baltimore: The Johns Hopkins University Press, 1994) 113.
14. Dorothy Sayers, "Introduction" to *The Omnibus of Crime* (1929) 18.
15. Richard P. Benton, "The Mystery of Marie Roget'--A Defense," *Studies in Short Fiction*, VI, ii (Winter, 1969).
16. T.O. Mabbott, ed. *Collected Works*, III, 715.
17. Richard Fusco, "Poe's Revisions of 'The Mystery of Marie Roget'—a Hoax?," in *Poe the Craftsman: The Changing Fiction*, ed. Benjamin Franklin Fisher IV (Philadelphia: Friends of the Library/ University of Pennsylvania, 1976) 91-92.
18. Martin Roth, "Mysteries of 'The Mystery of Marie Roget'," *Poe Studies,* Vol. 22, No. 2 (December 1989): 27-34.
19. *Letter,* I, 200.
20. Epigraph to the tale.
21. *Letters,* I, 200.

22. W.K. Wimsatt, analyzing eight contemporary newspapers and all the many later articles he found, traces (through "confused and contradictory journalism" the course of events by listing the principal documents inchronological sequences and by citing, with critical comments, newspaper accounts of the offical proceedings, as well as influential journalistic theorizing, from July 28 to October 10, 1841. See W.K. Wimsatt, "Poe and the Mystery of Mary Roget," *PMLA*, LV (March, 1941): 230-48. Also see John Walsh, *Poe the Detective* (1968) for excerpts from newspapers. T.O. Mobbott feels these two studies are fundamental to any serious consideration of Poe. (*Collected Works,* III, 716n).
23. Arthur H. Quinn, 358.
24. *Letters*, II, 356.
25. T.O. Mabbott, *Collected Works,* III, 722.
26. T.O. Mabbott, ed. *Collected Works,* III, 972.
27. *Letters,* I, 258.
28. Robert A.W. Lownders tells us that Poe perfected the genre of detective fiction, taking certain elements from his forerunners and adding his own. See "The Contribution of Edge Allan Poe," in *The Mystery Writer's Art,* ed: Francis M. Nevins (Bowling Green: Bowling Green University Popular Press, 1970) 1-36.
29. See Jacques Lacan, "Seminar on 'The Purloined Letter'," *French Freud: Structural Studies in Psychoanalysis* (Yale Frech Studies, No. 48). (Milwood, N.Y. Kraus Reprint, 1984). "The Frame of Reference: Poe, Lacan, Derrida" in *The Critical Difference: Essays in the Contemporary Rhetoric of Reading* (Baltimore: Johns Hopkins University Press, 1980). John T. Irwin, "Mysteries we Reread, Mysteries of Rereading: Poe, Borges, and the Analytic Detective Story'," *MLN*, Vol. 101, No. 5 (December 1986): 1170-1188. John P. Muller and William J. Richardson, *The Purloined Poe: Lacan, Derrida & Psychoanalytic Reading* (Baltimore: The Johns Hopkins University Press, 1988).
30. Quoted in John T. Irwin, 1170.
31. *Ibid.,* 1173.
32. Quoted in Michael Foster, *Mystery and Philosophy* (London: SCM Press, 1957) 18ff.
33. See Barton Levi St. Armand, "Poe's Sober Mystification': The Uses of Alchemy in 'The Gold-Bug'," *Poe Studies*, IV, i (June, 1971): 1-7.
34. As Frank Luther Mott says, *Charles Alexander's Weekly Messenger* (January 1836-1848) was published in Philadelphia, and to its December 18, 1839 number Poe contributed "Enigmatical and

Conundrum-ical" and offered to solve cryptograms submitted by the readers. Frank Luther Mott, *A History of American Magaziners* (Cambridge, Mass.: Harvard University Press, 1938-1939) I, 803. See also Arthur H. Quinn, *Poe,* 326. For an interesting study of Poe as a cryptographer see W.K. Wimsatt, "What Poe Knew about Cryptography," *PMLA*, LVIII (September, 1943): 754-79. Even Poe's correspondence reveals his comments on cryptograms submitted by his reader. Letters like the one to Charles G. Percival of January 3, 1846 reveal this. See *Letter,* II, 309. Also *Letter,* I, 172-73, 177, 253-36, 288.

35. Quoted in T.O. Mabbott, ed. *Collected Works*, III, 799.
36. "The Gold Bug" is based on the life of the most commonly known of all pirates, the notorious Captain William Kidd (c. 1645-1701).
37. Margaret Alterton and Hardin Craig, eds. *Edgar Allan Poe: Representative Selection,* cvi.
38. See *Letter,* I, 280.
39. Arthur H. Quinn, 392.
40. See Poe's letter of May 28, 1844 to James R. Lowell. *Letters,* I, 253. In his letter of January 4, 1848 to George W. Eveleth, Poe says, that the tale obtained. The Dollar Newspaper Prize "it obtained the premium and made a great noise." *Letter,* II, 356.
41. George E. Woodberry, *Life*, II, 109.
42. William Bittner, *Poe: A Biography* (Boston: Little, Brown and Company, 1962), 191.
43. Arthur H. Quinn, 422.
44. See Stuart Levine, *Edgar Poe: Seer and Craftsman,* 51-68.
45. Richard Fusco, 93.
46. A.E. Murch, *The Development of the Detective Novel* (London: Peter Owen Limited, 1958) 83.
47. George E. Woodberry says that the period April 1841 to June 1842 of Poe's authorship "is especially distinguished by a remarkable quickening of his powers of analytical reasoning, by virtue of which he struck out a new vein of fiction." (George W. Woodbery, I, 303). This analytical vein continued well into 1844-1845 when "The Purloined Letter" appeared. Duyckinck did not include "'Thou Art the man'" (1844) in the *Tales* of 1845 published by Wiley & Putnam: he included init all other tales of ratiocination including "The Gold Bug" (See A.H. Quinn, 464-66). It is significant however, to note Poe's private remarks to George W. Eveleth about this selection: "Those selected are *not* my best, nore do they fairly represent me in any respect." (Quoted

in Woodberry, II, 148). Poe's objection to the selection was on the ground that there was a "wide diversity and variety" in his tales (Letter to P.P. Cooke, August 9, 1846, *Letters*, II, 329). Thus the fact that "Thou Art the Man" was not included in the *Tales* of 1845 does not minimize the importance of the tale. Published in 1844, the tale falls in the fertile period of Poe's analytical story-writing and constitutes a distinct type of the detective story. During the period when this tale was published, Poe's analytical powers were still at their height and he was serious about the business of crimianl detection.

48. In February 1841, Poe wrote a review of Dickens' novel for *Graham's* in which he foretold the plot of the story which was then appearing serially. His successful perdictions caused Dickens to exclaim that "the man must be the devil" (*sic*). See Hervey Allen, *Israfel: The Life and Times of Edgar Allan Poe,* 410.
49. See Revie of Dicken's *Barnaby Rudge, Works,* VII, 49-52.
50. N. Bryllion Fagin, *The Histrionic Mr. Poe* (Baltimore: The Johns Hopkins University Press, 1949) 224n, 233.
51. Mary E. Phillips calls this tale "the poet's stong conscience story." Mary E. Phillips, *Edger Allan Poe the Man* (Chicage: The John C. Winston Co., 1926), II, 920.
52. T.O. Mabbott, ed. *Collected Works,* III, 919.
53. George E. Woodbery, *Poe*, 1885, 220.
54. Arthur H. Quinn, 422.
55. T.O. Mabbott, ed. *Collected Works of Edge Allan Poe.*
56. David Daiches, *Critical Approaches to Literature* (London: Longmans, Green and Co. Ltd., 1956) 195.
57. Northrop Frye, *Anatomy of Criticism: Four Essays* (Princeton: Princeton University Press, 1957) 46.

6

THE VISIONARY AND THE BEAUTIFUL

"the singular wrought into the strange and mystical"

(Letter to Thomas W. White
August 30, 1835)

The Romantic and Symbolist critics generally tend to look for the visionary and the beautiful in poe's Gothic tales, including the repulsively horrible ones.[1] The character and atmosphere in tales of terror like "The Fall of the House of Usher" and "Ligeia" are no doubt removed from the world of everyday reality. The heroes of these tales are normally taken as visionaries on account of their propensity for dream visions, and the tales are interpreted as being primarily poetic. However, the visions of these characters are caused by abnormal states of mind resulting from either inexpressible guilt or a passionate yearning for the impossible. And the kind of beauty that critics see in these Gothic tales is incompatible with Poe's own idea expressed in "The Poetic Principle." The really visionary and the beautiful in Poe's writing is not something that takes the reader into the world of the abnormal, but is one that elevates his soul, transporting him into the ideal world of the Beautiful. As Poe says in "The Poetic Principle," Beauty should predominate over all other elements like Passion and Truth: "...but the true artist will always contrive to tone them down ['the incitements of Passion, the precepts of Duty, or even the lessons of Truth'] in proper subjection to that *Beauty* which is the atmosphere and the real essence of the poem" (VI, 13). Having thus eliminated Passion from the truly Beautiful and the Poetical, Poe describes the sense of the Beautiful which is "an immortal instinct, deep within the spirit of man":

> This it is which administers to his delight in the manifold forms, and sounds, and odors, and sentiments amid which he exists. And just as the lily is repeated in the lake, or the eyes of Amaryllis in the mirror, so is the mere oral or written repetition of these forms, and sentiments, a duplicate source of delight (VI, 11).

It is contemplation of the Beautiful in human and natural life that causes the "pleasurable elevation, or excitement, *of the soul*, which we recognize as the poetic sentiment" (VI, 12). In the light of such views expressed by Poe himself, it is difficult to see the embodiment of the truly Beautiful and the Poetical in all the types of tales he has written.

Critics have overpraised "Ligeia" as a poetic tale. It falls apart between the Poetic and the Gothic, the ultimate effect on the reader being one of confusion.[2] It is true that Poe employs in his tales certain motifs already used in his poems. He incorporates poems in the tales. But he does that for sheer dramatic effect. Not all of his tales are poetic or intended to be poetic. We have to respect the distinction that Poe himself makes between the subject of poetry. i.e., Beauty and that of the tale proper, i.e., Truth. Thus in his review of Hawthorne's *Twice-Told Tales*, he says:

> We have said that the tale has a point of superiority even over the poem. In fact, while the *rhythm* of this latter is an essential aid in the development of the poem's highest idea--the idea of the Beautiful---the artificialities of the rhythm are an inseparable bar to the development of all points of thought or expression which have their basis in *Truth*. But Truth is often, and in very great degree, the aim of the tale. Some of the finest tales are the tales of ratiocination... (VII, 32).

The very fact that Poe calls the tales of ratiocination "the finest tales" in that they embody Truth, speaks for Poe's idea of Truth as being different from the poetic Truth. Poe also brings the sarcastic or the humorous under Truth which is "the satisfaction of the intellect" (VII, 32). Hence Poe's idea of Truth comes close to the neo-classical standard of truth and fitness. In a recent article entitled "Poe's concept of Truth," J. Lasley Dameron takes issue with Richard A. Fogle who declares Poe to be a fine critic but a "heretic who upsets the balance of organic doctrine by exaggerating and misapplying truth."[3] Dameron examinees the ramifications of Poe's concept of truth, a concept whose most mature statement is in *Eureka*. He describes four main schools of philosophical thought, namely, the Correspondence theory, the Pragmatic theory, the Intuitionist theory, and the Coherence theory and maintains that Poe's theory, is suggestive of the Coherence theory of truth. Poe cites truth as that form of knowledge associated with the intellect or reason. Maintaining that Poe is consistent in being both prescriptive and formalistic, Dameron says that Poe's concept is Aristotelian in its "communication of truth to the reader."[4]

Poe applies the standards of empiricism even to a group of tales in which the beauties of nature are described. These tales--sketches, to be properly designated--are "The Domain of Arnheim," "Landor's Cottage," "The Island of the Fay," and "Morning on the Wissahiccon," wherein the settings are different from those of the Gothic tales. The empirical aspect of these sketches is evident in that they depict nature as Divine structure, man's constructions being parallel to it. However, these sketches embody Poe's poetic sentiment, appealing more to the heart than to the head. However flimsy in narrative framework, they exemplify Poe's aesthetic vision. Despite all that he says about the organic structure, Poe in these pieces takes us into the realm of the poetic, the truly beautiful. Hence these sketches, rather than the Gothic, the Ratiocinative, and the Comic tales, should be more appropriately read as exemplifications of Poe's concept of Beauty. In them there is a pretext of character and incident.

The atmosphere is serene and poetic. The artistic principle behind these sketches finds its objective correlative in the interior decoration and landscape garden. Man's work here parallels the Divine.

In fact, the compositions under consideration in this chapter are so few in number and offer such slender material that they do not perhaps deserve a separate treatment. Nevertheless, their classification as an independent category would be justified when judged strictly on the basis of their effect. Arthur H. Quinn is correct in grouping them under "Descriptive Sketches." These pieces do not really deserve to be called tales since the narrative structure in them is slender and serves as a kind of framework for descriptions or for poetic visions. Yet they possess an independent interest of their own since in some ways they illustrate Poe's idea of the poetic sentiment. In "The Poetic Principle," he says: "The Poetic sentiment, of course, may develop itself in various modes—in Painting, in sculpture, in Architecture, in the Dance—very especially in Music—and very peculiarly, and with a wide field, in the composition of the Landscape Garden" (VI, 11-12). Two of the pieces considered in this chapter deal with a poetic conception of the Landscape Gardening. "Landor's Cottage" is interesting for the theory it propounds of the structure of an artistic composition. In *Eureka* Poe has said that the structure of an artistic compostion parallels the structure of the Divine composition. In these landscape sketches he means to show that the man-made landscape garden or interior decoration parallels his literary structures in terms of the unity of effect. "The Island of the Fay," "Morning on the Wissahiccon," and "Silence" are essentially poetic visions and produce a distinct effect of their own. Thus these compositions illustrate the distinction that Poe has made between a poem and a fictional composition. Beauty, the true province of the poem, can be seen illustrated in these sketches more than in the Gothic tales. Truth, in the sense of the psychological rather than the merely factual or the poetic, is more appropriately rendered in the Gothic tales. However, Truth as meaning the truth of natural experience can also be seen illustrated in these landscape sketches. These sketches constitute an impressive transition from Poe's poetry to his tale-writing. It is in this respect that they are relevant to an understanding of Poe's fictional method. Poetic effect is but one of the innumerable effects that Poe intends to achieve in his work and these sketches—among his prose writings--illustrate the particular effect of the poetic.

Robert D. Jacobs has sought to find the origins of Poe's aesthetics in Archibald Alison and traces the preponderance Alisonian ideas into Poe's landscape tales.[5] Also several other scholars like Hans Huth, John Conron, Edwin H. Fussell, Elizabeth Philips, Kent Ljungguist and Catherine Rainwater have commented upon Poe's interest in the American Landscape.[6] The more recent among these commentators are Ljungquist and Rainwater. Referring to Poe's knowledge of a popular aesthetic controversy "Picturesque moment" between 1750 and 1800, Rainwater says: "Poe's landscape works reflect his now well-documented tendency to develop hoaxes and parodies which bedevil the credulous reader."[7] Such an approach misses the central focus of the aesthetics of Poe's Landscape tales which illustrate his theory of Beauty and Poetry. Ljungquist, however, is more convincing when he maintains: "Poe's treatment of landscape oscillates between the grand on one hand and the fair on the other--the 'grand' standing for wilderness in its artless, unenhanced state, the 'fair' representing nature subject to the artist's craft or executive skill. The outward drive to confront landscape in its beaming majesty and the centripetal impulse toward order and artistic control constitutes the twin rhythms of Poe's landscape fiction and criticism."[8] However, one wonders whether Ljungquist is justified in treating the "picturesque" in Gothic tales like "Usher" and the Visionary and the Beautiful in sketches like "Landor's Cottage" on the same level. The effects in the two types of tales differ. While the Gothic tales produce an effect of terror, the poetic pieces produce an effect less terrible and more poetic. Joan Dayan goes a step further in a recent linguistic study in emphasizing the provisional quality in the narrator's descriptions, the winding path matching his sinuous syntax and linguistic dodges.[9]

In another recent study, John Michael maintains that "In tales like 'The Domain of Arnheim' and 'The Power of Words' Poe both participates and subverts the grounding of thought in subjectivity. In these tales Poe explores the problem of reflection and finds the act of narration to be essential to it. In Poe the necessity of narration reveals the coherence and the indispensability of attempts to ground certainty in an unmediated relationship of self to self."[10] The story-line as such in "The Power of Words" is less than in " The Domain of Arnheim." In "The Power of Words" Agathos and Oinos discuss the power of creation in an elevated spiritual sense. In "The Domain of Arnheim," there is an attempt to realize Beauty on earth. Poe is, however, presenting the character as a seeker after poetic beauty more in external terms than in the depths of subjectivity as it happens in Gothic tales. Despite the reference to "semi-Gothic, Semi-Saracenic structure" in the concluding paragraph, Poe's emphasis is more on "the mortal or human *point of view.*" Ellison is basically in quest of a "fulfillment, not only of his own destiny as poet, but the august purposes for which the Deity had implanted the poetic sentiment in man."[11] J. Gerald Kennedy is more convincing when he says that "The Doman of Arnheim" represents "the author's own intermittent desire to abolish or surmount mortality."[12]

"The Domain of Arnheim" (1847)[13] and "Landor's Cottage" (1849) are of a piece, as intended by the author himself, who calls "Landor's cottage" "A Pendant to the Domain of Arnheim." Both the pieces develop a common theme and motive: the poetry of a Landscape Gardening, or the landscape gardener as a poet (i.e., a maker in Greak). Despite the air of circumstantial reality, they project an entirely imagined vision of beauty and portray the protagonists Ellison and Landor as creators of supernal beauty of a pictorial as distinguished from a musical order. Both the men are "painters" of genius gifted with rare powers of combining the forms of Nature into the configurations of art. Painting techniques play a considerable part in Poe's theory and practice of tale-writng.[14]

Just as a painter combine various colors to bring out an aesthetic piece, so also the writer of the tale combines the various components of the tale to make it an organic structure. What Ellison and Landor do is to take this power of synthesis to the level of Nature herself. For Ellison "the creation of the landscape-garden offered to the proper Muse the most magnificent of opportunities. Here, indeed, was the fairest field for the display of imagination in the endless combining of forms of novel beauty" (II, 97). On approaching Ellison's domain, the visitor feels that he is "enwraps in an exquisite sense of the strange." Ellison's idea of a landscape is a combination of vastness, magnificence, beauty and strangeness. This makes the atmosphere truly poetic. Both Ellison and Landor have a vision of their own destiny as poets, of fulfilling "the august purposes for which the Deity had implanted the poetic sentiment in man" (II, 98). They are both seekers after perfection in the beautiful and see that "in landscape arrangement alone is the physical nature susceptible of exaltation, and that, therefore, her susceptibility of improvement at this one point, was a mystery" (II, 99). Referring to "Landor's Cottage," T.O. Mabbott says: "This charming description of a beautiful little home in the country has in it a pervading element of poetic autobiography. It is laid in a part of our country that Poe knew well, for he was living amidst the scenery that inspired the many artists of the Hudson River School."[15] Thus Poe's sketch is reminiscent of a beautiful painting. Both the landscape garden of Ellison and the cottage of Landor embody the supernal vision of their author-- a vision that at the same time as it imposes upon Nature the elements of human art, combines it with a magnificence and strangeness conveying "the sentiment of spiritual interference." They represent the "architecture" of the creative imagination. Poe's concern as a creative writer has alway been an aspiration from the physical to the spiritual. The architectonics of imagination is perhaps his greatest preoccupation. And this is evident in the Landscape sketches too. Of landor's cottage, the narrator remarks that "this house, like the infernal terrace seen by Vathek, 'etait d'une architecture inconnue dans les annales de la terre, '..'' (II, 99). It is an act of poetry. It is matched only by the natural perfection and romance of Annie, the lady who opens the door of the cottage for him. In a passionate letter of October 18, 1848 to Sarah Helen Whitman, Poe says that "The Domain of Arnheim" "expresses much of my soul."[16] The atmosphere of the sketch is comparable to the ideal atmosphere of Nature and Beauty Poe imagines to have been inhabited by himself and Helen:

> I suffered my imagination to stray with you, and with the few who love us both to the banks of some quiet river, in some lovely valley of our land. Here, not too far secluded from the world, we exercised a taste controlled by no conventionalities, but the sworn slave of a Nature Art, in the building for ourselves a cottage which no human being ever passed without an ejaculation of wonder at its strange, weird, and incomprehensible yet most simple beauty.[17]

Poe's landscape sketches are concerned with this "strange, weird, and incomprehensible yet most simple beauty."

"The Domain of Arnheim" and "Landor's Cottage" are not tales in the real sense. The narrative framework of these pieces merely serves as a springboard for the author for lengthy discourses on his theory of art and beauty and on creative imagination itself. It is the merest pretext for his cognitions. The characters of Ellison and Landor, no doubt, possess an independent interest as they embody a certain conception of the ideal artist and poet. But the characterized in both cases does not issue in an action of the narrative kind; nor do these compositions develop any plot interest. They are better characterized as poetic or artistic visions. They propound a theory of artistic composition--a theory that the arrangement of landscape gardens should exhibit a perfect "adaptation" of their constituent parts. Whether it is in fictional composition or in the cosmic arrangement, poe insists upon the same kind of adaptation, logical interrelatedness of the parts of the work contributing to unity of effect.

T.O. Mabbott calls "The Island of the Fay" (1841) a "charming fantacy."[18] Burton R. Pollin says that the piece should not be taken seriously as a symbolic narrative because it was a "plate story" written to interpret an engraving made by John Sartain for *Graham's*.[19] John Sartain greatly altered and adapted a drawing by John B. Martin, who had been Sartains's teacher, Burton R. Pollin calls it a Poe hoax in many ways in its presentation.[20] The sketch, like the two preceding pieces, concerns a certain imaginative vision, though thematically it is different from them. In the discursive opening paragraphs the author tells us of "the happiness experienced in the contemplation of natural scenery" (II, 85), and of the effects of solitude on the human spirit, comparable in its influence to the effects of music. The narrator records his journey into the island of the Fay and the dreamy vision induced in his mind as he contemplates the scene. His entire experience amidst the awesome solitude of the island partakes the quality of a vision. In recording this vision the narrator assumes absolute reality of the world of imagination as opposed to commonsense world of every day experience. This is no doubt one of the basic beliefs of Poe as a poet and tale-writer. But the vision on the island of the Fay also takes on a symbolic significance for the narrator:

> I Fancied that each shadow, as the sun descended lower and lower, separated itself suddenly from the trunk that gave it birth, and thus became absorbed by the stream; while other shadows issued momently from the trees, taking the place of their predecessors thus entombed (II, 89).

The Fay's circuiting of the island in her canoe passing from light into shade suggests to the narrator a sense of tragic mystery; it symbolizes the eternal cyclic process of life and death:

> "The revolution which has just been made by the Fay," continued I, musingly, "is the cycle of the brief

year of her life. She has floated through her winter and through her summer. She is a year nearer unto Death; for I did not fail to see that as she came into the shade, her shadow fell from her, and was swallowed up in the dark water, making its blackness more black" (II, 90).

As in the other sketches, in "The Island of the Fay" also the narrative serves as a convenient framework for containing a certain dream vision. And the three pieces considered so far are significant in that they constitute Poe's concern for the reality of imaginative vision.

"Morning on the Wissahiccon" ("The Elk"), first published in 1843, is similar to "The Island of the Fay" as it also deals with a brief dreamy vision induced in the narrator's mind in the course of his visit to the Wissahiccon. This sketch is perhaps different from "The Island of the Fay" in that the descriptions of the scene are more naturalistic and imaginative. Whatever visionary element the composition contains has been subordinated to the matter-of-fact tone of the naturalistic description.

The author devotes several paragraphs to a survey of the American landscape before coming to a description of the region of Wissahiccon, a brook falling into the Schuylkill, about six miles west of Philadelphia.[21]

> Now, the Wissahiccon is of so remarkable a loveliness that, were it flowing in England, it would be the theme of every bard, and the common topic of every tongue, if, indeed, its banks were not parcelled off in lots, at an exorbitant price, as building-sites for the villas of the opulent (II, 80).

Poe's attempt to capture the natural beauty of Wissahiccon is remarkable. In describing the beautiful in such idyllic surroundings he comments not only on the beauty of the virgin land but warns civilized man of the consequences of disturbing the natural beauty. The surrounding scene with its extraordinary beauty prompts in him "half-slumberous" fancies in the light of which he contemplates the animal with its "attitude indicative of profound and melancholy inquisitiveness."

Another tale that is somewhat different from the landscape sketches but visionary and poetic in its effect is "Silence--A Fable" (1838). Even though this is called a companion piece to "Shadow," it is considered in the present chapter on account of the predominance of the poetic element over the other aspects. The fabulous character of the piece is clearly brought out by the author in the course of the sketch. The entire fable may be an attempt to represent an informing idea--a state of mind and attitude: in this case the sense of desolation, "of sorrow, and weariness, and disgust with mankind, and a longing after solitude" (I, 244). The man upon the summit of the rock is the type of this situation. The Demon narrator may be just a narrative device or he may represent the inner spirit of the listener in the tale. The fable-like structure of the tale is rendered conspicuous not only by the character of the man upon the summit but by the other details of description such as the inscriptions upon the rock: "DESOLATION AND SILENCE." The presentation of the idea of the tale is more direct than subtly suggestive. The significance of character and incident is stated in so many words. The method employed by the author in this tale is not of psychological presentiment but one of concreteness of presentation typical of the fable. According to John Gardner, "In the fable we are concerned with men and animals not as human beings or human-like beings but as representatives of particular values or modes of behavior."[22] In Poe's fable the concreteness of presentation, moralistic element and representation of particular values or modes of behavior are very much present.

In its choice of image and in its repetition of certain phrases and motifs, "silence" becomes what Arthur H. Quinn calls "a piece of imaginative prose."[23] Rhythmically, the narrative is close to a ballad. Each paragraph in the tale reads like a poetic stanza with the refrain-like repetition of the last line (in most of them) as in a poem: "And the man trembled in the solitude;--but the night waned, and he sat upon the rock." The repetition of the conjunction "And" and certain groups of words within the individual paragraphs evokes poetic mood. Words like "desolation" and "silence" are often repeated with effect. Furthermore, images like the tempest, and the under-water foliage contribute to the poetic atmosphere of the tale.

Finally, the conclusion of the tale in which the double-narrator opening is disentangled and the narrator presents himself before us, completes the fable-like structure of the tale by giving us a situation in which the Demon tells him the story of "silence." The tale suggests resemblances to some of the Biblical visions like that of Ezekiel or of Moses; and the highly imaginative quality of the prose confirms these resemblances.

On the whole, "Silence" does not possess a strong narrative core. Its Fable-like character becomes too palpable. The narrative framework is but a pretext for presenting an idea as in a typical fable. Another significant aspect of the tale is that while using certain Gothic features like desolation and an unusual state of mind, it evokes a definite poetic atmosphere unlike the major Gothic tales like "Ligeia" wherein the poetic is overwhelmed by the Gothic.

NOTES

1. See Edward H. Davidson, *Poe: A Critical Study* (Cambridge, Mass.: The Belknap Press of Harvard University Press, 1957) and Patrick F. Quinn, *The French Face of Edgar Poe* (Carbondale: Southern Illinois University Press, 1957).
2. See D. Ramakrishna, "Poe's LIGEIA," *The Explicator,* XXV, No. 2 (October, 1966), Item 19.
3. Richard H. Fogle, "Organic From in American Criticism, 1840-1870," in *The Development of American Literary Criticism,* ed. Floyd Stoval (Chapel Hill: University of North Carolina Press, 1955) 100.
4. J. Lasley Dameron, "Poe's Concept of Truth," *Mississippi Quarterly,* XLIII, i (Winter 1989-90), 17.
5. See Robert D. Jacobs, *Poe: Journalist and Critic* (Baton Roughe: Louisiana State University Press, 1969).

6. Hans Huth, *Nature and the American: Three Centuries of Changing Attitudes* (Berkely: University of California Press, 1957); John Conron, ed. *The American Landscape* (New York: Oxford University Press, 1973); Edwin H. Fussell, *Frontier: American Literature and the American West* (Princeton: Princeton University Press, 1965); Elizabeth Phillips, "The Imagination of Great Landscape," in *Edgar Allan Poe: An American Imagination* (Port Washington, N.Y.: Kennikat Press, 1979) 53-96; Kent Ljungquist, *The Grand and the Fair: Poe's Landscape Aesthetics and Pictorial Techniques* (Potomac, Md: Scripta Humanistica, 1984); Catherine Rainwater, "Poe's Landscape Tales and the 'Picturesque' Tradition," *Southern Literary Journal,* 16, i (Spring 1984): 30-43; Joan Dayan, "The Road to 'Landor's Cottage': Poe's Landscape of Effect," *University of Mississippi Studies in English*, 3 (1982): 136-54.
7. Catherine Rainwater, 31.
8. Kent Ljungquist, 10.
9. See Joan Dayan.
10. John Michael, "Narration and Reflection: The Search for Grounds in Poe's 'The Power of Words' and 'The Domain of Arnheim'," *Arizona Quarterly,* Vol. 45, No. 3 (Autumn, 1989): 1-22.
11. "The Domain of Arnheim," *Edgar Allan Poe: Pottery and Tales,* ed. Patrick F. Quinn (New York: The Library of America, 1984) 859.
12. J. Gerald Kennedy, *Poe, Death, and the Life of Writing* (New Haven: Yale University Press, 1987) 208-209.
13. A revised and rewritten version of the earlier "The Landscape Garden" (1842) and which superseded the earlier version.
14. Poe's taste for music and painting is well known. In his letter of May 1847 to Marie Louise Shew he expresses immense admiration for beauty of the paintings of Raphael and the arrangement of musical instruments like guitar adding to the overall beauty of the drawing room (*Letters,* II, 350).
15. T.O. Mabbott, ed. *Collected Works,* III, 1326. Poe obviously intends to portary in these landscape sketches his own conception of ideal beauty, as evident from his letter to Annie L. Richmond: "Not long ago I sent one ['article'] to the *Metropolitan* called 'Landor's Cottage': it has something about Annie in it"... In this letter Poe expresses his love for Annie L. Richmond (*Letters,* II, 419).
16. Letters, II, 397.
17. *Ibid.*, 396. Poe's Letter of October 18, 1848 to Mrs. Whitman.

T.O. Mabbott tells us that Poe wrote on the copy of the New York *Columbian Magazine* sent to Mrs. Whitman: "This story contains more of myself of my inherent tastes and habits of thought than anything I have written" (*Collected Works,* III, 1266).

18. T.O. Mabbott calls it "charming fantasy" (*Collected Works*, II, 597).
19. Burton R. Pollin, "Poe as Probable Author of 'Harper's Ferry'," *American Literature,* XL (May, 1968): 169-70. Kent Ljungquist says that the composition of the sketch followed the rather common practice of writing a prose piece to accompany pictures in eary nineteenth century magazines. Kent Ljungquist, *The Grand and the Fair: Poe's Landscape Aesthetics and Pictorial Techniques.* (Potomac, Md.: Scripta Humanistica, 1984) 112. See also F. DeWolfe Miller, "The Basis for Poe's The Island of the Fay'," *American Literature,* 16 (1942): 135-40. Burton Pollin, "Poe's Illustration for 'The Island of the Fay': A Hoax Detected," *Mystery and Detection Annual* (Baverly Hills, California: Donald Adams, 1972) 33-35. Charies Sanford, "Edgar Allan Poe: A Blight Upon the Landscape," *American Quarterly,* 20 (1967): 54-56. Sanford sees the sketch as an expression of the American Adam theme.
20. See Burton R. Pollin, "The Hoax in Poe's illustration for 'The Island of the Fay'," *Insights and Oulooks: Eassys on Great Writers* (New York: Gordian Press, 1986) 173-88.
21. The sketch is called the "quiet landscape sketch of the environs of Philadelphia." Mabbott, III, 860.
22. John Gardner and Dunlap, ed. *Forms of Fiction*, 26-27.
23. Arthur H. Quinn, 215.

7

THE PITFALLS OF SUSTAINED NARRATION

"The ordinary novel is objectionable, from its length,...As it cannot be read at one sitting, it deprives itself, of course, of the immense force derivable from totality. Worldly interests intervening during the pauses of perusal modify, annul, or counteract, in a greater or less degree, the impressions of the book. But simple cessation in reading would, of itself, be sufficient to destroy the true unity."

(Review of Hawthrone's Twice-Told Tales, May, 1842)

"If any literary work is too long to be read at one sitting, we must bc content to dispense with the immensely important effect derivable from unity of impression; for, if two sittings be required, the affairs of the world interfere, and everything like totality is at once destroyed."

("The Philosophy of Composition," April, 1846)

The Narrative of Arthur Gordon Pym (1838) and The Journal of Julius Rodman (1840) are Poe's attempts at sustained narration. "The Light House," brought to light by T.O. Mabbott, is an unfinished piece of writing in this category. But *Pym* is Poe's only significant attempt at writing a novel. Whatever his success in such an attempt, the narrative has been a model for adventure story writers since Jules Verne.[1] Burton R. Pollin calls is "the sea-adventure novel, "and says that it" showed the growing interest of Americans in expanding their maritime knowledge and their national control over the still unexplored oceans and lands of the world, even to the limits of the Antarctic and the Pacific."[2]

J. Gerald Kennedy calls *Pym* a "satire of the popular novel of adventure"[3] Lisa Gtelman says: "the very status of *Pym* as a novel is enforced throughout by Poe's parodic representation of the discursive (ditinctly non-novelistic) conventions of exploration accounts and the generic constraints evidently experienced by explorers eager to present the 'facts' of geographic discovery in a believable manner."[4]

In his letter of June 1, 1840 to William E. Burton Poe says, "You once wrote in your magazine (a sharp critique) upon a book of mine--a very silly book--*Pym*."[5] Whether Poe called *Pym* "a very silly book" on account of Burton's adverse criticism or he himself felt that the book was inadequate remains to be examined. In view of this own preference for the shorter tale, Poe might not be quite at home in the composition of the longer narrative.

Jeffrey Meyers, groups *Pym* with "Hans Pfaall" and *Julius Rodman* as "imaginary journeys,"[6] obviously in agreement with Burton R. Pollin in Vol. I of *Collected Writings of Edgar Allan Poe*. Poe published two installments of *Pym* under his own name in the *Messenger* of January and February 1837 but he continued it through 1837 for the book Publication in 1838. After being fired from the magazine, he abandoned the novel. He resumed work on it while living in New York that year, but reached an imaginative deadened with his hero adrift in Antarctic waters. Unable to find a way to bring Pym back to Nantucket after his trip further South, to get him out of the fantastic realm and back into the real world, Poe left the book unfinished,[7] and devised a mysterious, semi-mystical conclusion.

The Narrrative of Arthur Gordon Pym is an admirable blend of realism and fantasy. Even though the narrative acquires symbolic overtones toward the conclusion, it is also realistic in its details. Poe's central motive in tho narrative seems to be the creation of a world of make-believe about the then unknown South Polor region. He does it not only through minute and realistic detail but also by means of a prefatory and a concluding note appended to the narrative. In these Poe devises an elaborate ruse to give his story an air of authenticity. The symbolic overtones of the passages dealing with hieroglyphics and the final shrouded figure cause immense confusion for any clear understanding of Poe's meaning, especially among modern critics. In its day, it was often greeted with skepticism that derision.

The introductory note under the signature of A.G. Pym explains the very interesting manner in which the narrative got written. Pym the narrator explains the reasons why he deputed Mr. Poe with the task of writing an account of the earlier portion of his extraordinary series of adventures in the South Sea. He (Pym) would not do it himself because of a distrust in his own abilities as a writer, and also because

> I feared I should not be able to write, from mere memory, a statement so minute and connected as to have the *appearance* of that truth it would really possess, barring only the natural and unavoidable exaggeration to which all of us are prone when detailing events which had powerful influence in exciting the imaginative faculties. Another reason was, that the incidents to be narrated were of a nature so positively marvelous that, unsupported as my assertions must necessarily be (except by the evidence of a single individual, and he a halfbreed Indian), I could only hope for belief among my family, and those of my friends who have had reason, through life, to put faith in my veracity,--the probability being that the public at large would regard what I should put forth as merely an impudent and ingenious fiction. (V, 3-4).

So, in order to give his account complete credibility as one of real happenings, he persuades Mr. poe to publish it "*under the garb of fiction.*" But, finding that the reading public is not disposed to receive it as a fable and to give complete credence to his account, Pym himself undertakes to relate the latter part of the narrative in his own writing. Having now nothing to fear on the score of popular incredulity, Pym even says that the difference in point of style between Mr. Poe's and his own writing should be evident to the readers. Nevertheless, it is clear that all this is a very ingenious ruse on the part of the author to invest his fictitious account with verisimilitude. While Pym tells us that he planned a ruse to secure credulity for his narrative by presenting what is a real account under the garb of fiction, thus giving it an appearance of truth, Poe's own ruse is to present what is essentially a piece of fiction under the garb of an authentic account, to give it the appearance of truth. All this is very ingenious of course, and the concluding note (supposedly of the editor of the journal) further strengthens the make-believe. While it is erroneous to take Poe's account as factual, what makes *Pym* of absorbing interest is the author's creation of a neutral zone of the mind (mingling fact and fiction) to re-enact an imaginative drama with multiple significance. This style of presentation reminds us of the one adopted by Jonathan Swift in *Gulliver's Travels*. Poe seeks to justify the incomplete end of the narrative by explaining the circumstances of Mr. Pym's sudden death and the loss of the remaining chapters. However, it is promised that "the papers, if ultimately found, will be given to the public." It is by such means that the author attempts to achieve the effect of complete authenticity for his narrative. This is supported by a sustained realism of descriptive detail in the course of the narrative itself. As John H. Ingram says,

> The truthful air of "The Narrative," and the circumstantiality of the title-page and preface, doubtless attracted attention, but indeed the whole romance is detailed with such Defoe-like minuteness-with such an apparent want of art—especially in lengthy, almost tedious, citations from presumable

> kindred works--that the reading public was bound to submit to the temporary fascination, and accept the vraisamblance for truth itself. The abrupt termination of "The Narrative," and the pretext alleged for it, both contributed greatly to the apparent fidelity to fact.[8]

In addition to the Defoe-like minuteness that Ingram finds in *Pym*, the narrative reminds us of Swift's *Gulliver's Travels* in that it is externally a tale of adventure with a serious message. As in Swift's *Travels*, in Poe's *Pym* too, one notices the kind of historical authenticity and simplicity of narration describing an adventure. Probably in Poe's narrative also one can see some satiric intention, though milder than swift's. It is, however, at the level of allegory that Poe's narrative looks dull in comparison with Swift's. The final paragraphs of *Pym*, with some obvious symbolic overtones, are an attempt on the part of the author to convey a serious message. What remains to be seen on a close study of the method of *Pym* is the extent to which Poe is able to carry out his intentions.

While *Pym* achieves *vraisemblance* at the level of physical reality, the unusual experiences of the narrator are presented at the level of psychological realism. The psychological realism relates mainly to three incidents. The first of these is Pym's experience in the ship's hold, the second relates to his fall from the cliff and the third is the rushing of Pym's canoe toward the cataract at the end of the story. In the vivid portrayal of these experiences, *Pym* anticipates the method of "The Pit and the Pendulum" (1843) and "The Premature Burial" (1844). In the first instance of Pym's experiences in the ship's hold, Poe describes with extreme vividness and realism the sensations of being entombed alive. The inner frontiers of fear and nightmare on the part of the protagonist have been rendered with superb craftsmanship. The description of Pym's descent from the cliff is one breathless moment for the reader. In fact, the success of Poe's rendition in this part of the story consists in the manner in which he *bodily* transfers the narrator's experience to the reader so much so that the reader actually feels the sensation of the fall:

> ...I threw my vision far down into the abyss. For one moment my fingers clutched convulsively upon their hold, while, with the movement, the faintest possible idea of ultimate escape wandered like a shadow through my mind; in the next my whole soul was pervaded with a *longing to fall;* a desire, a yearning, a passion utterly uncontrollable. I let go at once my grasp upon the peg, and, turning half round from the precipice, remained tottering for an instant against its naked face. But now there came a spinning of the brain; a shrill-sounding and phantom voice screamed within my ears; a dusky, fiendish, and filmy figure stood immediately beneath me; and, sighing, I sunk down with a bursting heart, and plunged within its arms (V, 238).

Critics have interpreted the "filmy figure" as the mother image. However, the whole experience of the narrator at the precipice getting dizzy and becoming semi-conscious due to the threatened fall is rendered with extreme psychological realism. The incident is rendered so skillfully that the reader is likely to identify himself with the narrator as in a tale like "A Descent into the Maelstrom." Referring to Defoe's *Robinson Crusoe*, Poe speaks of this "Identification" which contributes to the effect of the narrative:

> Indeed the author of "Crusoe" must have possessed, above all other faculties, what has been termed the faculty of *Identification*--that dominion exercised by volition over imagination, which enables the mind to lose its own in a fictitious individuality (VII, 301).

In his letter of March 8, 1849 to Evert A. Duyckinck, Poe gives his own conception of verisimilitude. Thus, he says, "In 'Robinson Crusoe' the design was far more to please, or excite, than to deceive by verisimilitude..."[9] The sense of "identification" results in the pleasure or the excitement experienced by the reader in his perusal of the narrative. The extreme vividness and dramatic immediacy of the presentation of Pym's experiences are striking. The incident of Pym's canoe rushing headlong into the cataract is another instance of Poe's mastery of psychological realism:

> The summit of the cataract was utterly lost in the dimness and the distance. Yet we were evidently approaching it with a hideous velocity. At intervals there were visible in it wide, yawning, but momentary rents, and from out these rents, within which was a chaos of flitting and indistinct images, there came rushing and mighty, but soundless winds, tearing up the enkindled ocean in their course.
>
> ....The darkness had materially increased, relieved only by the glare of the water thrown back from the white curtain before us. Many gigantic and pallidly white birds flew continuously now from beyond the veil, and their scream was the eternal "Tekeli-li" as they retreated from our vision. Hereupon Nu-Nu stirred in the bottom of the boat; but upon touching him, we found his spirit departed. And now we rushed into the embraces of the cataract, where a chasm threw itself open to receive us. But there arose in our pathway a shrouded human figure, very far larger in its proportions than any dweller among men. And the hue of the skin of the figure was of perfect whiteness of the snow (V, 250).

This passage makes it evident that in *Pym* the author attempts to blend realistic presentation with symbolic configuration. The Nantucket vessel which has set sail for the South Seas embodies Poe's fascination with the imaginary described in realistic detail. On the one hand the adventures of Pym and Augustus through mutiny, delirium, and the harrowing experiences with the seagulls constitute adolescent fantasy. But, on the other hand, the horrors of whiteness at the conclusion of the tale--as the voyagers drift into the Antarctic—remind us of Coleridge's albatross and Melville's "Whiteness of the Whale."[10] While being chased by the savages on the island of Tsalal, Pym and Peters get trapped in the narrow fissure. As the walls caved in, they experience being "entombed alive." The "living inhumation" is most painful. As Poe Puts it, "The blackness of darkness which envelopes the victim, the terrific oppression of lungs, the stifling fumes from the damp earth, unite with the ghostly considerations that we are beyond the remotest confines of hope, and that such is the allotted portion of *the dead*, to carry into the human heart a degree of degree of appalling awe and horror not to be tolerated--never to be conceived." (Ch. XXI, *Pym* II Para.)

Harry Levin rightly says, tracing the origin of the phrase "blackness of darkness," that Poe's imagery should be viewed in the light of the aesthetics of his period and that the *Chiaroscuro* in "The Pit and the Pendulum" characterizes Gothic fiction dealing with the horror of darkness.[11] However, Kent Ljungquist suggests that the supporting aesthetics of such fiction was presented by Burke's *Enquiry*, a work which had gained currency by the time of the tale's composition.[12] But, there is no evidence to prove that Poe knew about Burke and his views.[13]

The recent Deconstructionist interpretations of *Pym* are interesting. In his 1986 dissertation, "Architects of the Abyss: The Indeterminate Fictions of Poe, Hawthorne and Melville," Dennis Pahl is concerned with the "indeterminate boundaries between fiction and criticism." The narrators of "The Fall of the House of Usher," "The Assignation," and *Pym* "cannot define themselves outside a world of textuality and so must inevitably fail in their romantic quest for truth, presence and origins" (*DAI*) Pahl's third chapter, published first as "Poe/Script: The Death of the Author in *The Narrative of Arthur Gordon Pym*" (1987) aims to demonstrate that "the truth of the self...is not discovered but invented. In....*Pym* Poe challenges whatever authenticity, or truth value, the narrator might lend to his narrative by putting in question the narrator's self--that is, his ability to stand outside his own system of representation, total and present to himself" (51). Foucault on writing and the death of the author is quoted in support, and later Lacan's theory is applied to the mirror scene aboard the *Jane Guy*.

J. Gerald Kennedy's study, "Unreadable Books,

Unspeakable Truths" in *Poe, Death, and the Life of Writing* (1987) constitutes the first sustained attempt with regard to Poe to combine history—essentially of the old sort--with deconstructive theory. Kennedy explores *Pym's* "implications of illegibility, focusing first on the nature of the hermeneutic dilemma which the reader shares with *Pym*, and then shifting attention to the metaphysical crux of this impasse. The narrator's abortive quest for meaning seems ultimately related to his progressive immersion in the phenomenology of death" (145-146). Kennedy pairs the note from Augustus, "a paradigm of unreadability" (153), with an equally unreadable event in the book's narrative world, the death ship episode. This "frame" is comparable in importance to that provided by the "Preface" and the concluding "Note," which Kennedy also stresses. However, we must remember that Poe always derides what he termed (in his own coinage) "metaphysicianism." (See Burton R. Pollin, *Poe, Creator of Words*, 31)

The incidents of the narrative are related in an episodic manner (with intermittent digressions, at times tedious) without logical consequence; one incident does not "beget" another. But in a story of this type we do not perhaps look for a dramatic structure. In the way the incidents follow one another, perhaps there would not be the kind of dramatic conclusion or climax one finds in the conventional narrative. The conclusion of the narrative is simply the termination of the adventures. The series of adventures might go on endlessly or they might be brought to a close whenever the author chooses to do so. Normally the adventurer returns home to tell his tale. In the case of *Pym*, the author tries to explain certain things by means of a "Note." Even in an adventure tale there is perhaps a kind of unity that can legitimately be expected: the entire story should relate to and center round one character. This happens in Defoe's *Robinson Crusoe*, a novel that obviously impressed Poe.[14] But in *Pym* there is no such central unity. The story is apparently that of two adolescents who set out on a globe-trotting adventure. They are in pursuit of nothing and are getting nowhere. This has been interpreted by critics like

Edward H. Davidson and Patrick F. Quinn as a journey into the interior, a quest for self-identity. However, the journey of Pym is less organized than captain Ahab's in *Moby-Dick* or Huck Finn's in the novel by Mark Twain. The initial adventure of Pym's getting locked up in the ship's hold is one of those accidents with no momentous reason for its happening. Poe, however, does an excellent job of dramatizing Pym's experiences during his confinement, anticipating the incarceration in some of his more successful Gothic tales like "The Pit and the Pendulum," (1843). The story of Pym's adventures might have ended with his rescue by the *Jane Guy* at the end of the thirteenth chapter. Structurally the story reaches a point of completion here. But the protagonist starts out on another adventure into the South Sea islands on board the *Jane Guy*. This adventure is a separate story altogether and does not arise from the circumstances of the preceding one. Through the absence of the logical development of plot or of inevitability, Poe seems to suggest the endless fortuitousness of experience.

The abrupt termination of the narrative offers a major difficulty of interpretation. There have been attempts both to defend and to condemn the tale on this score. Arthur H. Quinn thinks that the ending is not really inconclusive, but is made highly suggestive by the reference to the mysterious shrouded figure:"

> There have been critics who object to what they are pleased to call an inconclusive ending. But when the details of the voyages have long been forgotten, the picture of the mysterious figure remains, stimulating the imagination of those readers who do not have to have everything explained to them in words of one syllable.[15]

Charles O'Donnell defends the present form of the tale saying that Poe deliberately leaves the story inconclusive. He calls attention to the special significance of the miniature episode of the Ariel adventure in the beginning for the conclusion of the narrative. Pym and Peters in the latter half are actually rescued in the manner in which Pym and Augustus are rescued earlier by the ship after the Ariel hit it. The white shrouded figure, according to O'Donnell, is not some mysterious supernatural form but the "sail, or prow of the ship being blown toward him by the new winds from the South."[16] Edward H. Davidson seems to find in the irresolute ending of the narrative the very essence of its meaning. For him Pym represents the unfinished continuing quest of the character after self and reality.[17] The story has an organic structure with a proper beginning and an end: "....somewhere in the amplitude of its growth there is a middle, and that may rest on infinity."[18] John H. Ingram, on the other hand, finds the termination indefensible and thinks that the supernatural final paragraph was a mistake "wisely" omitted in the London reprint of 1841).[19] Much has been said by recent critics on the ending. Joseph J. Moldenhauer and William Peden take the figure as "death."[20] Paul John Eakin takes it as a death-conquering Lazarus figure.[21] Charles O'Donnel considers it as emblematic of knowledge.[22] According to Todd M. Leiber. The imagination is suggested by Pym's enigmatic vision.[23] J. Gerald Kennedy maintains that the narrative is imbued by that vision.[24] Kent P. Ljunquist reads the figure as a Titan.[25] Marie Bonaparte and Leslie Fiedler treat the figure as a divinity.[26] John T. Irwin argues that the "shrouded human figure" is Pym's white shadow."[27] On the whole, there are two extreme stands taken by critics about the conclusion of *Pym*. The seeming inconclusiveness of the ending could be explained only by the fact of the fragmentary nature of the composition, many say. Poe has invented the pretext of the concluding note to justify this state and explain still obscure points. However, the narrative does not have the same suggestiveness as an open ending. The reader is left with the feeling that Poe is trying to say something but fails to achieve his end.

It might be worthwhile to examine if there is also a symbolic structure in the narrative operating as an undercurrent. This aspect has been emphasized by critics, perhaps at the expense of its narrative structure. For instance, Patrick F. Quinn has drawn attention to the strong oneiric elements present in the narrative.[28] There is no doubt that Pym and his companions go through certain experiences which in their nightmarish horror resemble the world of dreams. Pym's experiences in the ship's hold and his fall from the cliff are of this nature. The Ariel episode and the final experience of the impending descent into the cataract, too, have a strong oneiric element in them. The entire description of the horror and agony of Pym and his companions aboard the wrecked ship, the appearance of the death ship, and the incident of cannibalism partake of the nature of some dream experience. After being rescued by the *Jane Guy* and recovered from the agony of those experiences Pym feels that he has awakened from some frightful dream:

> I have since found that this species of partial oblivion is usually brought about by sudden transition, whether from joy to sorrow or from sorrow to joy--the degrees of forgetfulness being proportioned to the degree of difference in the exchange. Thus, in my own case, I now feel it impossible to realize the full extent of the misery which I endured during the days spent upon the hulk (V, 157).

It is the presence of this strong imaginative element that has led critics to read the tale not for its surface value as a sea-adventure but as a powerful psychological and symbolic narrative. Baudelaire himself sees the tale not only as a "purely human" story--a story of adventure or an exciting yearn--but as a psychological rendering of the deepest fears and yearnings of its author and of readers. The French psychological critics, who have taken the cue from Baudelaire, similarly find in *Pym* a reflection of the character and mind of Poe. Patrick F. Quinn, while he does not quite agree with the psychologists, reads the narrative as a symbolic drama. He not only finds a coherent structure in the narrative in terms of certain thematic patterns and motifs that are recurrent in all of Poe's major tales, but thinks that the significant movement and direction of Pym's voyage is that of an imaginary voyage. He grants numerous mistakes and improbable events and descriptive details, but he thinks that these limitations are more than offset by the deeper imaginative content that is present in the story as a strong undercurrent. Thus Quinn says,

> If Pym's voyage is not interpreted as a voyage of the mind, then it must appear as just one more sequence of adventures at sea, suitable for the adolescent readers of Stevenson and Verne but hardly worth the attention of anyone else.[29]

Again,

> For *Arthur Gordon Pym,* which on the surface is an episodic tale of improbabilities, is fundamentally, at the submerged level of intuition, a truly *imaginary* voyage.[30]

While the psychological content of certain episodes described in the narrative might not be denied, one wonders whether it is possible to read into *Pym* the kind of profound symbolic meaning that Quinn and others have attributed to it. However, Burton R. Pollin maintains that Poe *did* regard *Pym* as his juvenile novel–for a very popular and mixed audience.[31] It is interesting to sea parallels with the work of an earlier Gothic writer, Charles Brockden Brown. Pym's experiences in the rocks remind us of Edgar Huntly's in the hilly tracks in Brown's *Edgar Huntly.*[32] The "subterranean prison"[33] of Huntly is similar to Pym's hold in the ship or the passes in the mountains wherein he undergoes intense psychological experience. In fact, the mind of the character in a novel should record a certain degree of change and development. But in *Pym* it is difficult to see any such change or development. The incidents in the narrative, in addition to their disconnectedness, evoke a certain Gothic atmosphere. Epithets like "cramped," "disquietude," "disorder," "close atmosphere," "oppressed," "gloomy," and "forced," employed by the author while describing Pym's experiences in the *Grampus*, establish the "Gothic" tone of the narrative. The incidents of the narrative do not flow from character, nor do they in any sense express it. As we go through Poe's narrative, we are reminded of Melville's *Redburn* which abounds in the imagery of disease, disaster, and death. In Melville's narrative too we have a voyage of the adolescent hero. The *Highlander* collides with another vessel as in Poe's story. The protagonist sees a dismantled, waterlogged schooner in the Irish sea, with dead men lashed to the taffrail, the victims of storm and starvation.

Despite the presence of the Gothic element, there is no suggestion anywhere in the narrative that Pym, like Captain Ahab, is out on a "psychological" exploration or even that he has embarked on a dramatic confrontation with an inner reality. Whatever the technical lapses of the narrative, Poe here attempts to exploit fully the Gothic potentialities of the sea. This is in contrast to Melville's use of the sea in *Moby-Dick*. Whereas Poe uses certain extraneous aspects of the sea insisting upon realistic detail, Melville fuses his own personal experiences as a maritime writer into his creative art. While melville's novel succeeds in integrating the realistic details, adventure, and Rabelaisian and metaphysical digressions into an architectonic whole, the loose episodes of Poe's narrative disturb a rapt absorption or enthrallment by most readers not preconceived of its allegorical meaning. In *Moby-Dick* the themes of treachery, meaning violence, and death are elevated into materials of epic and tragedy. Pym's experiences border more on the psychological (in the tradition of Brockdn Brown) than on the oneiric. This is further evident in the Gothic tales published after *Pym*, in which the develops motifs and ideas. The narrative cannot be read as a parable of regeneration either, since there is no strict pattern of deception, self-loss, death, and rebirth. Edwin Fussell calls *Pym* a "tale of Western adventure and exploration." He refers to Poe's review of Irving's Astoria, and says that Poe drew heavily on Astoria for a whole series of mishaps and perhaps even for formal elements.[34]

While Poe uses certain documents to hoax the reader by

producing an effect of verisimilitude, Melville discovers great truths latent in the historical facts and out of them he shapes a powerful cosmic drama. Hence Patrick F. Quinn's comparison of *Pym* and *Moby-Dick*[35] might be valid only to a limited extent. It is difficult to agree with Quinn's view that Pym's voyage suggests Rimbaud's symbolic voyage in the "Bateau Ivre." Julian Symons is more convincing in asserting that the strength of *Pym* "lies in the excitement and horror of the narrative. Considered as an allegory or fable of death and rebirth it is trivial, because the symbols are altogether inadequate to the theme."[36]

Pym and his companions are upon an adventure in a strange region of the earth and they see strange phenomena (like the white sea-animal and the island with its trees, rocks and resinous water and the hieroglyphic structures). John T. Irwin focuses on the relationships between writing, doubling, and an interest in hieroglyphics resulting from Jean-Francois Champollion's success in the 1820's in deciphering Egyptian hieroglyphic writing. The author attempts to cheat death by way of writing the creation of a double or dark shadow.[37]

In a recent conference on *Pym*, critics have offered new interpretations. Alexander Hammond discusses the figure of food as literary product.[38] J. Gerald Kennedy treats the figure of decomposition as suggestive of the limits of language.[39] However, in adventure tales the travellers bring back accounts of incredible and fantastic things, seen by them in the dark unexplored regions of earth. Certain other episodes of the tale like the protagonist's experiences in the ship's hold and in the mountains have a strong psychological appeal. But these episodes do not by themselves point to the operation of an overall psychological drama. There is no inner experience of the character here as in the Gothic tales. The digressions, often tediously elaborate, serve to strengthen the impression of realism.[40] As a tale of adventure, *Pym* is not as compact in its structure as Mark Twain's *Huckleberry Finn*. Like Twain's narrative, Poe's story is the account of an adolescent adventurer. Twain's work is a sustained effort to convey the message of freedom of the human spirit, but *Pym* is fragmentary, falling between the symbolic and the realistic. Despite the fact that certain elements like the hieroglyphics and the shrouded figure (with probable symbolic implications) are not properly developed and integrated into the mainstream of the narrative, *Pym* makes an interesting reading on account of its verisimilitude. The story cannot be interpreted as a journey into the interior. A typical instance of the journey into the interior is "The Fall of the House of Usher." In the character of Pym one cannot find the inexplicable subjective experience of an Usher. Pym is exposed to a series of fantastic experiences rendered with increasing intensity untill the final rushing into the cataract.

The Journal of Julius Rodman (1840) is even more fragmentary than *Pym*. According to Burton R. Pollin, it is "the unfinished story" of an expedition of 1792 up the Missouri river, compiled by Poe from many travel accounts by Zebulon Pike, Lewis and Clarke, Captain Bonneville via Irving and Alexander Mackenzie.[41] He also shows it to be exactly in the style of Poe's hoax tales, full of bonafide facts (mostly taken from Lewis & Clarke's *Jowenals*) so that the Library of Congress even closed it, for a time, as a *true* account.[42] In his "Preface," Poe says that *Julius Rodman* "embodies a relation of *the first* successful attempt to cross the gigantic barriers of that immense chain of mountains which stretches from the Polar Sea in the north, to the Isthmus of Darien in the South" (V, 257). Thus for all practical purposes this fragment is to be read as another true account. *Pym* too was listed in the London *Gentlemen's Magazine* as a narrative of a real journey. It may be profitable to compare this with *Pym* in an attempt to assess the extent of its technical success as a longer tale.

While the Gothic tales explore the human psyche with the backdrop of the mysterious chambers of darkness, the tales of adventure take the protagonist away toward the vastness of nature and into the unknown. Thus Rodman talks about his "burning love of nature and of the unknown." Like Pym, Rodman too attempts "to get, if possible, beyond the extreme bounds of civilization." If *Pym* is a voyage to the end of the ocean, *Julius Rodman* is a journey into the wilderness on land. In both the narratives, in an attempt to give the semblance of credibility and historical authenticity to the account of a journey, Poe resorts to the journal method, styling himself as editor (although only toward the end of *Pym*). Frequent references to the adventures of Lewis and Clarke[43] give *Julius Rodman* an air of veracity. Poe's story is supposed to be similar to the *Journals* of Lewis and Clarke about the Westward expansion. While presenting Rodman's journal date-wise, Poe adds commentary in order to connect the loose strands. In spite of all that, *Julius Rodman* remains a patchwork, even less interesting than *Pym*.

Whatever the drawbacks of *Julius Rodman*, it transports the reader into the Frontier, re-creating Fenimore Cooper's atmosphere of the trappers and Indians.[44] Poe's narrative abounds in descriptions of the Indians, their wars, and customs.[45] In addition, the description of the rivers and the wild animals brings out Poe's own burning love of nature. However, Poe's description is not as engaging as Cooper's account of the Prairies with their evocation of vastness, giving the reader a sense of spiritual experience.

The adventures of Rodman's party with the attacking Indians down the river constitute the action of the narrative.[46] The members of the party are quite cordial to each other, but they are mere fellow-travellers. There is no interaction of character and the resultant psychological interest: "we were all like brothers, and a dispute, of any importance, never occurred. One interest seemed to bind all: or rather we appeared to be a band of *voyageurs* without interest in view—mere travellers for pleasure" (V, 325). The personal relationship between Rodman and Thornton is referred to, but again there is no psychological interest. However, Poe attempts to sketch Rodman's character, ascribing certain traits to it:

> The peculiar character of the gentleman who was the leader and soul of the expedition, as well as its historian, has imbued what he has written with a vast deal of romantic fervor, very different from the lukewarm and statistical air which pervades most records of the kind (V, 258).

It is the instigation of the "hereditary hypochondria" that "led him to attempt the extraordinary journey." Poe does not quite succeed in striking a proper balance between character-depiction and realistic detail. In *Pym* he tries, though not successfully, to depict the character of Pym by placing him in a series of unusual adventures, but in *Julius Rodman* no meaning of characterization is evident. What finally turns out in the narrative is precisely the kind of "lukewarm and statistical air" which the author sets out to avoid. Even though Poe says that Rodman's "hereditary hypochondria" results in his "extraordinary Journey," the subsequent events do not show that incidents are determined by character or that character emerges out of the incidents. Also there is no sustained effort at depicting character: we are presented only with a few strokes by way of introducing Rodman and party.

Rodman's journal is supposed to have been extensively edited by Poe whose commentary connects the various parts of the account, giving it the semblance of unity. By means of footnotes he verifies the authenticity of the historical details presented.[47] This of course somewhat relieves the reader of the boredom of wading through innumerable commonplace details. There are occasional incidents like the confrontation of the party with the Indians, description of natural phenomena, and the prairies re-creating the Frontier scene.

Despite these purple patches, Rodman's journey is the adventure of a man with no definite objective, even though early in the narrative he talks of his "burning love...of *the unknown*" (V, 326). This "unknown" remains on the plane of physical reality and the narrative does not warrant deeper psychological or symbolic interpretation. We are, however, provided with an insight into the customs of the Indians and their relations with the Whites. There is an occasional Cooper-like situation in the confrontation of the Whites with the Indians.

While there is an attempt in *Pym* to explore the unknown by means of symbolism, whatever its success, there is no such thing in *Julius Rodman*. The character's exploration of the "unknown" remains on the plane of objective reality. And the conclusion of the narrative sounds like the matter-of-fact ending of a tale of adventure. At the most it suggests a possible continuation of misadventures. Rodman's adventures, as Poe tells the reader in the "Preface," are no doubt "entertaining," but not "unusual," as he seems to assert.[48] In this respect there is in *Pym* something more "unusual."

In spite of Poe's own preference for the shorter form, *Pym* and *Julius Rodman* are two longer narratives that meant critical scrutiny. In both the narratives, however, certain aspects—like the protagonist's adventures in *Pym* and the conflicts between the Indians and the Rodman party in *Julius Rodman*—engage the reader's attention. Episodic in structure, the narratives do not contain incidents logically related to each other. In these narratives Poe's ostensible purpose is to achieve verisimilitude. However, his attempt in *Pym* at juxtaposing physical reality with Gothic fantasy and symbolism is interesting despite the fragmentary nature of his writing. Certain parts of the narrative have fictional elements in them that find elaboration in the subsequent Gothic tales. But *Julius Rodman* is more disappointing in terms of narrative strategy. As we have observed, Poe had no time and inclination to write longer fiction or he was temperamentally not suited to write novels of novelettes.

NOTES

1. William T. Bandy says that Jules Verne acknowledged Poe's influence on him and that Verne dedicated to Poe his "Sphinx of the Ice Fields," a sequel to *The Narrative of Arthur Gordon Pym*. See Bandy's Lecture, "The Influence and Reputation of Edgar Allan Poe in Europe" at the Thirty-seventh Annual Commemoration Program of the Edgar Allan Poe Society in October 1959. (Baltimore: The Edgar Allan Poe Society, 1962) 11.

2. Burton R. Pollin, Foreword to Vol. I, *The Imaginary Voyages: The Narrative of Arthur Gordon Pym, The Unparalleled Adventure of one Hans Pfaall, The Journal of Julius Rodman, Collected Writings of Edgar Allan Poe.* xiii.
3. J. Gerald Kennedy, "The Preface as a key to the Satire in *Pym,*" *Studies in the Novel,* 5 (1937): 192, 195.
4. Lisa Gitelman, "Arthur Gordon Pym and The Novel Narrative of Edgar Allan Poe," *Nineteenth-Century Literature,* Vol. 27, No. 3 (December, 1992): 350.
5. *Letters,* I, 130.
6. Jeffrey Meyers, *Edgar Allan Poe: His Life and Legacy.* New York: Charles Scribner's Sons, 1992.
7. *Ibid.*, 96.
8. John H. Ingram, *Edgar Allan Poe: His Life, Letters, and Opinions* (London: John Hogg, Paternoster Row, 1880), I, 147-48.
9. *Letters,* II, 433.
10. For a comparison of "whiteness" in Poe's work with the "whiteness" in Melville's; see Patrick F. Quinn, *The French Face of Edgar Poe,* 213-14. Also see Edward Stone, *Voices of Despair: Four Motifs in American Literature,* 92-93.
11. *The Power of Blackness* (New York: Knopf, 1956) 26. David Hirsch discusses its origin in Jude: 13 in his article, "The Pit and the Apocalypse", *The Sewanee Review,* 76 (1968): 632-52. The phrase also appears in Carlyle's *Sartor Resortus,* a work Poe and Melville knew well. Herr Diogenes Teufelsdrockh plumps the mysterious riddles of the universe and comments: "In red streaks of unspeakable grandeur, yet also in the blackness of darkness, was Life, to my too unfurnished though unfolding itself"—*Sartor Resortus* (New York: Scribner's, 1931), I, 102.
12. Kent Ljungquist, *The Grand and the Fair: Poe's Landscape Aesthetics and Pictorial Techniques* (Potomac, Md.: Scripta Humanistica, 1984) 195-96.
13. See Burton R. Pollin *Poe, Creator of Words* (Bronxville, New York: Nicholas T. Smith, 1980) 31.
14. See *Works,* VII, 301.
15. Arthur H. Quinn, 266.
16. Charles O'Donnel, "From Earth to Ether: Poe's Flight into Space," *PMLA*, LXXVII (March, 1962) 90.
17. Edward H. Davidson, 160.
18. *Ibid.*, 159.

19. John H. Ingram, I, 148.
20. Joseph J. Moldenhauer, "Imagination and Perversity in *The Narrative of Authur Gordon Pym," Texas Studies in Literature and Language,* 13 (1971): 207; William Peden, "Prologue to a Dark Journey: The 'Opening' to Poe's *Pym,*" in *Papers on Poe: Essays in Honor of John Ward Ostrom,* ed. Richard P. Veler (Springfield, Ohio: Chantry Music Press, 1972) 89.
21. Paul John Eakin, "Poe's Sense of an Ending," *American Literature,* 45 (1973): 15-22.
22. Charles O'Donnell, "From Earth to Ether: Poe's Flight into Space", *PMLA*, 77 (1962): 87-89.
23. Todd M. Leiber, "The Apocalyptic Imagination of A. Gordon Pym," in *Endless Experiments—Essays on the Heroic Experiences in American Romanticism* (Columbus: Ohio State University Press, 1973) 188.
24. J. Gerald Kennedy, *Poe, Death, and the Life of Writing* (New Haven: Yale University Press, 1987) 172-73.
25. Kent P. Ljungquist, *The Grand and the Fair: Poe's Landscape Aesthetics and Pictorial Techniques* (Potomac, Md: Scripta Humanistica, 1984) 56-72. See also Ljungquist's "Speculative Mythology and the Titan Myth in Poe's *Pym* and Melville's *Pierre," The Sphinx*, 4 (1985): 250-57.
26. Marie Bonaparte, *The Life and Works of Edgar Allan Poe: A Psychoanalytic Interpretation,* trans. John Rodker. London: Imago, 1949) 350-51; Leslie Fiedler, *Love and Death in the American Novel* (1960; rpt. New York: Stein and Day, 1975) 394-400.
27. John T. Irwin, *American Hieroglyphics: The Symbol of the Egyptian Hierogyphics in the American Renaissance.* (New Haven: Yale University Press, 1980) 205-35.
28. See Patrick F. Quinn, 169-215.
29. *Ibid.,* 201-202.
30. *Ibid.,* 204.
31. See Burton R. Pollin, "Introduction," to *Pym, Collected Works,* Vol. I.
32. Charles Brockden Brown, *Edgar Huntly* (New York: The Macmillan Company, 1928) 105.
33. *Ibid.*, 221.
34. Edwin Fussell, *Frontier: American Literature and the American West* (Princeton: Princeton University Press, 1965) 150.
35. Patrick F. Quinn, 205-14.
36. Julian Symons, *The Tell-Tale Heart: The Life and Works of Edgar Allan Poe.* (London: Faber and Faber, 1978) 219.

37. See John T. Irwin, *American Hieroglyphics: The Symbol of the Egyptian Hieroglyphics in the American Renaissance.* (New Haven: Yale University Press, 1980) 64-235.
38. Alexander Hammond, "Consumption, Exchange and the Literary Marketplace: From the Folio Club Tales of *Pym," Poe's Pym: Critical Explorations*, ed. Richard Kopley. (Durham: Duke University Press, 1992)153-66.
39. J. Gerald Kennedy, "*Pym* Pourri: Decomposing the Textual Body," *Ibid.,* 167-174.
40. The interest of the *Narrative* for its adventure and verisimilitude is evident from the fact that it influenced adventure story writers like Jules Verne. See William T. Bandy.
41. Burton R. Pollin, *Discoveries in Poe* (Notre Dame: University of Notre Dame Press, 1970) 154.
42. See Pollin's Introduction and Commentaries on *Julius Rodmen in Collected Writings,* Vol. I.
43. See *Works,* V, 328n and 342n.
44. Edwin Fussell makes an interesting study of Poe's knowledge of the literature of the West and refers to the Western element in *Arthur Gordon Pym* and *Julius Rodman.* See Edwin Fussell, 149-62.
45. See *Works*, V, 321.
46. See *Works*, V, 148-49.
47. See *Works*, V, 328, 342.
48. *Works*, V, 258.

8

CONCLUSION

In order to make a judicious estimate of Poe as a tale-writer it is essential to keep in mind what he says in his review of Hawthorne's *Twice-Told Tales* concerning "a vast variety of modes." I have scrutinized Poe's critical principles and analyzed the tales in the light of these principles. The essence of Poe's meaning as a writer emerges from a study of the craft of his tales grouped into categories suggested by Poe himself. The "vast variety of modes" of Poe's tales are geared toward producing a variety of effects on the reader's mind, in his Gothic, Ratiocinative, Comic, and Visionary tales. It is difficult to evaluate the variety of Poe's tales if the critic adopts unitary concepts. Poe scholarship during the past two decades has been largely concerned with studying the tales from the Poetic, Romantic, or the Symbolistic points of view. Critics have been particularly fond of seeing the kind of unity sought by Poe in *Eureka* in the tales and poems. Robert D., Jacobs has argued that Poe was writing in nineteenth-century America under the influence of the Scottish Commonsense philosophers. Even though Poe was writing in the Romantic Age employing certain romantic themes and motifs borrowed extensively from contemporary periodicals, the empirical attitude usually, he days, determines his craft as a tale-writer. I have attempted to bring out the essential drama of his tales arising out of the empirical and the romantic, the objective and the subjective. The "subjectivity" in Poe's tales is not his own but the character's. Such an approach to the dramatic element in Poe is somewhat different from N. Bryllion Fagin's, according to which, Poe's "own face and mood haunt his creation."[1] Poe's emphasis on a carefully planned effect by means of a manipulation of the reader's response establishes the rhetorical nature of his writing. In the particular emphasis laid on effect and the causal connection of incidents, his theory and practice come closer to the dramatic than to the poetic or the symbolistic. Symbolism in tales like "The Fall of the House of Usher" and "The Masque of the Red Death," instead of creating poetic vagueness, contributes to dramatic effect.

As William Charvat has stated, Poe had no tradition of American short-story writing before him. It was Poe who gave a definite shape to the short story in theory as well as in practice. The great variety of modes of tale-writing is evident both in his theory and practice. No other American writer of the nineteenth century, except perhaps Henry James, has had a clearer conception of his aims and has striven to realize them in his own writing with a more conscious artistry.

Poe has given a somewhat detailed theory concerning the Gothic and the Ratiocinative tales, but speaks relatively less about the Comic tale and the Landscape sketch. The Gothic tales are poe's experiments in varied point of view, openings and endings, and atmosphere. Even though he says that in a tale no character development is possible, he has written tales like "Ligeia" which are primarily tales of character. In tales like "the Black Cat" and "The Tell-Tale Heart" he records changes in the characters. These changes are dramatic in significance. This drama, of course, is less effective than the drama in tales like "The Pit and the Pendulum" and "The Cask of Amontillado." In "The Fall of the House of Usher" and "A Descent into the Maelstrom" reason and irrational fear contribute to the tension of the tales.

Poe's concern for reason as the governing principle in both ciritcism and creation is well known. Even while dealing with irrational characters in the Gothic tales he seems to be in search of a sense of order in the midst of chaos. This sense of the rational order finds its fullest exemplification in his tales of mystery and ratio cinastion. "The Man That Was Used UP," ridiculing the merely mechanical in human life, shows Poe's comic sense as close to the bergsonian. Even the poetic and beautiful atmosphere of the Landscape Sketches is imbued with the sense of order. These tales embody Poe's idea of the poetic and the beautiful as defined in "The Poetic Principle." Here the sense of the beautiful is different from the beautiful in the Gothic tales that critics have so much over emphasized.

In his letter of November 2, 1844 to Charrles Anton, Poe says that a great number of his tales "might be termed Phantasy Pieces." Fantasy is present in different forms in different types of Poe's tales like the Gothic, the Grotesque, the Ratiocinative, and the Visionary and the Beautiful. However, in all these tales fantasy is juxtaposed with the actual. In trying writing. The tension between the fantastic and the realistic in tales like "A Descent into the Maelstrom" and "William Wilson" and is different from what happens in lighter pieces like "The Balloon Hoax" and "Hans Pfall" which also employ a sort of fantasy coupled with verisimilitude.

Poe's skill as a tale-writer consists in treating the same material for both serious and comic purposes. Even the methods of tale-writing based on his reading of the magazines like Blackwood's have been employed for both serious and comic effects. Such a manipulation of his materials shows the writer's skill as craftsman. As T.O. Mabbott has observed, Poe "has too carelessly been called a hoaxer in some tales when he was using selected materials with an artist's design for effect."[2] Daniel Hoffman, in his interesting study of Poe, treats his work in a somewhat light-hearted vein, seeing "Hoaxie-Poe" even in his serious tales.[3] But hoax, as Poe himself says in his letter to Arch Ramsay of Scotland, is intended by him deliberately only in certain pieces like "M. Valdemar's Case," "Von Kempelen and His Discovery," and "The balloon Hoax" for comic purposes.

Poe as a tale-writer makes conscious efforts to put his

critical principles into practice. While he succeeds in his objective in some tales, in some his performance is faulty. There are sometimes technical lapses resulting from an imperfect application of his own theory. These weaknesses are discernible in both the major and the minor tales. As I have tried to prove in the second chapter, some of the minor tales of the Gothic are dismal failures. Even in a major tale like "Ligeia," Poe is not entirely convincing in the management of his effect. However, where he achieves success–and his successes out number his failures–he does so with absolute calculation. A much-neglected tale like "'Thou Art the Man'" shows the author as a pioneer in presenting an amateur detective engaged in a dramatic hunt for the criminal. A tale like "William Wilson" is unique in striking a balance between fantasy and realism. In comic tales like "The Balloon Hoax," "Dr. Tar and Prof. Fether," "Von Kempelen and His Discovery," and "The Man That Was used Up," Poe is very realistic, commenting directly on topics of contemporary importance.

Poe admits that it is possible to write longer narratives of interest. While in *Pym* the author tries to establish character and incident in terms of symbol, in *Julius Rodman* he does not make even that effort. On the whole, both are essentially fragmentary in nature. However, due to his preoccupation with tale-writing and his correction that a proper effect can he produced on the reader only in a composition that can be read in a single sitting, Poe is not driously serious about writing the longer narrative.

NOTES

1. N. Bryllion Fagin, "Preface," *The Histrionic Mr. Poe* (Baltimore: The Johns Hopkins Press, 1949) x.
2. T.O. Mabbott.
3. Daniel Haffman.

BIBLIOGRAPHY

I. POE'S WORKS

Alterton, Margaret, and Craig, Hardin, eds. *Edgar Allan Poe: Representative Selections*. New York: American Book Company, 1935.

Auden, W.H. ed. *Edgar Allan Poe: Selected Prose and Poetry*. New York: Rinehart and Co., Inc., 1950.

Davidson, Edward H., ed. *Selected Writings of Edgar Allan Poe*. Riverside Edition, New York, 1956.

Harrison, James A. *The Complete Works of Edgar Allan Poe*. (Virginia Edition) 17 Vols. New York: T.Y. Crowell and Co., 1902. rpt. New York: AMS Press, Inc., 1965.

Mabbott, T.O. ed. *Collected Works of Edgar Allan Poe*. Cambridge, Mass: The Belknap Press of Harvard University Press, 1978. 3 Vols.

Ostrom, John W. ed. *The Letters of Edgar Allan Poe*. New York: Gordian Press, Inc., 1966. 2 Vols.

Pollin, Burton R. ed. *Collected Writings of Edgar Allan Poe: The Imaginary Voyages: The Narrative of Arthur Gordon Pym, The Unparalleled Adventure of one Hanspfaall, The Journal of Julius Rodman*. Boston: Twayne Publishers, 1981.

___________. *Edgar Allan Poe: Writings in the Broadway Journal, Non-Fictional Prose, Part I, Text*. New York: Gordian Press.

___________. *Edgar Allan Poe: Writings in the Broadway Journal, Non-Fictional Prose, Part II, Text*. The Annotations. New York: Gordian Press, 1986.

Quinn, Arthur H. and O'Neill, Edward H., eds. *The Complete*

Poems and Stories of Edgar Allan Poe. New York: Alfred A. Knopf, 1946. 2 Vols. rpt. New York: Alfred A. Knopf, 1971.

Quinn, Patrick F. ed. *Edgar Allan Poe: Poetry and Tales.* New York: The Library of America, 1984.

Stedman, Edmund C., and Woodberry, George E., eds. *The Works of Edgar Allan Poe*. London: Lawrence and Bullen, 1895, 10 Vols. rpt. New York: Charles Scribner's Sons, 1914.

The Complete Tales and Poems of Edgar Allan Poe. New York: Modern Library, 1938.

Thompson, G.R. ed. *Edgar Allan Poe: Essays and Reviews.* New York: Library of America, 1984.

II. BIBLIOGRAPHIES

Benton, Richard P. "Current Bibliography on Edgar Allan Poe," *The Emerson Society Quarterly*, 47 (II Quarter, 1967), 84-87.

Dameron, J. Lasley, and Stagg, Louis C. *An Index to Poe's Critical Vocabulary*. Hartford, Conn: Transcendental Books, 1966.

Dameron, J. Lasley, and Cauthen, Irby B. *Edgar Allan Poe: A Bibliography.* Charlottesville: University of Virginia Press, 1974.

Frank, Frederick S. "Poe's Gothicism: An Analytic Bibliography," *Sphinx*, 4[4(16)], 1985, 277-301.

Fisher, Benjamin Franklin. "Poe," *American Literary Scholarship: An Annual, 1988.* Durham, N C: Duke University Press, 1990.

Hyneman, Ester F. *Edgar Allan Poe: Annotated Bibliography of Criticism on Poe, 1827-1972 and His Contemporary Reputation*. Boston: G.K. Hill and Co., 1972.

Moldenhauer, J.J. "Descriptive Catalog of Edgar Allan Poe's Manuscripts in the Humanities Research Center Library of the University of Texas at Austin," *Texas Quarterly,* XVI, v-xxi (Autumn, 1973), 1-89. (Subsequently issued by University of Texas Press in 1973 as a hardbound edition).

Dameron, J. Lasley, *et al. Current Poe Bibliography. Poe Studies,* Vol. 16, No. 2 (December 1983): 34-37.

Dameron, J. Lasley. *Edgar Allan Poe: A Bibliography of Criticism, 1827-1967.* Charlottesville: University Press of Virginia, 1974.

Kopley, Richard. "Fugitive Poe References: A Bibliography," *Poe Studies*, 18, i (June 1985): 9-12.

Lawson, Lewis A. "Poe and the Grotesque: A Bibliography," *Poe Newsletter,* I (April 1968): 9-10.

Quinn, Arthur H. and Hart, Richard H. ed. *Edgar Allan Poe: Letters and Documents in the Enoch Pratt Free Library.* New York: Scholars' Facsimiles and Reprints, 1941.

III, POE CRITICISM AND BIOGRAPHY

Allen, Harvey. Israfel: *The Life and Times of Edgar Allan Poe*. New York: Holt, Rinehart and Winston, 1926, 2 Vols.

Allen, Michael. *Poe and the British Magazine Tradition*. New York: Oxford University Press, 1969.

Alterton, Margaret. "Origins of Poe's Critical Theory," *University of Lowa Studies,* II, No. 3 (April 1925).

Andriono, Joseph. "Archetypal Projection in 'Ligeia': A Post-Jungian Reader," *Poe Studies*, 19, ii (Dec. 1986): 27-31.

__________. *Our Ladies of Darkness: Feminine Daemonology in Male Gothic Fiction*. University Park: The Pennsylvania State University Press, 1993.

Astrov, Vladimir. "Dostoyesky on Edgar Allan Poe," *American Literature,* XIV, March 1942: 70-74.

Auerbach, Jonathan. "Poe's Other Double: The Reader in Fiction," *Criticism*, XXIV, iv (Fall, 1982): 341-61.

__________. *The Romance of Failure: First Person Fictions of Poe, Hawthorne, and James*. New York: Oxford University Press, 1989.

Bailey, J.O. "What happens in 'The Fall of the House of Usher'," *American Literature,* 35 (January 1964): 445-66.

Baldwin, Summerfield. "The Aesthetic Theory of Edgar Allan Poe," *The Sewanee Review*, XXVII (April 1918): 210-21.

Barthes, Roland. "Textual Analysis of a Tale of Poe," in *On Signs*, ed. Marshall Blonsky. (Baltimore: Johns Hopkins University Press, 1985): 84-97.

Barton Levi St. Armand. "The 'Mysteries' of Edgar Poe: The Quest for a Monomyth in Gothic Literature," *The Gothic Imagination: Essays in Dark Romanticism,* ed. G.R. Thompson. (Pullman: Washington State University Press, 1974): 65-93.

Basler, Roy P. "Poe's Ligeia," *PMLA*, LXXVII (December 1962): 675.

Baskett, Sam S. "A Damsel with a Dulcimer: An Interpretation of Poe's 'Eleonora'," *Modern Language Notes,* LXXIII (May 1958): 332-38.

Beaver, Harold. ed. *The Science Fiction of Edgar Allan Poe* (Harmondsworth: Penguin Books Ltd., 1976): vii-xxi.

Bell, Michael Davitt. *The Development of American Romance: The Sacrifice of Relation.* Chicago: The University of Chicago Press, 1981.

Bennett, Maurice J. "Edgar Allan Poe and the Literary Tradition of Lunar Speculation," *Science-Fiction Studies,* Vol. 10, Part 2 (July 1983): 137-47.

Benton, Richard P. "The Mystery of Marie Roget'—A Defense," *Studies in Short Fiction*, VI, ii (Winter 1969): 144-51.

Bittner, William. *Poe: A Biography*. Boston: Little, Brown, 1962.

Blair, Walter. "Poe's Conception of Incident and Tone in the Tale," *Modern Philology*, XLI (May 1944): 228-40.

Bloom, Clive. *Reading Poe Reading Freud: The Romantic Imagination in Crisis.* New York: St. Martin's Press, 1988.

Bloom, Harold. ed. *Edgar Allan Poe.* New York: Chelsea House Publishers, 1987.

Bieganowski, Ronald. "The Self-consuming Narrator in Poe's 'Ligeia' and 'Usher'," *American Literature*, Vol. 60, No. 2 (May 1988): 175-87.

Blythe, Hal and Sweet, Charlie. "The Reader as Poe's Ultimate Dupe in 'The Purloined Letter," *Studies in Short Fiction,* Vol. 26, No. 3 (Summer 1989): 311-16.

Buranelli, Vincent. *Edgar Allan Poe.* New York: Twayne Publishers, 1961.

Burke, Kenneth. "The Principle of Composition," *Poetry*, XCIX, No. 1 (October 1961): 46-53.

Campbell, Killis. *The Mind of Poe and Other Studies.* Cambridge, Mass.: Harvard University Press, 1933.

Carlson, Eric W. ed. *The Recognition of Edgar Allan Poe.* Ann Arbor: The University of Michigan Press, 1966.

__________. ed. *Critical Essays on Edgar Allan Poe.* Boston, Mass.: G. K. Hall and Co., 1987.

Cassuto, Leonardo. "The Coy Reaper: Unmasque-ing the Red Death," *Studies in Short Fiction*, Vol. 25, iii (Summer 1988): 317-20.

Cecil, L. Moffitt. "Poe's Arabesque," *Comparative Literature*, XVIII (1966): 55-70.

Chai, Leon. *The Romantic Foundations of the American Renaissance.* Ithaca: Cornel University Press, 1987.

Chiari, Joseph. *Symbolism from Poe to Mallarme: The Growth of a Myth.* London: Rockliff, 1956.

Clemen, John. "Irresistible Impulses: Edgar Allan Poe and the insanity Defense," *American Literature.* Vol. 63, No. 4, (December 1991): 623-40.

Cobb, Palmer. *The Influence of Ernest theodore Hoffman on the Tales of Edgar Allan Poe.* Chapel Hill: University of North Carolina Press, 1908.

Clough, Wilson O. "The use of color words by edgar Allan Poe," *PMLA*, XV (March 1930): 598-613.

Clifton, Michael. "Down Hecate's Chain: Infernal inspiration in three of Poe's tales," *Nineteenth-Century Literature,* 41, ii (September 1986): 217-27.

Cosken, Robert. "'William Wilson' and the disintegration of self," *Studies in Short Fiction*, 12, ii (Spring 1975): 155.

Crisman, William. "'Mere Household Events' in Poe's 'The Black Cat," *Studies in American Fiction.* Vol. 12, i (Spring 1984): 87-90.

Daniel, Robert. "Poe's detective God," *Furioso,* VI (Summer 1951), 49.

Davidson, Edward H. *Poe: A Critical Study.* Cambridge, Mass: the Belknap Press of Harvard University Press, 1957.

Dauber, Kenneth. "The problem of Poe," *The Georgia Review,* XXXII, iii (Fall 1978): 645-57.

Dameron, J. Lasley. "Poe's concept of Truth," *Mississippi Quarterly*, XLIII, i (Winter 1989-90): 11-21.

Dayan, Joan. "The identity of Berenice, Poe's idol of the mind," *Studies in Romanticism*, Vol. 23, No. 4 (Winter 1984): 491-513.

__________. *Fables of Mind: An Inquiry into Poe's Fiction.* New York: Oxford University Press, 1987.

Eakin, Paul John. "Poe's sense of an ending," *American Literature*, XLV, i (March 1973): 1-22.

Egan, Jr., Kenneth V. "Descent to an ascent: Poe's use of perspective in 'A Descent into the Maelstrom'," *Studies in Short Fiction*, XIX, ii (Spring 1982): 157-62.

Eddings, Dennis W. ed. *The Naiad Voice: Essays on Poe's Satiric Hoaxing.* Port Washington, N.Y. : Associated Faculty Press, 1983.

__________. "Poe, Dupin, and the Reader," *University of Mississippi Studies in English*, 3 (1982): 128-35.

Elmer, Schenkel. "Disease and Vision: Perspectives on Poe's 'The Sphinx'," *Studies in American Fiction*, Vol. 13, No. 1 (Spring 1985): 97-102.

Engel, Leonard W. "Identity and Enclosure in Edgar Allan Poe's 'William Wilson'," *College Language Association Journal,* 29, i (September 1985): 91-99.

Eliot, T.S. "From Poe to Valery," *The Hudson Review,* II (Autumn, 1949): 327-42.

Fagin, N.Bryllion. *The Histrionic Mr. Poe.* Baltimore: The Johns Hopkins University Press, 1949.

Finholt, Richard D. "The Vision at the brink of the Abyss: 'A Descent into the Maelstrom' in the light of Poe's Cosmology." *The Georgia Review*, XXVIII, iii (Fall 1973): 356-66.

Fisher IV, Benjamin Franklin. "Poe's 'Metzengerstein': Not a

Hoax", *American Literature*, XLII, IV (January 1971): 487-94.

__________. *Poe at Work: Seven Textual Studies.* Baltimore: The Edgar Allan Poe Society, 1978.

__________. ed. *Poe and His Times: The Artist and his Milieu*. Baltimore: The Edgar Allan Poe Society, Inc. 1990.

__________. "Devils and Devilishness in Comic Yarns of the Old Southwest," *ESQ*, Vol. 36, No. 1 (I Quarter 1990), 39-60. Vol. 46, iv (Winter 1980): 1-26.

Foster, Dennis A. "Re-Poe Man: A Problem of Pleasure," *Arizona Quarterly*, Vol. 46, iv (Winter 1980): 1-26.

Gargano, James W. "The Question of Poe' Narrators," *College English*, XXV, iii (December 1963): 177-81.

__________. "The Theme of time in 'The Tell-Tale Heart'," *Studies in Short Fiction*, V, 1968: 378-82.

Garrison, Joseph M. "The Function of Terror in the Work of Edgar Allan Poe," *American Quarterly,* XVIII, ii (Summer 1966): 136-50.

__________. "The Irony of 'Ligeia'," *New Approaches to Poe: A Symposium*, ed. Richard P. Benton. Hartford: Transcendental Books, 1970.

Gitelman, Lisa. "Arthur Gordon Pym and the Novel Narrative of Edgar Allan Poe," *Nineteenth-Century Literature*, Vol.27, No.3, (December 1992): 349-61.

Goldhurst, William. "The Self-Reflective Fiction by Poe: Three Tales," *Modern Language Studies*, 16, iii (Summer 1986): 4-14.

Greenlaw, Edwin. "Poe in the light of literary history," *The Johns Hopkins Alumni Magazine*, XVIII, iv (June 1930): 273-90.

Griffith, Clark. "Poe's 'Ligeia' and the English Romantics," *University of Toronto Quarterly*, XXIV (October 1954): 8-25.

Gruesser, John C. "'Ligeia' and Orientalism," *Studies in Short Fiction*, Vol. 26, No. 2 (Spring 1989): 145-49.

Halliburton, David. *Edgar Allan Poe: A Phenomenological View*. Princeton: Princeton University Press, 1973.

Harrowitz, Nancy, "The body of detective model: Charles S. Peirce and Edgar Allan Poe," in *The Sign of Three: Dupin, Holmes, Peirce*, ed. Umberto Eco and Thomas A. Sebcok. (Bloomington: Indiana University Press, 1983) 179-97.

Harvey, Kenneth A. "Critical Provincialism: Poe's Poetic principle in Antebellum context," *American Quarterly*, Vol. 39, No. 3 (Fall 1987), 341-54.

Hellar, Terry. "Poe's 'Ligeia' and the pleasures of terror," *Gothic*, 2 (1980), 39-49.

Hirsch, David H. "The Pit and the Apocalypse," *The Sewanee Review*, LXXV, iv (Autumn 1986): 632-52.

Hoffman, Daniel. *Poe Poe Poe Poe Poe Poe Poe*. Garden City, N. Y.: Doubleday and Company, Inc., 1972.

Howard, Leon. "Artificial Sensitivity and Artful Rationality: Basic Elements in the creative imagination of Edgar Allan Poe," *Poe Studies*, Vol. 20, i (June 1987). 1-9.

Howes, Craig. "Burke, Poe, and 'Usher': The Sublime and Rising Woman," *ESQ: A Journal of the American Renaissance*, 31 (1985): 173-89.

Hubbs, Valentine C. "The Struggle of the Wills in Poe's 'William Wilson'," *Studies in American Fiction*, Vol. II, No. 1 (Spring 1983): 73-79.

Hubert, Thomas. "The Southern Element in Poe's Fiction," *The Georgia Review*, XXVIII, ii (Summer 1974): 200-11.

Hudson, Ruth L. "Poe and Disraeli," *American Literature,* VIII (January 1937): 402-416.

Hungerford, E. "Poe and Phrenology," *American Literature*, II (November 1930): 209-31.

Irwin, John T. *The Mystery to a Solution: Poe, Borges, and the Analytic Detective Story.* Baltimore: The Johns Hopkins University Press, 1994.

Jay, Gregory S. "Poe: Writing and the Unconscious," in *The American Renaissance : New Dimensions*, ed. Garvin,

Harry R. (Lewisburg: Bucknell University Press, 1983) 144-69.

Jacobs, Robert D. *Poe: Journalist & Critic*. Baton Rouge: Louisiana State University Press, 1969.

__________. "Poe's Earthly Paradise," *American Quarterly*, XII, iii (Fall 1960): 404-13.

Johansen, Ib. "The Madness of the Text: Deconstruction of Narrative Logic in 'Usher,' 'Berenice,' and 'Dr.Tarr and Prof. Fether'," *Poe Studies*, Vol. 22, No. 1, (June 1989): 1-9.

Johnson, Barbara. "The Frame of Reference: Poe, Lacan, Derrida," *The Critical Difference: Essays in the Contemporary Rhetoric of Reading* (Baltimore: Johns Hopkins University Press, 1980) 110-54.

Kehler, Joel R. "New light on the genesis and progress of Poe's Landscape Fiction," *American Literature*, 47, ii (May 1975): 173-83.

Keller, Mark. "Dupin in the 'Rue Morgue': Another form of madness," *The Arizona Quarterly*, 33, No. 3 (Autumn 1977): 249-55.

Kelly, George. "Poe's Theory of Beauty," *American Literature*, XXVII (January 1956): 521-36.

__________. "Poe's Theory of Unity," *Philological Quarterly*, XXXVII, i (January 1958): 34-44.

Kennedy, J. Gerald. *Poe, Death, and the Life of Writing*. New Haven: Yale University Press, 1987.

__________. "The Limits of Reason; Poe's Deluded Detectives," *American Literature*, No. 47, No. 2 (May 1975): 184-96.

Kempton, Daniel. "The Gold/Goole/Ghoul Bug," *ESQ*, I Quarter 1987, 33 (1): 1-19.

Knapp, Bettina L. *edgar Allan Poe*. New York: F Unger Pub. Co., 1984.

Klein, Kathleen Gregory and Keller, Joseph. "Deductive Detective Fiction: the Self-Destructive Genre," *Genre*, XXX, ii (Summer 1986): 155-72.

Kopley, Richard, ed, *Poe's Pym: Critical Explorations*. Durham: Duke University Press, 1992.

Ketterer, David. "Devious Voyage: the Singular *Narrative of A. Gordon Pym*", *The American Transcendental Quarterly,* No. 37, (Winter 1978): 21-34.

__________. *The Rationale of Deception in Poe.* Baton Rouge: Louisiana State University Press, 1979.

Krutch, Joseph W. *Edgar Allan Poe: A Study in Genius.* New York: Alfred A Knopf, 1926.

Levin, Harry. *The Power of Blackness: Hawthorne, Poe and Melville.* London: Faber and Faber, 1958.

Levine, Stuart. *Edgar Poe: Seer and Craftsman.* Deland: Everett/Edwards, Inc. 1972.

__________. "Poe's *Julius Rodman:* Judaism, Plagiarism, and the Wild West," *Midwest Quarterly*, I, iii, (Spring 1960): 245-59.

Lind, Sidney E. "Poe and Mesmerism," *PMLA*, LXII, (December 1947): 1077-94.

Lawes, Rochie. "The dimensions of terror: Mathematical imagery in 'The Pit and the Pendulum'," *Poe Studies*, Vol. 16, No. 1, (June 1983): 5-7.

Lacan, Jacques. "Seminar on 'The Purloined Letter'," in *French Freud: Structural Studies in Psychoanalysis.* Millwood, N.Y.: Kraus Reprint, 1984, (Yale French Studies, No. 48).

Lawler, James. "Daemons of the Intellect: the symbolists and Poe," *Critical Inquiry*, Vol. 14, No. 1 (Autumn, 1987): 95-110.

Lawson, Lewis A. "Poe's conception of the Grotesque," *Mississippi Quarterly*, XIX (Fall 1966): 220-25.

Lee, A. Robert, ed. *Edgar Allan Poe: the Design of Order.* Totowa, N J: Barnes & Noble, 1987.

Liebman, Sheldon W. "Poe's Tales and His Theory of the Poetic Experience," *Studies in Short Fiction*, VII, iv (Fall 1970): 582-96.

Ljungquist, Kent. *The Grand and the Fair: Poe's Landscape Aesthetics and Pictorial Techniques.* Potomac, Md: Scripta Humanistica, 1984.

Lowndes, Robert A.W. "The contributions of Edgar Allan Poe," *The Mystery Writer's Art,* ed. Francis M. Nevine. (Bowling Green: Bowling Green University Popular Press, 1970) 1-36.

Lubbell, Albert J. "Poe and A.W. Schlegel," *Journal of English and Germanic Philology*, LII (1953): 1-12.

Lynen, John F. *The Design of the Present: Essays on Time and Form in American Literature.* New Haven: Yale University Press, 1969.

Mabbott, T.O. "On Poe's Tales of the Folio Club," *The Sewanee Review,* XXXVI (April 1928): 171-76.

__________. "Poe's 'The Man that was Used up," *The Explicator,* XXV (1967), Item 70.

__________. "Poe's 'The Cask of Amontillado'," *The Explicator*, XXV (1966), Item 30.

MacAndrew, Elizabeth. *The Gothic Tradition in Fiction*. (New York: Columbia University Press, 1979) 191-202.

Malloy, Jeanne M. "Spocalyptic Imagery and the Fragmentation of the psyche: 'The Pit and the Pendulum'," *Nineteenth-Century Literature*, Vol. 46, No. 1 (June 1991): 82-95.

Marks, Emerson R. "Poe as a literary theorist: A Reappraisal," *American Literature*, XXXIII (November 1961): 296-306.

Martin, Terrence. "The Imagination at play: Edgar Allan Poe," *Kenyon Review*, XXVII (1966): 194-209.

May, Charles E. *Edgar Allan Poe: A Study of the Short Fiction.* Boston: Twayne Publishers, 1991.

McElderry, B.R. "T.s. Eliot on Poe," *Poe Newsletter*, II, ii (April 1969): 32-33.

Mead, Joan Tyler. "Poe's 'The Man that was Used up': Another Bugaboo Campaign," *Studies in Short Fiction*, Vol. 23, No. iii (Summer 1986): 281-86.

Meyers, Jeffrey. *Edgar Allan Poe: His Life and Legacy.* New York: Charles Scribner's Sons, 1992.

Michelson, Bruch F. "Richard Wilbur: The Quarrel with Poe," *The southern Review*, XIV, ii (April 1978): 245-61.

Miller, Perry. *The Raven and the Whale: the war of words and wits in the era of Poe and Melville*. New york: Harcourt, 1956.

Moldenhauer, Joseph J. "Murder as a Fine Art: Basic Connections between Poe's Aesthetics, Psychology, and Moral Vision," *PMLA*, LXXXIII (May 1968): 284-97.

__________. "Imagination and Perversity in *The Narrative of Arthur Gordon Pym," Texas Studies in Language and Literature*, XIII (1970): 267-80.

Mooney, Stephen LeRoy. "Poe's Grand Design: A study of theme and unity in the tales," *Dissertation of University of Tennessee*, 1960.

__________. "The Comic in Poe's Fiction," *American Literature*, XXXII (January 1962): 433-44.

More, Paul Elmer. "The Origins of Hawthorne and Poe," *Shelburne* Essays, I series. New York, 1904: 51-70.

__________. "A Note on Poe's Method," *Studies in Philology*, XI (1923): 302-309.

Moffitt, Cecil L. "Poe's Arabesque," *Comparative Literature*, XVIII (1966): 55-70.

Moss, Sidney P. *Poe's Literary Battles: The Critic in the Context of his Literary Milieu,* Durham, N.C: Duke University Press, 1963.

Michael, John. "Narration and Reflection: the search for Grounds in Poe's 'The Power of Words' and 'The Domain of Arnheim'," *Arizona Quarterly*, Vol. 45, No. 3 (Autumn 1989): 1-22.

Muller, John P William J. Richardson, eds. *The Purloined Poe: Lacan, Derrida and Psychoanalytic Reading*. Baltimore: The Johns Hopkins University Press, 1988.

Nelson, Dana D. "The Haunting of White Manhood: Poe, Fraternal Ritual, and Polygenesis," *American Literature*, Vol. 69, No. 3 (Sept. 1997): 515-46.

Nettels, Elsa. "Poe and James on the Art of fiction," *Poe Studies*, 13 i (1980): 4-8.

O'Donnell, Charles. "From earth to ether: Poe's flight into space," *PMLA*, LXXVII, No. 1 (March 1962): 85-91.

Pahl, Dennis. "Poe/script: The death of the author in *The Narrative of Arthur Gordon Pym," Northwest Ohio Quarterly,* Vol. 14, No. 3 (Fall 1987): 51-60.

__________. *Architects of the Abyss. The Indeterminate Fictions of Poe, Hawthorne, and Melville.* Columbia: University of Missouri Press, 1989.

Persons, Jr., Leland S. *Aesthetic Headaches: Women and a Masculine Poetics in Poe, Melville, and Hawthorne.* (Athens: The University of Georgia Press, 1988) 19-47.

__________. "Poe's Composition of Philosophy: Reading and Wriitng 'The Raven'," *Arizona Quarterly*, Vol. 46, iii (Autumn 1990): 1-16.

Parks, Edd Winfield. *Edgar Allan Poe as Literary Critic.* Athens: University of Georgia Press, 1964.

Parkes, Henry B. "Poe, Hawthorne, Melville: An Essay in Sociological Criticism," *Partisan Review*, XVI, ii (February, 1949): 157-65.

Paul, Raymond. *Who Murdered Mary Rogers?* Englewood Cliffs, N.J: Prentice-Hall, 1971.

Peterson, Dewayne A. "Poe's Grotesque Humor: A Study of the Grotesque Effects in his Humorous Tales," Diss. Duke University, 1962.

Pollin, Burton R. "Names used for humon in Poe's fiction," *Proceedings of Names Institute* at East Texas State University, (Fall, 1972): 51-57.

__________. *Discoveries in Poe.* Notre Dame: University of Notre Dame Press, 1970.

__________. "Poe's Tale of Psyche Zenobia: A Reading for Humor and Ingenious Construction," *Ostrom Festchrift Papers on Poe* (Wittenberg, Ohio), March 1972: 92-93.

__________. *Poe, Creator of Words.* Baltimore: Enoch Pratt Free Library and the Edgar Allan Poe Society, 1974; revised and augmented ed. Broneville, N.Y. 1980.

__________. *Insights and Outlooks: Essays on Great Writers.* New York: Gordian Press, 1986.

__________. "'The Spectacles' of Poe-Sources and Significance," *American Literature* 38 (May 1965): 185-90.

Quinn, Arthur H. *Edgar Allan Poe: A critical Biography.* New York: Appleton-Century-Crofts, Inc., 1941.

Quinn, Patrick F. *Th French Face of Edgar Poe.* Carbondale: Southern Illinois University Press, 1957.

__________. "Four Views of Edgar Poe," *Jahrbuch for America Studien* V (1960): 136-46.

Ramakrishna, D. "Poe's LIGEIA," *The explicator*, 2 (October 1966), Item 19.

__________. "The Conclusion of Poe's LIGEIA," *The Emerson Society Quarterly*, II Quarter, 1967, No. 47, Pt. II: 69-70.

Rainwater, Catherine. "Poe's Landscape Tales and the Picturesque Tradition," *Southern Literary Journal,* 16, ii (Spring 1984) : 30-43.

Railton, Stephen. *Authorship and Audience: Literary Performance in the American Renaissance.* Princeton, NJ: Princeton University Press, 1991.

Regan, Robert, ed. Poe: A Collection of Critical Essays. Englewood Cliffs, NJ.: Prentice-Hall, 1967.

Rea, J. "Poe's 'The Cask of Amontallado'," *Studies in Short Fiction*, IV (1966): 57-69.

Richards, Sylvia L.F. "The Eye and the Portrait: The Fantastic in Poe, Hawthorne, and Gogol," *Studies in Short Fiction*, Vol. 20, No. 4 (Fall 1983): 307-15.

Ringe, Donald A. "Edgar Allan Poe," *American Gothic: Imagination and reason in Nineteenth-Century Fiction.* (Lexington: The University Press of Kentucky, 1982): 128-51.

Robinson, Douglas. "Trapped in the Text: 'The Pit and the Pendulum'," *Journal of the Short Story in English*, 7 (Autumn, 1986): 63-75.

__________. "Reading Poe's Novel: A Speculative Review

of *Pym* Criticism, 1950-1980," *Poe Studies*, Vol. 15, No. 2 (December 1982): 47-54.

Roth, Martin. "Poe's 'Poe's 'Three Sundays in a Week'," *Sphinx*, 4[4(16)],1985: 258-67.

__________. "Mysteries of 'The Mystery of Marie Roget," *Poe Studies*, Vol. 22, No. ii (December 1989): 27-34.

Ross, Donald H. "The Grotesque: A Speculation," *Poe Studies*, IV, I (June 1971): 11.

Robinson, E. Arthur. "Order and Sentience in 'The Fall of the House of Usher'," *PMLA*, Vol. 76. No. 1 (March 1961): 68-81.

__________. "Poe's 'The Tell-Tale Heart'," *Nineteenth-Century Fiction*, XIX (1965): 369-78.

Rocks, James e. "Conflict and Motive in 'The Cask of Amontillado'," *Poe Studies*, V, ii (December 1972): 50-51.

Ridgely, J.V. "The Continuing Puzzle of *Arthur Gordon Pym*: Some Notes and Queries," Poe *Newsletter*, III, i (June 1970): 5-6.

Roppolo, Joseph P. "Meaning and 'The Masque of the Red Death'," *Tulane Studies in English*, XVIII, 1963: 59-59.

Rouge, Bertrand. "Irony and Ventriloquism: Notes toward an interpretation of Edgar Allan Poe' 'Thou Art the Man',' *Interface: Essays on History, Myth, and Art in American Literature,* ed. Daniel Royot. (Montpellier Pubs. de la Kecherche, Univ. Paul Valery, 1985) 21-30.

Rosenzweig, Paul. "Dust within the Rock': The Phantasm of Meaning in *The Narrative of Arthur Gordon Pym," Studies in the Novel*, XIV, ii (Summer 1982): 137-51.

Ruddick, Nicholas. "The Hoax of the Red Death: Poe as Allegorist", *Sphinx*, 4[4(16)], 1985: 268-76.

Saliba, David R. "The Nightmare in Miniature: 'Ligeia'," *The American Transcendental Quarterly*, No. 40 (Fall 1978): 367-78.

__________. *A Psychology of Fear: The Nightmare Formula of Edgar Allan Poe*. Lanham, Md: University Press of America, 1980.

Scharnhorst, Gary. "Another Night-Sea Journey: Poe's 'Ms. Found in a Bottle'," *Studies in Short Fiction,* Vol. 22, No. 4 (Fall 1985): 203-208.

Sanford, Charles L. "Edgar Allan Poe: A Blight on the Landscape," *American Quarterly*, XX (1968): 54-66.

sinclair, David:. *Edgar Allan Poe.* Totowa, N.J: Rowman, 1977.

Smith, Horatio E. "Poe's extension of his theory of the tale," *Modern Philology*, XVI (August 1918): 195-203.

Smith, Ronald L. *Poe in the Media: Screen, songs, and Spoken Word Recordings.* New York: Garland Publishing, Inc., 1990.

Stochr, Taylor. "Unspeakable Horror in Poe," *The South Atlantic Quarterly*, 78, iii (Summer 1979): 317-32.

Stovall, Floyd. "Poe's Debt to Coleridge," *University of Texas Studies in English*, X (1930): 70-127.

__________. "Poe as a poet of idea," *University of Texas Studies in English,* XI (1931): 56-62.

__________. "The Women of Poe's Poems and Tales," *University of Texas Studies in English*, V (1925): 197-209.

__________. "The Conscious Art of Edgar Allan Poe," *College English*, XXIV vi (March 1963): 417-21.

Stewart, Kate. "The Supreme Madness: Revenge and the Bells in 'The Cask of Amontillado'," *University of Mississippi Studies in English*, V (1984-1987): 51-57.

Stone, Edward. "Usher, Poquelin, and Miss Emily: The Progress of the Southern Gothic," *The Georgia Review*, (Winter 1960): 433-43.

__________. "Poe in and out of his time," *ESQ*, XXXI (1963): 14-17.

Schroeter, James. "Poe's 'Ligeia'," *PMLA*, LXXVII (December 1962): 675.

Swanson, Donald R. "Poe's 'Conqueror Worm'," *The Explicator*, XIX, No. 7, Item 52.

Sweeney, Gerald M. "Beauty and Truth: Poe's 'A descent

into the Maelstrom'," *Poe Studies,* VI, i (June 1973): 22-25.

Sippel, Erich W. "Bolting the Whole shebang Together: Poe's predicament," *Criticism*, XV, iv (Fall 1973): 289-308.

Snell, George. "First of the New critics," *Quarterly Review of Literature*, II (1946): 333-40.

Stroupe, John H. "Poe's imaginary voyage: Pym as hero," *Studies in Short Fiction*, IV (1967): 315-21.

Steele, Jeffrey. *The Representtion of the self in the American Renaissance*. Chapel Hill: University of North Carolina Press, 1987.

Symons, Julian. *The Tell-Tale Heart: The Life and Works of Edgar Allan Poe*. London: Faber & Faber, 1978.

Sutherland, Judith L. *Te Problematic Fictions of Poe, James, and Hawthorne*. Columbia: University of Missouri Press, 1984.

Tate, Allan. *The Man of Letters in the Modern World: Selected Essays*, 1928-1955. 1936; rpt. New York: Meridian Books, 1955.

__________. *The Forlorn Demon*. Chicago: Regnery, 1953.

__________. "Three Commentaries: Poe, James, and Joyce," *The Sewanee Review*, LVIII (1950): 1-15.

Thompson, G.R. " 'Proper Evidences of Greatness': American Gothic and the Interpretation of 'Ligeia'," *The Emerson Society Quarterly*, XVIII (1972): 30-49.

__________. "Unity, death, and Nothingness—Poe's 'Romantic Escapism'," LXXXV (1970): 297-300.

__________. "The face in the pool: Reflections on the Doppelganger motif in 'The Fall of the House of Usher'," *Poe Studies*, V, i (June 1972): 16-20.

__________. *Poe's Fiction: romantic Irony in the Gothic Tales*. Madison: The University of Wisconsin Press, 1973.

__________. "Literary Politics and the 'Legitimate Sphere': Poe; Hawthorne, and the 'Tale Proper'," *Nineteenth-*

Century Literature, Vol. 49, No. 2 (September 1994): 167-95.

Thomas, Dwight and Jackson, David K. *The Poe Log: A Documentary Life of Edgar Allan Poe, 1809-1949*. Boston: G.K. Hall, 1987.

Turner, H.a. "A Note on Poe's *Julius Rodman," University of Texas Studies in English* (July 1930): 147-51.

Taylor, Wlter F. "Israfel in Motley," *The Sewanee Review,* XLII (July-September 1934): 330-40.

Trieber, J. Marshall. "The Scornful Grin: A Study of Poesque Homor," *Poe Studies*, IV, ii (December 1971): 32-34.

Varner, Cornelia. "Notes on Poe's use of Contemporary Materials in certain of his stories," *The Journal of English and Germanic Philology,* XXXII (January 1933): 77-80.

Vitanza, Victor J. "'The Question of Poe's Narrators': Perverseness Considered Once Again," *The american Transcendental Quarterly*, No. 38 (Spring 1978): 137-50.

Voller, Jack G. "The Power of Terror: Burke and Kant in the House of Usher'," *Poe Studies,* Vol. 21, No. 2 (December 1988): 27-35.

Voloshin, Beverly R. "The Explanation in 'The Fall of the House of Usher'," *Studies in Short Fiction*, 23, iv (Fall 1986): 419-28.

__________. "Poe's 'The Fall of the House of Usher'," *The Explicator*, 46 (3), Spring 1988: 13-15.

Wagenknecht, Edward. *Edgar Allan Poe: The Man Behind the Legend*. New York: Oxford University Press, 1963.

Walker, I. M. ed. *Edgar Allan Poe: The Critical Heritage*. London: Rowtledge and Kegan Paul, 1986.

Ware, Tracey. "The Two Stories of 'William Wilson'," *Studies in Short Fiction*, Vol. 26, i (Winter 1989): 43-48.

weiner, Bruce I. *The Naiad Voice: Essays on Poe's Satiric Hoaxing*. Port Washington, N.Y.: Associated Faculty Press, 1983.

Witherington, Paul. "The Accomplice in 'The Tell-Tale Heart'," *Studies in Short Fiction*, Vol. 22, iv (Fall 1985): 622-32.

Williams, Michael J.S. "Poe's 'Shadow-A Parable' and the problem of Language," *American Literature*, 57.4 (December 1985): 622-32.

__________. *A World of Words: Language and Displacement in the Fiction of Edgar Allan Poe*. Durham: Duke University Press, 1988.

Wheat, Patricia H. "The Mask of Indifference in 'The Masque of the Red Death'," *Studies in Short Fiction*, XIX, i (Winter 1982): 51-56.

Whipple, William. "Poe's two-edged satiric tale," *Nineteenth-Century Fiction,* IX (September 1954): 121-33.

Wilbur, Richard. "The House of Poe" (Library of Congress Anniversary Lecture, May 4, 1959) rpt. in *The Recognition of Edgar Allan Poe*, ed. Eric W. Carlson (Ann Arbor: The University of Michigan Press, 1966) 256-77.

Weissbuch, T.N. "Edgar Allan Poe: Hoaxer in the American Tradition," *NYSHQ*, XLV (July 1961): 291-309.

Wilson, Edmund. "Poe at Home and Abroad," *The Shores of Light*. New York, 1952.

__________. "Poe as a Literary Critic," *Nation,* October 31, 1942.

Woodberry, George E. The Life of Edgar Allan Poe. 1909; rpt. New York: Biblo and Tannen, 1965. 2 Vols.

Winters, Yvor. "Edgar Allan Poe: A Crisis in the History of American Obscurantism," *American Literature*, VIII (January 1937): 379-401.

Wilt, Napier. "Poe's attitude toward his tales: A New Document," *Modern Philology*, XXV (August 1927): 101-105.

Wilson, James S. "Poe's Philosophy of Composition," *The North American Review*, CCXXIII (Dec/Feb 1926-27): 675-84.

__________. "The Devil was in It," *American Mercury*, XXV (October 1931): 215-20.

Wiletich-Brinberg, Sybil. *Poe: The Ratiopnale of the Uncanny*. New York: Peter Lang, 1988.

wimsatt, W.K. "Poe and the Mystery of Mary Rogers," *PMLA*. LVC (March, 1941): 230-48.

__________. "What Poe knew about Cryotography," *PMLA*, LVIII (1943): 754-79.

Young, Philip. "The Earlier Psychologists and Poe," *American Literature*, XXII (1950): 442-54.

Zanger, Jules. "Poe's Endless Voyage: *The Narrative of Arthur Gordon Pym", Papers on Language and Literature,* 22 (Summer 1986): 276-83.

Zweig, Paul. *The Adventurer: The Fate of Adventure in the Western World.* New York: Basic Books, 1974.

LITERARY THEORY

Abrams, M.H. *A glossary of Literary Terms,* New York: Holt, Rinehart and Winston, 1962.

Adams, Richard P. "Romanticism and the American Renaissance," *American Literature,* XXIII (1951-52): 431.

Aristotle's Theory of Poetry and fine Art with a critical text and translation of "The Poetics" by S.H. Butcher. New York: Dover Publications, Inc., 1951.

Attebery, Brian. *The Fantasy Tradition in American Literature: From Irving to LeGuin.* Bloomington: Indiana University Press, 1980.

Bagwell, J. Timothy. *American Formalism and the Problem of Interpretation.* Houston, Texas: Rice University Press, 1986.

Bell, Michael Davitt. *The Development of American Romance. Chicago:* University of chicago Press, 1981.

Benton, Richard P. ed. "The Gothic Tradition in Nineteenth-Century american Literature: A Symposium," *The Emerson Society Quarterly*, XVIII (1972): 5-123.

Beckson, Karl, and Ganz, Arthur. *A Reader's Guide to Literary Terms*. New York: The Noonday Press, 1960.

Bergson, Henri. "Laughter", *Comedy*, ed. Wylie Sypher. Garden City, N.Y: Doubleday and Company, Inc., 1956.

Booth, Wayne C. *The Rhetoric of Fiction.* Chicago: University of Chicago Press, 1961.

__________. *A Rhetoric of Irony*. Chicago: The University of Chicago Press, 1974.

Blair, Walter. *Native American Humor.* San Francisco: Chandler Publishing Company, Inc., 1960.

Brooke-Rose, Christine. *A Rhetoric of the Unreal: Studies in Narrative and Structure, especially of the Fantastic.* Cambridge: Cambridge University Press, 1981.

Brooks, Cleanth and Warren, Robert P. eds. *Understanding Fiction.* 2 ed. New York, 1959.

Burke, Kenneth. *The Philosophy of Literary Form: Studies in Symbolic Action.* 1941; rpt. New York: Vintage Books, 1957.

Canby, H.S. *The Short Story in English.* New York: Henry, Holt and Company, 1909.

Charvat, William. *The Origins of American Critical Thought, 1810-1835.* New York: A.S. Barnes and Company, Inc., 1936. A Perpetua Book, 1961.

Coad, Oral Sumner. "The Gothic Element in American Literature Before 1835," *The Journal of English and Germanic Philology*, XXIV (1925); 72-93.

Cohn, Robert G. "Symbolism," *The Journal of Aesthetics and Art Criticism*, XXXIII, ii (Winter 1974): 181-92.

Coleridge, Samuel Taylor. *Biographia Literaria*. 1906; rpt. London: Everyman's Library, 1967.

Cooke, Arthur L. "Some Side Lights on the Theory of the Gothic Romance," *Modern Language Quarterly*, XII (1951): 429-36.

Conron, John Joseph. "Poe and the theory of the Short Story", Diss. The University of Michigan, 1970.

Clark, Kenneth. *The Gothic Revival: An Essay on the History of Taste*. 1928; rpt. London: Constable, 1950.

Crane, R.S. "The Concept of Plot and the Plot of *Tom Jones," Critics and Criticism*. Chicago: University of Chicago Press, 1952.

Day, William Patrick. *In the circles of Fear and Desire: A Study of Gothic Fantasy.* Chicago: University of Chicago Press, 1985.

Fain, John T. and Young, Thomas D. *The Literary*

Correspondence of Donald Davidson and Allen Tate. Athens: University of Georgia Press, 1974.

Feidelson, Charles. *Symbolism and american Literature.* Chicago: the University of Chicago Press, 1953.

Ferguson, Suzanne C. "Defining the Short Story: Impressionism and Form," *Modern fiction Studies*, Vol. 28, No. 1 (Spring 1982): 13-24.

Forster, E.M. *Aspects of the Novel.* 1927; rpt. Harmondsworth: Penguin Books, Ltd., 1962.

Foerster, Norman. *American Criticism.* New York: Houghton Miffline Company, 1928

Freedoman, Ralph. "Interntionality and the Literary Object," *Contemporary Literature,* Vol. 17, No. 3, (Summer 1976): 430-452.

Frye, Northrop. *Anatomy of Criticism: Four Essays.* Princeton: Princeton University Press, 1957.

__________. "The Four Forms of Prose Fiction," *Hudson Review*, (Winter 1950): 582-95.

Foakes, R.A ed. *Romantic Criticism, 1800-1850* London: Edward Arnold Ltd., 1968.

Frankl, Paul. *The Gothic: Literary Sources and Interpretations Through Eight Centuries.* Princeton: Princeton University Press, 1960.

Freund, E. *The Return of the Reader: Reader-Response Criticism.* London & New York: Methuen, 1987.

Friedman, Norman. "Point of View in Fiction: The Development of a Critical Concept," *PMLA*, 70 (1955): 1160-84.

Gardner, John, and Dunlap, Lennis, eds. *The Forms of Fiction.* New York: Random House, 1962.

Gloversmith, Frank. ed. *The theory of Reading.* Totowa, N.Y.: Nobel Books, 1984.

Green, Deniel. "Metafiction and Romance," *Studies in American Fiction*, Vol. 19, No. 2 (Autumn 1991), 229-42.

Gullason, Thomas A. "The Short Story: Revision and Renewal," *Studies in Short Fiction*, Vol. 19, No. 3 (Summer 1982): 221-30.

Hardy, Barbara. "Towards a Poetics of Fiction," *Novel,* (Fall 1968): 5-14.

Haggerty, George. *Gothic fiction/Gothic Form.* University Park: Pennsylvania State University Press, 1989.

Highet, Gilbert. *The Anatomy of Satire.* Princeton: Princeton University Press, 1962.

Horton, R.W., and Edwards, H.W. *Backgrounds of american Literary Thought.* New York: Appleton, 1952.

Hirsch, David H. "Postmodernism and American Literary History," *The Sewanee Review*, XCIX, I (Winter 1991): 40-60.

Holub, Robert C. *reception Theory: A Critical Introduction.* New York: Methuen, 1984.

Hume, Robert D. "Gothic Versus Romantic: A Revaluation of the Gothic Novel," *PMLA*, 84 (1959): 282-90.

Irwin, W.R. *The Game of the Impossible: A Rhetoric of Fantasy.* Urbana, Ill: University of Illinois Press, 1976.

Jump, John D. *Burlesque.* London: Methuen, 1972.

Keech, James M. "The Survival of the Gothic Response," *Studies in the Novel,* VI, ii (Summer 1974): 130-44.

Kayser, Wolfgang. *The Grotesque in Art and Literature*, trans. Ulrich Weisstein. Bloomington: Indiana University Press, 1963.

Leavis, F.R. *The Common Pursuit.* 1952; rpt. Harmondsworth: Penguin Books, 1963.

Lovejoy, Arthur C. "The First Gothic Revival," *Essays in the History of Ideas.* 1948; rpt. New York: Putnam's, 1960.

Lubbock, Percy. *The Craft of Fiction.* London: Jonathan cape, Ltd., 1921.

MacAndrew, Elizabeth. *The Gothic Tradition in Fiction.* New York: Columbia University Press, 1979.

Mead, George H. *Movements of thought in the Nineteenth Century.* Chicago: University of Chicago Press, 1936.

Mailloux, Steven. *Interpretive Conventions: The Reader in the Study of American Fiction.* Ithaca: Cornell University Press, 1984.

Morrison, Claudia C. *Freud and the Critic: The Early Use of Depth Psychology in Literary Criticism.* Chapel Hill, N.C: University of North Carolina Press, 1968.

Malin, Irvin. *New American Gothic.* Carbondale: Southern Illinois University Press, 1962.

Murch, A.E. *The Development of the Detective Novel.* London: Peter Owen Limited, 1958.

Marler, Robert F. "From Tale to Short Story: The emergence of a New Genre in the 1850," *American Literature*, XLVI, ii (May 1974): 153-69.

McIntyre, Clara F. "Were the 'Gothic Novels' Gothic?" *PMLA*, XXXV (1921): 644-47.

Napir, Elizabeth R. *The Failure of Gothic: Problems of Disjunction in an Eighteenth-Century Literary Form.* New York: Oxford University Press, 1987.

Norman, Liane. "Risk and Redundancy," *PMLA*, Vol. 90, No. 2 (March 1975): 285-91.

Nelson, Lowry. "Night thoughts on the Gothic Novels," *The Yale Review*, LII, ii (Winter 1963): 236-57.

Nettels, Elsa. "Poe and James on the Art of Fiction," *Poe Studies,* 13, i (1980): 4-8.

Newberry, Frederick. "A New Perspective on the American Romance: A Review Essay," *Poe Studies*, 14, ii (December 1981): 33-39.

Nevins, Francis M. ed. *The Mystery Writer's Art.* Bowling Green: Bowling Green University Popular Pess, 1970.

Ong, S.J., Walter J. "The Writer's Audience is Always a Fiction," *PMLA*, Vol. 90, No. 1 (January 1975): 9-21.

O'Grady, Walter. "On Plot in Modern Fiction: Hardy, James, and Conrad," *Modern Fiction Studies*, XL, ii (Summer 1965): 107-15.

O'Faolain, Sean. *The Short Story.* New York: The Devin-Adair Company, 1951.

O'Connor, William Van. *The Grotesque, an American Genre.* Carbondale. Southern Illinois University Press, 1962.

Price, Martin. "The fictional Contract," *Literary Theory and Structure,* ed. Frank Brady, *et al.* New Haven: Yale University Press, 1973.

Platzner, Robert L. and Hume, Robert D. " 'Gothic Versus Romantic': A Rejoinder," *PMLA*, 86 (1971); 266-74.

Pritchard, John Paul. *Return to the Fountains: Some Classical Sources of American Criticism.* New York: Octagon Books, Inc., 1966.

__________. "Aristotle's Poetics and Certain American Literary Critics," The Classical Weekly, XXVII (1934): 81-85.

Peden, William. "The Recent American Short Story," *The Sewanee Review*, LXXXII, iv (Fall 1974): 712-29.

Rabkin, Eric S. *Narrative Suspense.* Ann Arbor: The University of Michigan Press, 1973.

Ringe, Donald A. *American Gothic: Imagination and Reason in Nineteenth-Century Fiction.* Lexington: University Press of Kentucky, 1982.

Richards, I.A. *Practical Criticism: A Study of Literary Judgment.* London: Rowtledge and Kegan Paul, 1929.

Robson-Scott, W.D. *The Literary Background of the Gothic Revival in Germany.* Oxford: Clarendon Press, 1965.

Rourke, Constance. *American Humor: A Study of the National Character.* 1931; rpt. New York: Doubleday Anchor Books, 1953.

Sayers, Dorothy L. "Introduction" to the third Series of *Great Short Stories of Detection, Mystery and Horror.* London: Gollancz, 1934.

Scholes, Robert and Kellogg, Robert. *The Nature of Narrative.* New York: Oxford University Press, 1966.

Schorer, Mark. "Technique as Discovery," *Hudson Review*, I, (Spring 1948): 67-87.

Stanton, Robert. *The Short Story and the Reader.* New York: Henry, Holt and Company, 1960.

Steig, Michael. "Defining the Grotesque: An Attempt at Synthesis," *Journal of Aesthetics and Art Criticism*. Vol. 29, No. ii (Winter 1970): 253-60.

Summers, Montague. *The Gothic Quest: A History of the Gothic Novel*. 1938; rpt. New York: Russell and Russell, 1964.

Thomson, Philip. *The Grotesque*. London: Methuen, 1972. Thompson, G.R. ed. *The Gothic Imagination: Essays in Dark Romanticism*. Pullman: Washington State University Press, 1974.

Thorburn, David & Hartman, Geoffrey. *Romanticism: Vistas, Instances, Continuities*. Ithaca: Cornell University Press, 1973.

Twitchell, James B. *The Living Dead: A Study of the Vampire in Romantic Literature*. Durham, N.C.: Duke University Press, 1981.

Varma, Devendra P. *The gothic Flame*. London: Arthur Baker Ltd., 1957.

Voss, Arthur. *The American Short Story: A Critical Survey*. Norman: University of Oklahoma Press, 1973.

Weber, Brom. ed. *An Anthology of American Humor*. New York: Thomas Y. Crowell Company, 1962.

West, Ray B. *The Writer in the Room*. Michigan State University Press, 1968.

Wellek, Rene. *A History of Modern criticism 11750-1950*, Vol. II, *The Romantic Age* (New Haven, 1955).

Wellek, Rene, and Warren, Austin. *Theory of Literature*, 1942; rpt. Harmondsworth: Penguin Books, 1973.

Williams, Valentine. "The Detective in Fiction," *The Fortnightly Review*, CXXVIII (September 1930): 381-92.

Wimsatt, W.K. and Beardsley, Monroe c. *The Verbal Icon: Studies in the Meaning of Poetry*. Kentucky: University of Kentucky Press, 1954.

Wimsatt, W.K. and Brooks, Cleanth. *Literary Criticism: A Short History*. New York: Vintage Books, 1967.

Winston, Mathew. "*Humor Noir* and Black Humor," *Veins of Humor*, ed. Harry Levin. Cambridge, Mass: Harvard University Press, 1972.

GENERAL

Adams, Robert M. *NIL: Episodes in the Literary Conquest of the Void during the Nineteenth-Century*. New York: Oxford University Press, 1966.

Brown, Charles Brockden. *Wieland*. Garden City, New York: Doubleday and Co., Inc., 1962.

__________. *Edgar Huntly*. New York: The Macmillan Company, 1928.

Brooks, Van Wyck. *The World of Washington Irving*. New York: E.P. Dutton and Company, Inc., 1944.

Chase, Richard. *The American Novel and its Tradition*. Garden City, N.Y.: Doubleday and Company, Inc., 1957.

Dostoyevsky, Fyodor. *The House of the Dead*. ed. Earnest J. Simmons. New York: Dell Publishing Co., Inc., 1959.

Eliot, T.S. *To Criticize the critic and Other Writings*. London: Faber and Faber, 1965.

Fiedler, Leslie. *Love And death in the American Novel*. New York: Criterion Books, 1960.

__________. *The Return of the Vanishing American*. New York: Stein and Day, 1968.

Crews, Frederick. *The Sins of the Fathers: Hawthorne's Psychological Themes*. New York: Oxford University Press, 1966.

Fussell, Edwin. *Frontier: American Literature and the american West*. Princeton: Princeton University Press, 1965.

Freud, Sigmund. *On Dreams*. trans. James Strachey. New York: Norton, 1952.

Holman, C. Hugh. *The Roots of Southern Writing*. Athens: University of Georgia Press, 1972.

Hoffman, frederick J. *The Mortal No: Death and Modern Imagination*. Princeton: Princeton University Press, 1964.

Howard, Leon. *Literature and the American Tradition*. Garden City, New York: Doubleday and Company, Inc., 1960.

Knight, G. Wilson. *The Wheel of Fire*. 1930, rpt. London: Methuen and Co., Ltd., 1968.

Lawrence, D.H. *Studies in Classic American Literature*. New York: doubleday and Co., 1923.

Minor, Benjamin B. *The Southern Literary Messenger: 1834-1864*. New York: Neale Publishing Co., 1905.

Mott, Frank Luther. *A History of American Magazines*. Cambridge, Mass.: Harvard University Press, 1938-1939, 3 Vols.

Reynolds, David S. *Beneath the American Renaissance: The Subversive Imagination in the Age of Emerson and Melville*. New York: Alfred A. Knopf, 1988.

Ruskin, John. *The Complete Works of John Ruskin*, ed. E T. cooke and Alexander Wedderburn, Vol. II, *The Stones of Venice*, Ch. IV, "The Nature of Gothic." London: G. Allen,1904.

Richardson, Lyon N ed. *Henry James: Representative Selections*. New York: American Book Co., 1941.

Shapiro, Morris. *Selected Literary Criticism: Henry James*. 1963; rpt. New York: McGraw-Hill Book Company, 1965.

Simpson, Lewis P. *The Man of Letters in New england and the South: Essays on the History of the Literary Vocation in America*. Baton Rouge: Louisiana State University Press, 1973.

Stovall, Floyd. ed. *walt Whitman: Representative Selections*. New York: American Book Company, 1934.

Stone, Edward. *Voices of Despair: Four Motifs in American Literature*. Athens: Ohio University Press, 1966.

__________. *A Certain Morbidness: A View of American Literature*. Carbondale: Southern Illinois University Press, 1967.

Tompkins, J.M.S. *The Popular Novel in England, 1770-1880*. 1932; rpt. Lincoln: University of Nebraska Press, 1961.

Tropp, Martin. "Dr. Jekyll and Mr. Hyde, Schopenhauer and the Power of the Will," *The Midwest Quarterly*, XXXII, ii (Winter 1991): 141-55.

Wilson, Edmund. *The shock of Recognition*. 1943; rpt. New York: The Modern Library, 1955.

Index